D0038626

Pies and Prejudice

Pies and Prejudice

In Search of the North

STUART MACONIE

EBURY
PRESS

11 13 15 17 19 20 18 16 14 12

Published in 2007 by Ebury Press, an imprint of Ebury Publishing

Ebury Publishing is a division of the Random House Group

Copyright © Stuart Maconie 2007

Stuart Maconie has asserted his right to be identified as the author of this work
in accordance with the Copyright, Designs and Patents Act 1988

All rights reserved. No part of this publication may be reproduced,
stored in a retrieval system, or transmitted in any form or by any means,
electronic, mechanical, photocopying, recording or otherwise,
without the prior permission of the copyright owner

The Random House Group Limited Reg. No. 954009

Addresses for companies within the Random House Group
can be found at www.randomhouse.co.uk

A CIP catalogue record for this book is available from the British Library

The Random House Group Limited makes every effort to ensure
that the papers used in our books are made from trees that have been
legally sourced from well-managed and credibly certified forests. Our paper
procurement policy can be found on www.randomhouse.co.uk

Typeset by seagulls.net

Printed and bound in Great Britain by Mackays of Chatham Plc

ISBN 9780091910228

Poetry extract from *Collected Poems* by Simon Armitage, Faber and Faber Ltd

Simon Armitage, *Zoom!* (Bloodaxe Books, 1989)

Extracts from *The Milltown Trilogy* by John Morrison, Pennine Pens

The Road to Wigan Pier by George Orwell (Copyright © George Orwell, 1936)
England Your England by George Orwell (Copyright © George Orwell, 1953)
By permission of Bill Hamilton as the Literary Executor of the Estate of
the Late Sonia Brownell Orwell and Secker & Warburg Ltd.

Extracts from *English Journey* by J.B. Priestley (Copyright © Estate
of J.B. Priestley 1934) are reproduced by permission of PFD
(www.pfd.co.uk) on behalf of the Estate of J.B. Priestley

For The Angels Of The North

Acknowledgements

For their help, encouragement, advice, love and hospitality, my heartfelt thanks to Eleanor, Bridget, John, Steph, Eddie, Suzanne, Martin, Kate (The Great Haldini), Lesley Douglas, Mark Byford, Paula Rogers, Rhys Hughes, John Leonard, Andrew Harrison, Peter Kay, Paul Rodgers, Judith Holder, my ever-patient editor Andrew Goodfellow, Mum and Dad, and of course Kirsty and Greggs the bakers.

'If you're an alien, how come you sound
like you come from the north?'

'Lots of planets have a north.'

Doctor Who, 2005

Contents

Prologue

A few years ago, I was standing in my kitchen, rustling up a Sunday brunch for some very hungover, very northern mates who were 'down' for the weekend. One of them was helping me out, finding essential ingredients like paracetamol and orange juice, and asked me, 'Where are the sun-dried tomatoes?'

'They're next to the cappuccino maker,' I replied.

A ghastly, pregnant silence fell. Slowly, we turned to meet each other's gaze. We didn't say anything. We didn't need to. Each read the other's unspoken thought; we had changed. We had become the kind of people who rustled up brunch on Sundays, passed around sections of the Sunday papers, popped down to little bakeries; the kind of people who had sun-dried tomatoes and cappuccino makers.

Southerners, I suppose.

Now before readers from Godalming and Sidcup, Aylesbury and Exeter hurl this book across the non-fiction section enraged, before they chuck it in the bin cursing the waste of a good book token when they could have got a nice Danielle Steel or Sven Hassel, let me explain. I don't like thinking this way, like a Pict in an animal pelt, face blue with woad. I'd rather be cosmopolitan, suave, displaying an easy confidence with pesto and fish knives and the Hammersmith and City Line. I have tried to change, really I have. I say 'lunch'. I say 'book' with an 'uh' not an 'oooh'. Though I draw the line at 'supper' and 'barth'.

But then again... Then again, I do have a cappuccino maker and some sun-dried tomatoes. Actually, moving with the times, of course, it's now some sun-blushed tomatoes (so much juicier, don't you think, and lovely tossed in with balsamic and feta). But on some level, I feel it should be a plate of tripe and a pound of lard, the sort of food you want after a hard day digging coal from a three-foot seam or riveting steel plates – proper jobs, in fact, as opposed to tapping effeminately at a keyboard for hours on end or talking to yourself in a radio studio.

This book, then, is an attempt to rediscover both the north itself and my own inner northerner. Does the north still exist? Are the hand-wringing cultural theorists right when they talk of a Britain of identikit prefab towns each with a Body Shop, Costa Coffee and Waterstones? Or is the north still more likely to rejoice in a flagship Cash Converters than a flagship Harvey Nicks, whatever the fashionistas of Leeds might think?

The north. What is it? Where is it? Where does it begin and end, what does it mean to be northern and why, in a country that you could drop and easily lose in one of the American Great Lakes, does that two and a half hour journey from London to Manchester or Leeds still feel like crossing time zones, political borders and linguistic and cultural frontiers?

When we say the north, what do we really mean? It's something both powerful (like Newcastle Brown) and attractively vague (like most Oasis lyrics). The north means the Lake Poets and Lindisfarne Island and at the same time sink estates, ASBOs and the AIDS capital of Britain (Doncaster, if you're interested). The north is big and complicated. Square metres of it are crowded, square miles of it are almost deserted. Surprisingly for an area so well covered by CCTV, it still says 'Here Be Dragons' on the *Daily Telegraph* and Radio 4's map of Britain.

And so, by supersaver and service station, by West Coast Main Line and M6, I began the journey back home. 'Home is the place,' wrote Robert Frost, 'where, when you have to go there, they have to take you in.' But would it still feel like home? Would they have to take me back? Would I want them to?

What kind of book is this that you have in your hand? I guess it's a travel book of sorts though it has little in common with many modern travel books. If you hang around the travel section of your local bookshop for a while you will notice how many modern travel books have titles that sing out with brisk and slightly wacky jauntiness: *Mind My Nose Flute! Bhutan on Three Dong a Day*, *To Tierra Del Fuego by Cement Mixer* or *Around Khazakstan with a Guinea Pig*. You can picture the authors, scrubbed-looking, enthusiastic men and women in big shorts and headscarves, pushing back the flaps of a tent on the Hindu Kush, inhaling deeply the desert air or emerging from a dilapidated shower block in a former Soviet Gulag and flicking the border guards with a towel.

By contrast I went to Harrogate. And Bury. And Haltwhistle. And Saddleworth. And Liverpool and Manchester. I went to a great many places, covered a lot of miles, saw a lot of gift shops and tearooms and city-centre regeneration displays and, boy, oh boy, a lot of high-visibility tabards and Greggs bakeries, as we shall see.

But even by the dire, apocalyptic, randomly privatised standards of the British transport system, a system so ill thought out that it takes longer to get to Norwich from Birmingham than from Birmingham to Moscow, these aren't epic journeys, and I knew many of the places quite well already. I didn't sleep under the stars with the Mujahideen, I slept in quite nice hotels most of the time, and the natives were largely friendly though getting a toasted teacake in Hexham proved dauntingly difficult.

Although I'm from Lancashire and this book is primarily about the north of England, I'd like to think it can be enjoyed by the fine people of the south of England too. My publishers are understandably as keen as mustard on this as well. I really hope that it's neither puff piece nor hatchet job. I just wanted to share some thoughts about the place I come from, its people and cities and music and food and humour and landscapes and stuff and how I feel about it. It isn't a guidebook in the sense that it isn't exhaustive. You will look in vain for much about Grasmere or Grimsby. It's my north and reflects both my centres of gravity, the directions that pulled me, the places that made me think, 'I wonder what that place is like now,' at the beginning of a shiny new millennium.

I hope this book is a love letter – one that makes you laugh, the best sort – but not just flannel and boasting about how bloody marvellous and decent and rugged and down-to-earth we are. Because we're not, not all the time. Like an old friend, I love the north of England dearly while recognising its many faults and I hope I don't shy away from them. They are part of its character. It can be grim up north, and heart-stoppingly beautiful.

It isn't all football and fags. It's politics and folklore, civil war and nuclear power, heavy industry and haute couture, poetry and Pina Colada, ships and shops, chips and fish, and football and fags, come to think of it.

And, of course, pies and prejudice.

The Beautiful South

The BBC has no South of England Correspondent. I say this without malice or anger. I wouldn't want you to think that I'm eaten up with corrosive rage over it or that I'm making my way to Broadcasting House with a flaming brand even as we speak. It's just a fact of nature, like glaciers or osmosis. The BBC has no South of England Correspondent because it would be silly, like having a Correspondent for Unicorns, or Spontaneous Combustion.

Because like unicorns or spontaneous combustion, there is no south of England, if we're honest. There's a bottom half of England, naturally, otherwise the country would get all unravelled and damp around Nuneaton. But there isn't a south in the same way that there's a north. As all of my old geography teachers used to say at some point, get out your atlases and turn to the page marked England and Wales.

Run your finger idly from left to right across the expanse below Birmingham and what do you find? Cardiff... Well, that's Wales, obviously; Tom Jones, Charlotte Church, the Manic Street Preachers, rugby union, miners and big hats with buckles on. Next is Bristol, home of two underachieving football teams, trustafarian DJs and the BBC Wildlife Unit. Salisbury Plain suggests bullied squaddies with tearful, boot-blacked faces and druids mooching about in Ku Klux Klan-style hoods. Oxford is Radiohead and dreaming spires. London? We'll come back to that. Basildon? Nothing. A void. Apart from Depeche Mode, of course, and then we are on to Margate and the sudden hot vinegary tang of bladderwrack and fish and chips.

Apart from disclosing my own rather juvenile frame of reference (football, bands, er, hats), this tells us nothing. It's like a coach driver's acid flashback, lurid and random. If there were a cohesive thing called the south of England, you'd expect to hear some swelling music in the back of your mind (Vera Lynn singing 'The White Cliffs Of Dover', perhaps, or one of The Wurzels' agricultural ditties) and to feel some unifying emotion. But none is forthcoming.

This is because there's no conception of the south comparable to the north. Good or bad, 'the north' means something to all English people wherever they hail from. To people from London – cheery costermonger, cravated fop or Shoreditch-based web designer on stupid scooter alike – it means desolation, arctic temperatures, mushy peas, a cultural wasteland with limited shopping opportunities and populated by aggressive trolls.

To northerners it means home, truth, beauty, valour, romance, warm and characterful people, real beer and decent chip shops. And in this we are undoubtedly biased, of course. When northerners think of the south, what do they think of? Well, let's try a little word association prompted by the word 'northern'.

OK then.

Northern ... Soul

Northern ... Lights

Northern ... Rock (it's a building society)

And now 'southern'. Let me see.

Southern ... Comfort

Southern ... Jessies

Southern ... Fried Chicken

Far from scientific but enlightening nonetheless. Soul and Lights and Rock versus Comfort, Jessies and Chicken. Even the most sophisticated northerner harbours an inner barbarian with a molten core of prejudice.

We like to think we're different. But what makes us different? What shapes us? Well, we like to think that some of the forces are elemental. The north-south divide was illustrated by a Trog cartoon in the *Observer* published during Thatcher's mid-eighties pomp: two smartly dressed yuppies are drinking champagne under a cloudless southern sky while at the other side of the frame, a dour middle-aged couple, rain-sodden beneath glowering clouds, are complaining, 'They've got their prime minister, why can't we have ours?' Crucially here, the difference between them is not just political or economic. It's climatic.

There's not much point me regaling you with statistics like Leeds being drier than Barcelona or Cornwall being wetter than Manchester or Sheffield's summers being generally warmer than Newquay's, true though these all are, apparently. What matters is perception and when we think of Brighton we think of nudists going gently pink, when we think of Devon we think of cream teas in the garden and when we think of Sunderland we think of a man with rime clinging to his beard leaning into a hail-peppered gale. In May.

The writer and TV producer Judith Holder has written that it's not that we get worse weather in the north, we just sort of get, well, more weather. Winds that take slates off in the night or have you asking someone two doors down for your dustbin back. Frosts that send old ladies skittling along pavements and kids mincing gingerly onto duck ponds despite what those scary public information films say. We relish our weather up north and we relish our capacity to endure it. A few years back I was at Highbury watching Arsenal play Sunderland and the difference in the two sets of supporters' apparel was hilarious. On a cold February day, the Gooners were togged up in car coats and parkas while at the away end, Mackems gathered happily in T-shirts and Fred Perrys. Watch Middlesbrough or Newcastle on their ventures into Europe and the camera will always find a gaggle of fat blokes with their shirts off, braving the Bratislavan winter's night, waving and laughing as if to say, 'Call this cold, man. I'm finding it oppressive!'

As much as we delight in our own capacity to endure the elements, we deride the softness of southerners in this regard. When a Cornish village gets flooded and a state of emergency is declared, we tut in sympathy but secretly we think, 'What do you expect? You live on the beach,' and after looking at the TV pictures conclude that they wouldn't cancel the racing at Thirsk for that drop of rain. We reserve most of our scorn for London, where an inch of powdery snow has taxi drivers weeping and ashen-faced TV reporters telling people to stay indoors, wait for help and don't panic-buy baked beans. HELLO! IT'S DECEMBER! BUY A CAGOULE!

Weather carves the landscape to a degree. Rain and wind scour and groove the hills through waves of ice ages, green the fields, smooth the coastline. Millennia of freeze-thaw scatter splintered boulders in valleys gouged by the tides of ice. Weather acts like an artist's hand but the canvas predates it. The canvas is geology.

In this, as in so many things, the north is well hard, we think. Not for us the soft feminine allure of Downs and Wolds, the rolling pasture, the chalky uplands. No, the north is built from Skiddaw slate and Borrowdale volcanics, granite and limestone. It's only rocks but people can get very emotional and florid about them. Read the great Cumbrian poet Norman Nicholson on the geology of his home town of Millom. Limestone even has its own Poet Laureate, the wonderful Wystan Hugh Auden.

When an undergraduate prodigy, Auden's limpid features, soft lips and dangling cigarette suggested every inch the southern intellectual. But he was born in York and called himself 'a son of the north', with a lifelong allegiance and kinship with the moorland of the North Pennines and the melancholic remains of the once-thriving lead-mining industry. Auden called it his 'Mutterland' and his 'great good place' and dated his artistic baptism to a moment of epiphany in 1922 at Rookhope, County Durham, when he dropped a stone down a flooded mineshaft and felt a calling to write. He often wrote about these districts, hills and people and actually turned his hand to a travel piece in 1954: 'England: Six Unexpected Days', a suggested driving itinerary through the Pennine Dales.

Auden, largely single-handledly, reintroduced the Anglo-Saxon metre into English verse and he employed it in 'In Praise Of Limestone', with the following chilly lines, among my favourites in modern poetry:

> *An older colder voice, the oceanic whisper:*
> *I am the solitude that asks and promises nothing;*
> *That is how I shall set you free. There is no love;*
> *There are only the various envies, all of them sad*

The oceanic whisper, eh? He was good, wasn't he? Later in life, the whey-faced Brideshead features hardened. Maybe it was the fags but he grew to look more northern, craggier, wrinkled as a walnut. His face famously was described as 'a cake left out in the rain', a phrase that Jimmy Webb borrowed for 'MacArthur Park'. One of my colleagues in the English department at Skelmersdale College, Val, once looked at a picture of him on the back of his collected poems and said, 'Good God, if that was his face, what must his testicles have been like?'

Skelmersdale, as we shall learn later, is a Viking name and up north we are proud of our Viking lineage. Now, I'm with Muriel

Gray on the subject of facial hair – 'Why bother growing a moustache? You could just write "I Am A Dickhead" on your top lip' – but if all thoughts of common sense and aesthetics desert me and I grow a beard, it will turn out to be ginger. Gingerish, anyway. I used to be embarrassed about this when I looked enviously at the dark if bum-fluffish sidies of my teenage mates but now I'm rather proud. My auburn whiskers I take as proof of my lineage right back to Eric Bloodaxe and evidence of the fact that my true calling is drinking from a giant horn at the prow of a longboat heading for a spot of pillage in Iceland. The country, not the discount freezer store, obviously.

Actually, the Vikings have had rather a bad press. True, they were not the gentle agrarians that some apologists say – *The Book of Common Prayer* had a bit in it about 'deliver us from the North Man' and for the 200 years up to the ninth century they were always popping over, helping themselves to local treasure, women and livestock – but they did do as much trading as raiding and eventually became absorbed into the racial mix, which is where my beard comes in. Their legacy is there as well as in all the dales and thwaites and leys in the region.

All of this makes us different, we think; harder, flintier, steelier. We are the ones who turn the air-conditioning down in the meeting room, who want to sit outside the pub in October, who order the hottest curries, the strongest beer, the most powerful drugs. We like to think we're different, and we cherish our prejudices.

But we can overcome these prejudices. When the resolutely northern pop group The Housemartins transformed themselves in the mid-eighties, they chose the new name The Beautiful South. Pretty much everyone thought this was a heavily ironic choice, to be said with a sneer. *The Sunday Times* simply assumed that it was 'a sarcastic dig at England's north-south divide'. In fact, singer Paul Heaton chose the name because 'it sounded nice, like a film'. And there are lots of things about the south of England that sound nice to me. There's the music of Vaughan Williams, with its heady scents of warm Gloucestershire afternoons, or The Clash, whose music is full of the even headier scents found beneath flyovers in west London. There's Powell and Pressburger's dreamlike films such as *A Canterbury Tale,* where Kent becomes a mythic Avalon. I like Cornish pasties and M. R. James ghost stories and Dorset Blue Vinny cheese.

But none of these things say 'the south' in the same way that certain things, good or bad, true or false, whippet or flat cap, say 'the north'. What would that mythical BBC South of England Correspondent be like? Bertie Wooster? Wurzel Gummidge? Mike 'Runaround' Reid? Prince Charles? What would he wear? A straw boater? Jodhpurs? A sheepskin jacket? Beefeater garb?

The BBC does have a North of England Correspondent and he conforms very much to type. He – and it is always he – is one of their more 'lived-in' presenters; a stocky man in his early fifties with jowls, a florid complexion and bullishly hetero moustache. He looks tough but somehow defeated, maybe an old rugby league pro with a messy, financially punishing divorce behind him and the beginnings of a drink problem (I suspect there may be a quarter of Bell's in the pocket of that Gore-Tex anorak). Fiona in the nice warm London studio will 'go over live' to him and he'll inevitably be found looking tense outside a courtroom in Bolton at the conclusion of a major drugs trial or by a burned-out Mondeo on a Yorkshire sink estate where some sort of armed siege is occurring. He never gets the heartwarming story about the unlikely friendship between the Doberman Pinscher and the hamster.

Where exactly is he? To many a south-based viewer, I guess he's in that vague but colourful region, 'Up North'. 'Up North' is a long way away. You wouldn't want to go there. It's a long trip, as in 'West Ham face a long trip to Hartlepool for the third-round tie'. Note it's never the other way round. It's OK too to be blithely approximate about northern geography. Some years ago, we northerners chortled when Des Lynam suavely announced on *Final Score*: 'Chesterfield 0, Chester 0. So no goals there in the local derby.'

A few years ago, I actually rang up Sky News frothing at the mouth to complain about a spectacularly half-arsed item they'd done on Rochdale, whose football team were enjoying a good Cup run and had drawn a big club in a glamour tie. A fresh-faced reporter had been despatched to the town. From his amused anthropological tone, you might have thought that he'd been sent to Burkina Faso rather than the second largest metropolitan borough of Greater Manchester with a population of more than 200,000. He ended his report, and I am not making this up, by saying, 'If the team win tomorrow, they will have put little Rochdale on the map.' No, I think you'll find the pioneers of the international co-operative movement did that back in 1844 when they changed the course of world history. News obviously hasn't reached the Sky centre in Hounslow yet, though. Perhaps I have a chip on my shoulder, but at least it's a proper chip, properly fried and served with gravy and mushy peas.

But let's not get too steamed up and tipsy on righteous indignation. If southerners do sometimes think it should read 'Here Be Dragons' on the map once you're past Watford, then we in the north can be just as sketchy about the south. What, for instance, does the south mean to me personally?

I am attractively vague about Suffolk, Sussex and Surrey. I routinely confuse them all though if I stop and think for a moment I can place Suffolk. As the name suggests, it's south of Norfolk. On one of my few trips to the area, the late John Peel picked me up at the station in his battered Mercedes. I couldn't get into the passenger seat, which was taken up with shopping or some such, so I sat in the back, taxi-style. As we moved through the decidedly staid and sweet environs of the town, Peel turned and over his shoulder said in broadest Manhattan cabbie-ese, 'So, how ya doin', bud? First time in Stowmarket?' We went to the village pub for steak pie (he and Sheila had the veggie lasagne) and it was all rather darling and slightly *Terry and June*. I've never been back to Suffolk; there's never been any need to. I guess that's precisely what Peelie loved about it.

Norfolk is a closed book to me. A closed book that has got some bad, rather sniggering reviews: Alan Partridge, Bernard Matthews, *Sale of the Century* and Delia Smith have conjoined like unlucky stars to make it a bit of a joke, a new shorthand for the rural sticks, sort of Crinkley Bottom goes *Deliverance*. I'm ashamed to say I have never been to Norwich though I'm told it's delightful. Even the supporters of Ipswich Town, though – hardly Los Angeles itself – mock Norwich folk for their yokelism in what is perhaps my favourite football chant, sung to the tune of *The Addams Family*:

Your sister is your mother
Your father is your brother
You all shag one another, the Norwich family

Bedfordshire and Hertfordshire are merely a gentle fog of airports and weddings. Middlesex conjures up only cricket and Russell Grant, the roly-poly astrologer who has campaigned tirelessly to get Middlesex reinstated as a county or made administrative capital of Europe or something.

Essex I do know a little about as I lived there briefly in the 1980s, courtesy of a girlfriend's hospitality at a time when

Margaret Thatcher was trying her hand at starving her enemies (students, miners, old people, children) into submission. My girlfriend lived in a place called Chadwell Heath; chiefly famous, if at all, for being the place where West Ham United train. Indeed, if Billy Bonds or Julian Dicks ever go out for an evening there, they will never have to put their hand in their pocket.

I went for several nights out there. I had to put my hand in my pocket an awful lot, it seemed to me. 'Southern prices,' we'd grizzle, after handing over most of our dole money for a pint of gaseous, urine-coloured but strangely tasteless liquid with an unconvincing cod-Hungarian name. Most of these nights out are etched in my mind and bring forth an involuntary shudder. This was the mid-1980s, after all, when a night out in Romford was a nightmarish blur of white stilettos, fun pubs and hair-gelled lotharios with earrings and plastic slip-ons who could turn nasty at any moment. Nights out soundtracked by Wham! and Luther Vandross, the banshee wail of car alarms and the whirring rotors of a police helicopter, girls cackling, fruit machines exploding with shrapnel and the mournful cry of 'Leave it, Gaz, he's not worth it'. Maybe it's still like that. I'm certainly not going back to find out.

It could be that my desperate emotional state has coloured my view of Essex. I met some lovely people there. Billy Bragg for one. But what struck me most, perhaps parochially, were the slight but powerful cultural differences. There was the happy hour, during which office workers in Top Man suits would neck cheap Löwenbräu and spritzers before falling asleep on the train and ending up in Southend with drool on their lapels and numb faces. Now I'd been brought up on a strict and manly regime of daily pub-going but this seemed wrong, immoral, against some natural law. Drinking at half past five? Everyone knew that you went straight home after work, fell asleep in front of *Blockbusters* with Bob Holness, had a Findus crispy pancake and a shower and met up again at half seven. It took me a while to realise that the happy hour, which had begun in Manhattan and migrated to Essex, fitted perfectly the drinking community it served, i.e. people who went to work in a suit or at least in regular clothes and thus would feel comfortable perched on a barstool with an overpriced lager. The thought of going straight out on the town (and possibly the pull) if you were black-faced with engine grease, wearing overalls and clutching an oily rag was less attractive. This was the north-south divide writ large via the licensed victualler trade.

Heading west, Wiltshire means little beyond maverick musician Julian Cope, who moved there to be nearer the ancient barrows, mounds and stone circles that he's frankly nuts about. I've visited him there a couple of times and once, while on the train back, I saw Princess Anne at Swindon station shouting about car parking. She was wearing a khaki body warmer, sporting that horrid hairstyle (clearly the royal family haven't heard of conditioner) and flanked by a huge vicious-looking dog and an armed guard. Now, she's a pillar of the community and Copey's the freak. But from where I was standing, it was hard to tell. What with the barking and braying.

Hampshire says practically nothing to me. I once spent several freezing hours at the impossibly grim Southsea terminal waiting for a ferry and, er, that's about it. Those Needles look great, though, rising from the Solent like dragons' teeth. And I do remember defence secretary Geoff Hoon using Hants as a reference during the early days of the invasion of Iraq when British soldiers were patrolling the city of Umm Qasr. 'Umm Qasr is a city similar to Southampton,' he informed the Commons, prompting one British squaddie to reply to an interviewer, 'He's either never been to Southampton, or he's never been to Umm Qasr. There's no beer, no prostitutes and people are shooting at us. It's more like Portsmouth.'

Dorset is a wild night out in Bournemouth with Blur's Alex James, a native of the once genteel, now almost lawless (according to the *Daily Mail*) seaside town. Weymouth is known as the Naples of Dorset. But is Naples the Weymouth of Italy? From my brief experience of Naples, it was violent, squalid, Mafia-run and at the time home to the world's best footballer. Perhaps Weymouth is actually like this, but I think not since the local newspaper for the day on which I write reads, and I quote, 'Pensioners book early to beat the rush for free bus passes.' I fancy they won't be remaking *The Godfather* there any day soon. Oh, and of course there's Thomas Hardy and some nice people I know called Wilf and Trish, who run a great little pub. The pub's in Cumbria, though.

Bristol is the gateway to cider and clichés. Rolling hills, seagull-haunted cliffs and long, long vowel sounds. I went on holiday to Minehead in Somerset frequently as a child but apart from a trip to Cheddar Gorge, this was spent in the confines of the Butlins holiday camp and, like airports and Hard Rock Cafes, Butlins is the same wherever you go – and reassuringly so to its many fans, an international language of donkey derbies, crazy golf and disco-dancing contests, at least in 1976. It had Britain's first – and therefore 'biggest and best' – dry ski slope. Despite this, Somerset's skiers have underachieved badly at the Winter Olympics.

In my desultory mental sketchbook, Devon is clotted cream, the Lib Dem heartland of the English Riviera and little cottages. On a recent trip to Plymouth, though, I saw at first hand in their native habitat that relatively new British social group, the urban yokel, or if you prefer, rural chavs – fifteen pimply youths in Burberry caps and Henri Lloyd jackets, racing their Golf GTIs at high speed round a deserted multi-storey car park in a mildly threatening manner. Once you get to Cornwall, it really is a foreign country and all the better for it, more Brittany than Britain, strange and remote, with names taken from witches' spells like Zennor and Mevagissey. Sadly, even this Arthurian land is not untouched by twenty-first-century malaises. If you visit Land's End, and well worth it it is, too, you can pay three quid to park your car and be ushered into 'a range of award-winning undercover exhibitions and attractions' or you can walk half a mile to the actual Land's End, get wet and blown about, look down at the churning waves (resisting that odd compulsion to leap off) and throw bits of sandwich to the gulls. On the day of my visit, every other car was unloading its visitors into the various Land's End 'experiences'.

That's about it for me and the south, then. Every generation, the people of the northern diaspora fan out across southern Britain, like the arrows at the start of *Dad's Army*, in search of work and the like, but unless we put down very deep and gnarly roots most of us never really get the hang of it and are always prone to Des-style mix-ups between Chippenham and Chipping Norton, Canning Town and Camden Town, Hertfordshire and Herefordshire.

There's one part of the south, however, that northerners do know, and are both simultaneously drawn to and repelled by like moths in cloth caps. It's a place they hate to love and love to hate. They may work there, play there, spend their lives there, but they are never really from there; their heart is in the misty north, as they will tell you in their flat and honest vowels, tears in their eyes, after a third rose-petal bellini at the Groucho Club.

Like Doctor Who, Doctor Fox and Miami Sound Machine's Doctor Beat, Doctor Johnson was not a real doctor. He'd have been no good with your plague, scurvy or ague though he would have undoubtedly been top of eighteenth-century medical league tables when it came to elegant aphorisms. One of his most famous is: 'When a man is tired of London he is tired of life.'

Not necessarily true, though, is it? Yes, you may be tired of life but you may just be tired of the Northern Line, the shit drivers, the overpriced paninis, the guns, the congestion charge, the automated ticket barriers, the Hanger Lane gyratory and Chelski.

Wordsworth famously said of the view from Westminster Bridge that 'earth has not anything to show more fair'. This is mental, particularly from someone who lived in the Lake District, where there is something more fair around every hummock. I mean, it's all right. There's a big, greasy-looking river and some tugs and the odd dredger. There's the London Eye, a piece of London that is forever Blackpool, and there's the rather handsome old GLC building. On the other side there's a couple of flash office blocks and Big Ben, of course. So, all in all, you know, pretty good but 'earth has not anything to show more fair'? Mental. And Wordsworth was the one who wasn't doing all the drugs. His mate Thomas De Quincey, who was whacked off his gourd on opium most of the time and didn't care who knew it, put it rather differently: 'A duller spectacle this earth of ours has not to show than a rainy Sunday in London.' Another Lake poet chum, Percy Bysshe Shelley, was even harsher: 'Hell is a city much like London.' I wouldn't go that far but I, like most northerners, maintain a cordial suspicion of 'the Smoke', even though I must have spent months of my life there since my first visit, which was on Saturday 28 April 1973.

Amazing powers of recall? Tragic hoarder of youthful diaries? Neither. Many northerners, maybe most, can tell you the date of their first trip to the capital. They can tell you what they were wearing as well – probably some multicoloured scarf, bobble hat, daft wig or replica shirt ensemble – because for most of us our first time is for the football. Up Wembley Way to the Twin Towers and thence inside a really quite crap football stadium.

That first trip to London, a formative experience for many a northerner, rattle in hand, full of wonder and optimism, is beautifully and memorably captured in an evocative short film of the 1970s. Late on a winter's Saturday evening, passengers disembark from a coach onto a darkened backstreet in Newcastle. Waiting relatives greet warmly; one welcomes a teenage boy cheerily. 'Four-nil at the Arsenal, what about that?' The boy walks on, hands in pockets, surly and uncommunicative. The relative tries again. 'Four-nil away to the Arsenal... You must be delighted.' The boy turns sourly and replies, 'Aye, but I had a packet of crisps a dog would have curled his lip at.'

All right, it wasn't an early effort by Peter Greenaway but an advert for leading Geordie snack comestible Tudor crisps, but it rang true. London would promise much to the provincial – excitement, glamour, sophistication – but this would turn out to be a chimera. Realising this, we'd return home soberly to regale school and work mates with news of London – much as we might have done in the Middle Ages – and they would listen, appalled, to our tales of people who didn't chat at bus stops, overpriced beer and crisps that canines would demur at.

My second trip to London was in the late 1970s when I went with the other precocious teenagers from Mr Spruce's first-year history of art 'A' level group from St John Rigby College. A few months' acquaintance with Modigliani and Rothko had made me quite the young bohemian and I stowed an illicit pack of Gauloises Disque Bleus in my clean underwear, one of the most vile cigarettes ever invented and must-have accessory of the seventies poseur. Armed with these, how could I fail to pull pale, winsome young women in the Tate café? That's if I could make them out through the noxious blue-green fug.

We stayed in Onslow Gardens, Kensington, and dined out in a variety of styles and cuisines. On the first night we went to the International House of Pancakes – oversold rather by its title, I always think – but on the second night, emboldened by our new familiarity with London, we went to a real Italian restaurant and ordered penne arrabiata and a carafe of the house red and chatted loudly about Fauvism and Matisse. I felt like James Bond or at the very least Brian Sewell. Later, though, we reverted to type by 'accidentally' setting off the sprinkler system in the hotel. Next day, Mr Spruce gave us a very public dressing down rich in expletives at Green Park Tube station.

Ah, the Tube. Before we first visit London, every northerner secretly fears the Tube; it sounds like something out of *Quatermass and the Pit* and the map at first glance looks like a Piet Mondrian or an autopsy diagram of one of a cow's four stomachs. Then we slowly become acclimatised to it and eventually we come to pride ourselves on our knowledge of it, wearing it as a badge of honour in a way no Londoner ever would. It's our version of The Knowledge, the arcane lore of the London cabbie: 'Royal College of Art, mate, no problem. Bakerloo to Embankment, across the footbridge, five stops to High Street Ken, stand in the rear carriage, the exit's right in front of you, lovely cappuccino at the café by the florist's. Tell Carlo I sent you...'

The Tube map, done in his spare time in 1931 by London Transport employee Harry Beck, is justly famous as a brilliant design concept. Beck grasped that since the railway ran mostly underground, the actual physical locations of the stations were irrelevant in knowing how to get to one station from another; only the topology of the railway mattered. London Transport didn't think it would catch on. Now, it's way more than a traveller's tool. It's iconic. You can buy posters and T-shirts featuring it and there's a very funny non-game based around it called Mornington

Crescent (tune in to *I'm Sorry I Haven't a Clue*, the funniest programme on the radio). It's even been turned into a rather sweet piece of art by Simon Patterson called 'The Great Bear'.

The Tube itself is quite brilliant in what it does, i.e. transporting people cheaply and efficiently from one bit of London to another. It's unsurpassed as a marriage of form and function. But for all the licensed buskers playing jazz guitar arrangements of Mozart and the poems on the underground and the tarted-up stations, it remains the unloveliest thing ever. Off-peak, it's soulless; at rush hour it's a fetid and dehumanising journey into hell which, as Jean-Paul Sartre nearly said, is other people's armpits. Last night's garlic and the thin hiss of an iPod wafts gently down the metal tube between the serried ranks of tired, anxious commuters seething with resentment at the relaxed laughter, radiant youth and gigantic wardrobe-sized rucksacks of the Italian teenagers standing by the doors.

Not even the most sentimental of Cockneys can ever have grown moist-eyed thinking of it. Unlike the Glasgow sleeper, no one could write a stirring John Buchan-style romantic thriller around it. They tried with *Sliding Doors* and it was unspeakable.

No one can ever be part of the queue traipsing up those steps at the Central Line at Tottenham Court Road looking blank-eyed at the adverts for *Chicago* and cut-price electrical stores without feeling part of some grim forced march or ritual sacrifice. The Goodge Street lifts – there are four of them and they wouldn't look out of place in an industrial-sized abattoir – always feel like a dispiriting social experiment into how rude, panic-stricken and dehumanised the average commuter can become. Glassy-eyed with fatigue and the fear that they may have to wait ten seconds for the next one, they charge in, crushing old ladies and tiny Japanese schoolgirls underfoot. Maybe they're all really keen to get out of London.

Periodically, different bits of London become fashionable. It was Camden back in the heady, buzzy Britpop boom of the mid 1990s when gaggles of trendy Japanese girls would go to the Good Mixer pub in search of Damon Albarn and find only three members of Menswear and a pool table. For the last few years, it has been the East End. Shoreditch, Hoxton and Hackney are three conceptual entities jostling to occupy the same physical space with residents of the area altering their addresses in line with current fashion. At the time of writing, Hoxton is winning and is the 'manor' de la mode. That said, Hackney is 'edgier'. If you crave the kudos of living somewhere 'edgy', i.e. with a high burglary rate and a good chance of getting mugged at a bus stop by a fifteen-year-old crackhead, you'll say you live in Hackney. 'Edginess' is another notion we northerners find hard to understand and rather laughable. Having often grown up in dangerous parts of hard towns rather than, say, Cheltenham, we're in no hurry to move back to such places, however good it is for our street cred.

I'm actually writing these words in Old Shoreditch station. It isn't a station any more, of course, but a rather chichi coffee bar where I'm playing with the froth of my vanilla latte. I think the man at the next table is the lead singer of a minor indie band on their third or fourth album. I catch a trailing strand of conversation from the table to my left. 'I'm, like, saving up like crazy cos I want to spend four months in South America.' It is all a very Shoreditch scenario.

The tiny alleys and spidery streets around ultra-fashionable Hoxton Square are crowded with Vietnamese kitchens, margarita bars and happening clubs whose flyers boast DJ sets by Gilles Peterson and all-night 'crunk' and 'grime'. It would seem next to impossible to buy anything useful, like a pair of pliers or an umbrella, but day or night you will never want for a plate of sushi or a twelve-inch dubplate. The older generation of taxi drivers will tell you that before its gentrification, this was a bad neighbourhood, a notorious den of rogues, a thieves' kitchen. At three quid for a milky coffee, I reckon it still is.

The East End, the quintessential London, is more conceptual than actual. Successive waves of Luftwaffe bombers, town planners, developers and immigrants have altered the shape and make-up of the area for ever but Cockney mythology and iconography hold some things very dear. They get all maudlin and tearful about some stuff while northerners view them with a mixture of boredom, mirth and hostility.

Chelsea Pensioners and Pearly Kings, for instance. What is it about London that even the old codgers and market traders have to ponce about in ridiculous costumes doing what can only be described as 'showing off'? Northerners – and I say this fully cognisant of exception-proving rule breakers like Liam Gallagher and Freddie Starr – are generally inoculated against showing off by slaps administered in childhood. 'Showing off', like 'showing us up', commits the cardinal sin of drawing attention to yourself. Pearly Kings and Queens: really, what is all that about? They are market traders, the people who sell you knock-off batteries and pressure cookers and snide versions of Nike tracksuits. Chelsea pensioners at least have served their country in the military; that's how they get the dubious honour of a three-quarter-length scarlet tunic and a stupid hat.

The north-south divide is not just geographical and cultural, it's temperamental. Northerners are often referred to from a southern perspective as dour, perhaps because we don't see the heartwarming side of the Kray Twins or because our fishmongers don't dress in rhinestones and throw parades. We secretly treasure this opinion of us and have even turned it into a cultural emblem, be it Les Dawson's bleak, grotesque humour, Joy Division looking miserable in long overcoats on a Hulme flyover or Alan Bennett's self-mocking melancholia. Take chimney sweeps. A northern Victorian chimney sweep would, very sensibly, feel that life had dealt him a poor hand and as he forced another urchin up the flue he'd probably utter a grim aphorism and hawk up some phlegm. Compare this with the London chimney sweep as portrayed by Dick Van Dyke, always grinning, tap-dancing and singing about how lucky he is to know 'Maori Parpens'.

Nothing about the Cockney proletariat sets our teeth on edge more than their 'cheeriness'. A few years back, I went to see *My Fair Lady* starring Martine McCutcheon at the National Theatre. Pretty good it was too. But halfway through, something really quite dreadful happened. The scene changed from Park Lane to what was unmistakably some theatre director's notion of a 'cheery' down-at-heel street scene in Lambeth or the Isle of Dogs. Slatternly women in shawls shrieked horribly as 'cheery' costermongers pinched them on the bum. Scamps and scallywags ran about nicking apples from barrows; chestnuts were sold and the contents of chamber pots flung about. Fear and apprehension began to grip me as it does when you hear the whine of the dentist's drill or the opening music to *Last of the Summer Wine*. But in this case, it was the fast-approaching whine and clatter of Dennis Waterman and a troop of choreographed 'geezers'. The clatter was the sound of the dustbin lids they had attached to their feet as they stomped and hoofed around. The whine was the awful version – I'm not sure there is a good one – of 'Get Me To The Church On Time'. When Dennis and co. got to the bit about 'having a whopper' and actually hooked their thumbs behind their lapels, that inexplicable Cockney gesture of, well, 'cheeriness', I could feel the blood drain from my face. I turned and was gratified to see that the journalist Tom Sutcliffe sitting next to me, a Yorkshireman, was similarly ashen and stricken. It took four or five strong drinks at the interval before I could be persuaded back in for the second half. At heart, northerners feel the Cockney lower orders shouldn't be so happy with their pathetic lot but organising a whelk stall strike and staging a violent revolution, whatever the Queen Mum might think.

We don't really get the Londoner's much-vaunted love of the royal family. I have never heard a northerner say 'Ma'am' except as a joke. We were really not that devoted to the Queen Mother. We never called her the Queen Mum and we didn't automatically say 'Gawd bless her' after mentioning her name, the way Catholics involuntarily nod after uttering the word Jesus. My dad used to say she was a game old thing but I think that was because she used to grin a lot and liked the odd Gordon's or twelve. True, though, the north did get as delirious with grief as anywhere in the semi-mystical passion over Diana's death. At the time, I saw a young man in a New Order T-shirt weeping openly over a newspaper in Manchester's Piccadilly Gardens. But I'm not sure we can draw any conclusions from that very strange episode in the nation's history. Think again of the scenario: a beautiful dead blonde princess being driven in a cortege of black cars along a deserted motorway while grieving subjects throw flowers, escorting her to her final resting place on a wooded island. It's closer to *Le Morte d'Arthur* than modern Britain.

A few hardy and devoted souls – harsher commentators may say 'nutters' – get up at dawn to take a coach down from Preston to stand in The Mall in a thin drizzle waving a plastic Union Jack on one of the Queen's birthdays but they are the exception rather than the rule. Why is this? Well, the royal family live smack in the middle of London, of course, and we see them as a world away from life in the north (although there's a persistent rumour that the Queen has a weekend place in the Forest of Bowland). Also, the north is awash with Irish immigrants, trade unionists, children of coal miners, factory workers and the like, a more generally leftist and anti-establishment stew than, say, the population of Woking.

But more than the Cockney's devotion to the royals, there is another London love affair we northerners find baffling and irritating. It is why, when I read this by Richard Littlejohn, writing in *The Spectator* in February 2006, I almost choked on my overpriced London panini:

> I'm always amused by the quaint expressions used to excuse criminality in certain communities. For instance, Scousers have the term 'scally' to describe someone who makes a career out of petty theft. 'He's a scally, our kid is. Nothing serious, just a bit of robbing.' This week I stumbled across a new one from Wales. 'Hobbling' is the word they use to describe the practice of working while simultaneously claiming unemployment or incapacity benefit. To hobble: a colloquialism meaning to commit fraud.

Now, while one should never expect common sense or humanity from the pen of Richard Littlejohn, least of all in the pages of *The Spectator*, this really does take the flipping biscuit. You will note that the certain communities of which he sniffily speaks are considerably, demonstrably, defiantly north of London. The reason this strikes me as the most diabolical liberty, guv, is that when it comes to glamorising the criminal classes, no one can beat the Cockneys.

Only yesterday, I saw a briefly fashionable young actor (his name escapes me but he was in *Layer Cake* or *Lock Stock* or *Snatch* or some other tedious bit of gangster porn) extolling his love for West Ham on some sports show, and proudly claiming, 'The East End – home of hardcore naughty people!'

Hardcore naughty people, geezers, wide boys, hard men, rogues, ducking and diving, a bit tasty, well handy; if anyone has cornered the market in euphemisms for scum it is the Londoner. For instance, it is apparently quite acceptable in the boozers and parlours of Stepney and Poplar for a grown man, when asked of his livelihood, to reply, 'Oh, bit of this, bit of that, bobbin' and weavin', you know.' In Halifax and Huyton, we call this 'being unemployed' or 'skiving' or perhaps even 'thievery'.

I have met people from London who genuinely like Vinnie Jones, actually think he's a 'diamond geezer'. No one north of the Blue Boar services has ever suffered from this particular insanity. The northern view of such 'geezers' is best illustrated by a character in that fine Geordie institution, *Viz*. In this particular strip, the central protagonist is a fat, ugly, balding man in a sheep-skin jacket, festooned with tacky gold jewellery. He's a swaggering bigot who speaks in rhyming slang, boasts of his criminal connections and bears an uncanny resemblance to former *EastEnder* Mike Reid. In each edition, he beats his wife and is disloyal to his friends while declaring his love of family, kiddies and country. He is called, with admirable succinctness and wit, 'Big Vern, Cockney Wanker'.

This Cockney cult of the criminal, though, reaches its zenith (or nadir maybe) in the veneration of two dead brothers, the enduring nature of which found me one winter's day in 2006 making my way gingerly through the shabby streets of Bethnal Green looking for Britain's most notorious pub.

If you were to find yourself at a loose end and thirsty on the Whitechapel Road, you could do worse than drop into the Blind Beggar, but I doubt it would detain you long. It's a reasonable enough pub with a couple of half-decent bitters and some rather old-fashioned 'hot pub fayre'. There are two cats called Pip and Molly that slink about looking proprietorial and the staff are friendly enough. But none of this is why the Blind Beggar is a tourist destination for the more morbid sightseer.

No, this is the pub where, in the summer of 1966, while Scott Walker in his honeyed baritone sang 'The Sun Ain't Gonna Shine Anymore', Ronnie Kray took out his Mauser and shot fellow crook George Cornell in the head at point blank range. Cornell had allegedly called him, unwisely I think, 'a fat poof'. The Krays were infamous local gangsters who have become as iconic in London mythology as the Queen Mum (Gawd bless her), beefeaters and Arthur Daley. The Krays, we are told, loved their mum, were always smart and polite and hardly ever killed anyone really except a few low-life of their own ilk. You may get a different view of the matter if you ask one of the many East End pub landlords, bookies, café proprietors and shopkeepers who, according to John Pearson's *The Profession of Violence*, all enjoyed the dubious and costly benefits of the Krays' 'protection'. But don't ask them over a pint in the Blind Beggar. They may not be especially forthcoming. The pub is actually known locally to some as The Tardis as apparently 50,000 people were there on the fateful night. Naturally none of them saw anything, guv. When Ronnie Kray died in 1998, the East End came to a standstill, plumed horses pulled the hearse through streets thronged with mourners and Barbara Windsor (predictably) and Morrissey (disappointingly) sent flowers.

I finished my pint of bitter and slunk off to the Tube, feeling somehow grubby and without checking for the bullet holes which some say remain in the bar woodwork. When I was next at a computer, I looked up on the internet some other people's impressions of the Blind Beggar. Most were complimentary, some were even gushing. One comment, posted at beerintheevening.com, read: 'One of the friendliest places I know. Bar staff are lovely and always welcoming. Never any trouble.'

Never any trouble? NEVER ANY TROUBLE? The only pub in England whose unique selling point is the fact that some poor sod got his brains blown out there? A pub that still has the pictures of the murderer on the wall where most pubs have a snap of Lulu or Frank Bough pushing over a pile of pennies? Never any trouble? Wouldn't a more accurate assessment have been: 'Never any trouble. Unless you count the infamous slaying.'

To try and get a more edifying take on London and its rich history and to perhaps dispel my now ingrained Lancastrian prejudices, I decided to visit the Museum of London. In this, I was seemingly unique among everyone I know, London native or not. No one knew where it was, or what it might entail. Even my cab driver was vague and despite their occasional bad press, London's famous cabbies are usually pretty knowledgeable and entertaining. Unlike their New York counterparts they aren't actually frightening and unlike their German brethren they don't consider it their patriotic duty to relieve you of all your money (I once saw the same Frankfurt traffic island three times before 'having a word').

Eventually, thanks to the nice brown tourist signs and one of those £1 maps you get from a dispenser, I found it in a squat neo-Brutalist structure behind the Barbican with an incongruously neat little garden and a doughnut-shaped balcony. As I arrived, three generations of a Spanish family were wheezing and panting up the stolidly unmoving escalator. It didn't seem auspicious. Nor did the snatch of conversation I overheard in the entrance hall between a kindly posh teacher and his young charge.

'Did you enjoy that, Rupert?'

'Yes, but I'd have enjoyed it more if so much of it hadn't been closed. And so dark. And confusing.'

Once inside, though, some of my fears are dispelled. There is no animatronic Dennis Waterman in costermonger garb doing a sinister clanking robotic knees-up. There are no short visual presentations on the history of pie and mash or rhyming slang. There is in fact a pretty bloody good visual representation of the growth of London as a settlement with lots of CGI cavemen with spears and the Ice Age in twenty seconds, that kind of thing. I don't know about you but I always start off round museums at an appropriately sedate pace with an expression of intense concentration but soon pick up speed and by the time I get to the gift shop I'm practically jogging. Thus I was soon into the section on early London civilisation. There was a tiny carved figure that had apparently been found in a mud flat in Dagenham, which was a stylised, sexualised representation of Odin. Small, sexy and from Dagenham, it could also have been the late Dudley Moore. In a charming tableau, a kaleidoscopically cosmopolitan class of eight-year-olds were listening with rapt attention to a young guide telling them about skeletons they'd found in nearby Cheapside. The riot of colour and headscarves, beads and braids and turbans, shapes and sizes of kid each asking eager questions in broad Cockernee said something profound and sweet about the city. There was no finer exhibit of real London life in the whole museum.

There was a great deal of signage which promised, thrillingly, The Great Fire of London Experience. Ascending a rather excessive ramp, I made my way into a tiny darkened room about the size of a prison cell. There was one other visitor already there – an Eastern European man judging by his muttered mobile phone calls – who behaved really rather oddly, shuffling around, rooting through his bag and generally looking everywhere but at the tableau presented behind glass along the far wall. Perhaps, in his Moldovan home, he was used to something more exciting. It was certainly inconceivable that anything could have been less exciting. The tableau consisted of a quite dull, very murky sort of architect's model of seventeenth-century London which, over the course of several tedious minutes, glowed very gently, almost imperceptibly, with an ochre hue. Far too gently, in fact, to see what was going on. With my face pressed firmly against the glass, I still couldn't make out even the River Thames let alone any major conflagration. In the background a tape played and someone, Martin Jarvis probably, read out period accounts lurid with disaster and mayhem and flames licking the sky, none of which was visible. Perhaps in a concession to political correctness they had tried to downplay the horror of it all. Or perhaps it was just broken. Whatever, I felt The Great Fire of London Experience was putting it somewhat grandly. The Great Fire Mild Diversion would be nearer the truth.

Emerging blinking into the strip-lighting of the museum, I found a display devoted to 'ordinary Londoners'. Prominent among this was one Arthur Harding, who turned out to be an East End criminal. Typical, I thought. It occurred to me that instead of talking up its thieves and thugs, its Jack the Rippers and Kray Twins, London should lionise the ordinary Londoners who marched down Cable Street against Oswald Mosley's Blackshirts. Or the Bryant and May match girls who went on strike in 1888 for better wages and conditions and succeeded against enormous odds in a landmark battle for women and the working class. You might not be able to find a part for Johnny Depp or the Kemp brothers in these films but London really does need to sort out its heroes.

On leaving the museum, I strolled down Cheapside itself. There were no skeletons there, I'm afraid to say, just the usual ubiquitous urban street panorama of Starbucks, Boots, Vodafone, Thomas Cook and Bovis construction work. (If the north is the land of Hovis, London is the land of Bovis, believe me.)

Tucked away unassumingly across from a branch of the Body Shop is Bow Church, at the heart of the financial 'City' and famous all over the world as the epicentre of Cockneydom. It's a nice little church too, good for a quiet moment in the middle of all that brisk trading in pork belly futures or whatever. But the most famous part about the church is its bells, which are, claims the noticeboard, 'woven into the folklore of the City of London'. In 1392 Dick Whittington, a Gloucester lad trying his luck in the big city, heard Bow Bells call him back to London to become Lord Mayor. The famous toll ends the medieval nursery rhyme 'Oranges And Lemons': 'I do not know say the Great Bells of Bow.' During the Second World War the BBC's World Service broadcast a recording of Bow Bells, made in 1926, as a symbol of hope to the free people of Europe. And most famous of all, to be born within the sound of Bow Bells is the mark of a true Cockney.

But, hurrah, the actual Bow Bells rang while I was there. Within the sound of them I heard hardly any actual Cockney accents. I heard American drawls, sensual Spanish, breathless Italian, Turkish and Latvian (I had to ask her, nice girl). The first Cockney I heard was from a newspaper vendor who seemed to be berating a customer for not having the right change. That would have been it, but for two surly youths, their pinched faces volcanic with pimples, dressed in the cheap, nasty uniform of the urban urchin: fake Nike, hoodies, flammable polyester trackie bottoms that would go up in a single whoosh, outsized jeans. They both smoked in that affected way that people who are trying really hard to be hard do; fag between crooked index and middle finger, eyes narrowed, sucking desperately as if trying to actually remove by suction the B&H logo. These two spoke the loud braying, lazy R-ed cockney of Loadsamoney, trying hard to intimidate those around them and signally failing. We were all too busy looking for St Paul's.

Prince Charles once described the buildings around St Paul's cathedral as 'a carbuncle on the face of a much-loved friend'.

Unusually, he was right. From Cheapside, it's obscured almost entirely by a grim octagonal sixties thing which houses Ricco Menswear on its street level. As I pass by, a 50% off sale is in full swing and Ricco is doing a brisk trade in anonymous polyester suits, presumably to the less stylish of the young men that make big money hereabouts.

A little further on, though, and you suddenly find the kind of thing that might have inspired Wordsworth to make his disloyal and intemperate remarks. You get a whiff, a real brackish, ozoney whiff, of what makes native Londoners hook their thumbs behind their lapels and tap dance on bin lids, singing 'Maybe It's Because I'm A Londoner' as they go. The riverside of the Thames at Bankside has blossomed these last few years; the old girl, or old Father if you prefer, has tarted itself up good and proper, 'had a makeover' in the modern parlance. A thin ribbon of steel flings itself from the St Paul's shore to the great brick cliff face of the Tate Modern. This is Richard Rogers' Millennium Bridge, which wobbled so terrifyingly under the weight of the opening-day crowds that they had to immediately close it again for six months. It's an impressive thing, though. There is, as we shall see, an even more impressive Millennium Bridge in Newcastle, but let's not be churlish. Credit where it is due. Walking across Millennium Bridge in either direction, between those two stunning buildings from two different eras, contemplating the vast muscular sweep of the river with Tower Bridge on the left and the vista from the Gherkin down to the Houses of Parliament on the right, with the launches and dredgers and river buses endlessly churning this majestic if slightly muddy waterway, you do feel at the centre of one of the world's undeniably great cities.

Unlike Wordsworth, who dashed off a stanza or two, I react as all awestruck modern travellers do. I take a picture with my mobile phone. London, on the right night in the right light, is truly fabulous.

At heart, though, the northerner is never too downhearted to leave London behind and head up country. As the old-fashioned train guards would say on old-fashioned trains that still plumed themselves in smoke as they strained out of Euston and King's Cross, 'All aboard...'

We are for the north.

All Change

According to legend, the north begins at the RAC Traffic Centre on the M6 just at the point where the road surface changes from tarmac to cobbles. Michael Winner believes that the north begins at Oxford Circus. 'Anything north of Oxford Street is just ridiculous,' he once said, probably with his mouth full of a rare and cruel pâté made from otters. According to a posting on the Leyton Orient website, the north begins at Barnet. Absurd, but of course if you think Leyton is the Orient, you evidently have Mark Thatcher's sense of direction.

It's more common – axiomatic, in fact – to say that the north begins at the Watford Gap. Not, note, north of Watford. 'North of Watford', used incorrectly by residents of Fulham, accompanied by a wave of the hand, means bad restaurants, restricted shopping, spears, wolves and woad. But it's a modern misnomer. The Watford Gap has nothing to do with the nondescript Hertfordshire town whose football team is beloved of Elton John.

No, this Watford is a little village in Northamptonshire on the B5385 just outside Daventry. Its famous Gap is not a branch of that American place that sells chinos but a low pass through the gentle Northamptonshire hills that's been used by the Romans, the first canal and railway engineers and more latterly the M1. Watling Street (now the A5) runs through it. So does the West Coast Main Line railway and the Grand Union Canal. For years this was the traditional crossing point between the

Midlands and the south-east and hence, by extension, the gate-way to the north as far as Londoners were concerned.

There used to be a well-known coaching inn here actually called the Watford Gap but you'd be hard pushed to get a pint there now; it was boarded up last time I looked. Instead, travellers going with heavy heart to London or with light step to the north can get a skinny decaf latte and a jaw-droppingly expensive pasty at the nearby Watford Gap service station located on the M1 between Junctions 16 and 17 and mildly celebrated as the first motorway service station in the UK. There's actually a plaque, just by the shelves full of lads' mags, gigantic cut-price quiz books and tins of speciality humbugs.

Motorway catering may begin here but as far as I'm concerned the north certainly doesn't. Northampton, despite its name, is not the north. It may not be exactly the south but it is undeniably, well, Midlands-ish. The accent is a sort of yokel Cockney. Des O'Connor comes from hereabouts, as do the goth group Bauhaus. Essentially I think Northampton is confused. But whereas Birmingham and Wolverhampton feel vaguely if inconclusively northern, Northampton's gravitational pull takes it south to the metropolis. In the eighties, the Northampton Development Council produced a really quite poor promotional seven-inch single in which aliens come to Northampton (Des O'Connor or Bauhaus fans, perhaps) and find that, as the cheesy chorus goes, 'It's only sixty miles by road or rail.' From where is never made clear but it doesn't have to be. Basically, whoop-de-do, it's sixty miles to London and that's a rather fawning, forelock-tugging gesture of kinship that no northern town would ever make.

The UK edition of the popular Lonely Planet travel guidebooks posits that the north begins in the Derbyshire Dales somewhere around Bakewell, home of Britain's most celebrated tart.

Now there may be some truth in this. Hereabouts the soft chalk-iness of southern England starts to stiffen with grit and lime-stone; there are proper ridges, escarpments and big bleak brawny moors. The grit is philosophical as well as conceptual; on Kinder Scout in April 1932, hundreds of ramblers wilfully 'trespassed' to reclaim ancient rights of way on to the mountain, a hugely significant event commemorated in song by Ewan MacColl and Chumbawamba. It should be said, though, that most of the tres-passers came from Manchester.

Head a little further north and a little further west and you reach the debatable lands of Staffordshire, perhaps England's most enigmatic county. It has pottery and a bull terrier. It has its own local delicacy, the oatcake, a sort of heavy-duty tortilla with the texture of flannel, which exiled 'clayheads' get all tearful about and is actually pretty good with cheese and bacon. Also, in Port Vale FC, it has the only football team in England not named after a place – it's actually in Burslem – but a building, Port Vale House, where the inaugural meeting took place. As I write these words, Vale's most famous supporter Robbie Williams has pledged an undisclosed but substantial sum of money to help the club. In doing so, he has shot up in my estimation, so much so that I have almost forgiven him for 'Angels'.

Burslem (along with Stoke, Longton, Hanley and Tunstall) is one of the five towns which make up what's thought of as Stoke-on-Trent. Say this in the pubs of Fenton, though (town number six) and you might get your head kicked in by local geography casuals, should they exist. From my experience of the denizens of Stoke-on-Trent, largely gleaned by the unscientific procedure of studying who gets on and off the train there as I pass through en route to Manchester, it would seem the people of the area need little encouragement to turn nasty. I always feel quietly relieved when we get to Macclesfield. Taken from a Stoke-on-Trent online forum comes this proud assertion, which I quote uncorrected: 'If your from there it is the friendliest city in the world which is great we dont want shitty southerners coming and telling us how shit our home is we know it already. Oh and the fact that were the hardest and Oatcakes.'

But for all the funny foods and simmering aggression, I'm still not having it that Staffordshire is the north. For one thing, the football teams aren't good enough. Sorry but it's true. Its sing-song accent is undeniably of a Midlands lilt. Wolverhampton is in Staffordshire, for God's sake, and how much more Midlands can you get than Dave Hill and kipper ties?

But go a little further north and you reach the spot where I would say that the north undeniably begins. Though it's in a very classy and grand county, it's far from classy and grand. It's an iconic structure though it isn't architecturally impressive or visually striking. For homecoming northerners it is the first sign that they are back in the right place, their moral and cultural compass righted. For southrons heading up country, it is here that the realisation begins that you may be in foreign country, as the vowels flatten and the skies grow leaden and the track curves away from you to the hills and moors and chimneys of the north. Welcome to Crewe station. Please make sure you have all your belongings with you before leaving the train.

As a non-driver without a desk job, I spend my life on trains. I have become skilled in reading every nuance of train travel. I can tell by the timbre of the intercom's chime whether it's good or bad news. I know by the way the engine dies just how long we'll be in this siding in Nuneaton. I know instinctively when we're going to be diverted via Leighton Buzzard. I can play the network like one of those American railway hobos Bob Dylan wanted to be, knowing just where to change for Penrith on a Friday night, which carriage to sit in to make the quickest time from platform six into the new Bullring shopping centre in Birmingham, how much the Opal Fruits are on the trolley. I have become immune to and philosophical about some railway irritants and increasingly irritated by others. I'm currently obsessed with the way the 'senior conductor', drunk with power and the sound of his own voice crackling through the PA, will declaim with the verbiage and prolixity of Larry Olivier doing Shakespeare, until something goes wrong, when he suddenly turns into Buster Keaton doing Harold Pinter, all mysterious pauses and menacing silences. They lovingly list, as if this were the 12.20 from Frankfurt to Dusseldorf circa 1938, all the things you can't do, the tickets you can't travel with, the noises you can't make, the things you can't eat, the places you can't put your bag and so on before becoming oddly mute and uninformative when you actually need to know something useful, like why we've been stuck in a tunnel near High Wycombe for three hours.

Sorry, where was I? Oh yes. Crewe. Balham may be the gateway to the south (an actual Southern Railway advertisement from 1926, later a legendary Peter Sellers sketch) but Crewe is surely the gateway to the north. It's from here that you head on to Manchester and Liverpool, the Lake District, Lancashire, the Pennines, Yorkshire and the bracing coast. Northerners come here on those first exciting trips to London. At some point, most people have found themselves on Crewe station, trying to get some kip on a hard bench or stamping their feet and watching their breath cloud the night air, waiting for a milk train and coppering up for a hot chocolate.

Making sure I have all my personal belongings with me, I detrain, as the current lingo has it, to find that the station clock reads 1398, which is more than a little disconcerting. I'm sure Jude Law and Kate Moss would find Crewe outré and behind the times but surely it's not still the end of the fourteenth century here. The clock, then, isn't working. The automatic doors at the information centre are broken. In fact the whole station is somewhat underwhelming, given its enormous strategic importance as a communication centre and the hub of the British rail network. Maybe it's just too busy to ponce about turning itself into a heritage site but it's a shame it's not as imposing as Grand Central or King's Cross. It's just as important. The Lemon Tree café seems to be doing well, though, and I note, with a little 'ahh', that two students are cuddled up fast asleep on rucksacks in the waiting room. If they do get round to a refurb, that would make a nice little statue, sweetly emblematic of Crewe.

Crewe is younger than America. Before 1837, when the Grand Junction Railway opened its station in fields near Crewe Hall, the population of the nearest village was just seventy, all of them probably wearing smocks. But a new town grew up alongside the increasingly busy station, with the population exploding to reach 40,000 by 1871. The GJR's chief engineer Joseph Locke helped lay out the town and railway money brought prosperity, schools, churches, a gasworks, a hospital, a public baths and a large park. Strolling here on a fine chilly spring morning, watching a young mum teaching a toddler to ride a trike and two elderly ladies sharing a bar of Dairy Milk, you wouldn't guess that this fine patch of civic greenery is a product of ruthless Victorian railway politics. The London and North Western Railway (the GJR's successor) bought the land and donated it to the town as a park designed by their own engineer Francis Webb in order to prevent the rival Great Western Railway from building a railway line through it.

Jonathan Glancey, the architectural writer, has spoken glowingly of Crewe's heritage, of it being one of the world's great workshops, building Rolls-Royce and Bentley cars as well as building the fine locomotives that sped expresses northward from

Euston and south from Glasgow, Edinburgh, Liverpool and Manchester, 'all of them pausing for water, tea and buns at Crewe'. He talks of a town bursting with civic pride, with workers' educational initiatives in every library and church hall, a true community 'that would have stayed a happily sustainable one if the railways hadn't been privatised a century on'. At Christmas 2005 (the timing of these things is always immaculate, don't you think?), the company that owns what remains of Crewe Works announced that a third of the 1,000 people still working there would be made redundant. At its peak, Crewe Works employed 20,000. Soon that figure will have dwindled to zero. It's the same old song with a bitter little refrain that you hear again and again in the blighted industrial towns of the north.

But away with such gloom and into Crewe, gateway to the north. Out of the station onto a confusingly anonymous bridge that gives no clue where the actual town might be. Turning left at random, I immediately find I am on Gresty Road, which, as anyone who's spent swathes of their life poring over Rothman's football yearbooks or glued to *Grandstand* will tell you, is home to the exotically named Crewe Alexandra Football Club and what must be the most easily accessible football ground in England.

Fairly quiet on a Thursday morning, though. Two youths in the ubiquitous hoodie style of the early twenty-first century are trying to be menacing by a bus stop but failing because of the utter ridiculousness of their appearance. I know it's a sure sign of middle age when you start chortling at how young people dress but, really, a hood worn over a flat cap. The effect is less lethal urban gangster than senile old bloke unaware that he's put two hats on.

A piece of venerable graffiti on a low wall claims 'Dario Gradi is God'. Now in case you think Crewe has a special affection for Italian film directors or left-wing playwrights, let me explain.

Milanese by birth, Dario Gradi is, as of 2006, the longest-serving manager in the football league, arriving at the club in 1983 when Betamax was still slugging it out with VHS and digital music for computers meant Gary Numan. In an industry that's become synonymous with venal greed and posturing, Gradi is renowned for nurturing young talent and for his good humour and loyalty. In Crewe, there's a street named after him (Dario Gradi Close) as well as a band, Dario G, who had a handbag house hit in 1997 with 'Sunchyme'. He has the freedom of the borough and probably never needs to buy a pint in south Cheshire ever again. Crewe seems to encourage loyalty: local MP, the redoubtable Gwyneth Dunwoody, has represented the town since 1974. Crewe and Nantwich have a joint council and because Nantwich is substantially posher, resentment simmers in Crewe. According to a Crewe website, 'the borough treats Crewe as a shithole and anything worthwhile (decent baths, skate park, roller hockey rink, etc...) goes to Nantwich'. One for Gwyneth, I think.

Out of Gresty Road, I am lured left by a sign on a lamp-post that promises excitingly the 'Nantwich Road Shopping Mile'. This would seem to be mainly of interest to people shopping for kebabs and Bacardi Breezers. I have never seen so many pubs and takeaways. The Station Hotel, oddly the focus for a recent novel by Alexei Sayle, has rooms for twenty-five quid a night and you might need them if you sampled the sundry wares of the Nantwich Road Shopping Mile. The Barrel is offering 2 for 1s on premium lagers, free birthday drinks and cut-price pitchers.

Feeling peckish myself, I decide to try something a little more traditional. Goodwin's chip shop is, like George Orwell's mythical pub The Moon Under Water, the sort of place you feared no longer existed. As well as the chippy bit with the glass counter and the battered sausages and cod in neat glistening rows and the red-hot metal strip perfect for burning your forehead on, there's an adjoining café section. This has tables and those glass sugar servers that miraculously pour just one teaspoon when you tilt them. There are red leather booklets with menus inside. There are nice pine chairs and tables, a kiddies' menu, cans of Vimto and jam roly-poly for afters. There are ketchup dispensers in the form of those comedically outsized plastic tomatoes that always have a congealed bit of red on the nozzle.

Elsie and Hazel behind the counter encourage me in the direction of the lunchtime special: fish, chips, mushy peas, mug of tea or soft drink and two rounds of bread and butter for four pounds. I take a seat feeling absurdly, childishly happy about having fish and chips for dinner in Crewe on a crisp February afternoon. And it was my dinner. Not my lunch. Gordon Gekko in *Wall Street* sneered that lunch was for wimps but it would have been more accurate to say that lunch is for southerners. Up north we have our dinner in the middle of the day and our tea at night. A little defiantly, my Scouse agent and I will still talk about going out 'for our tea' even if we're dining somewhere dreadfully chichi in the West End (which we don't do, obviously). And don't get me started on supper. A TV producer once invited me round for 'supper' and I was genuinely flummoxed. Supper means something very specific in the north and I was rather bemused by the prospect of going round to her house in Chiswick at half ten at night in my dressing gown to have digestive biscuits and cheese off my lap on the settee while watching the telly.

Dave Goodwin, eponymous proprietor of the fine chippy where I had my dinner, is from London but has lived everywhere and is now domiciled in Winsford, a town some seven miles away, built on the salt industry. He worked in retail for years. After seventeen years' loyal service he was made redundant by Littlewoods and the next day joined BHS. After seven years they made him redundant too. 'So I thought I'd buy a chippy.' After consulting the maps, drawing circles with compasses and scrutinising the competition, he bought this one, a great big gleaming place on Crewe's Nantwich Road, a thoroughfare apparently famous among Crewe's hungry revellers.

'There are forty-one takeaways on this street. Didn't you notice? Fish and chips are dying out. There'll always be some people who love their fish supper and won't have anything else but the glory days have gone.'

I can remember those glory days well. When I was a little kid in Wigan, seemingly everyone went to the chippy on a Friday night. I'm not sure why this was. Maybe something to do with being flush with the week's wages or not being bothered to cook if you were going out on the town or maybe because the Catholic church forbade meat on Fridays but took a pretty relaxed attitude to cod, plaice and whiting.

Whatever the reason, the Friday night chippy run was a ritual. They queued on the pavement. Some took bowls with them, the sort you might put on a child's head to help with a cheap haircut, and asked for them to be filled with chips, which they'd take home covered with a tea towel. (We didn't do this because my mum thought it was common.)

But as for Crewe, I didn't come here just to have a good feed. I came to find out whether, as I contend, Crewe is really the north. By one fabled criteria, it certainly is; namely the friendliness of the locals and their use of affectionate terms. Within twenty minutes of arriving, I have been loved by several women. Several more have petted me, lover-ed me, one or two even luvvie-d me. Mainly, it has to be said, by ladies of a certain age but twice by women in their twenties, which hopefully proves that this great northern tradition is not dying out.

If you're not used to being talked to in this way, it can be a little disconcerting at first but it's also utterly delightful. And if you want to be really disconcerted, go to Sheffield or Rotherham, where even brawny men will address you as 'love'.

But what do Dave and Elsie and Hazel think? Is Crewe the north? Dave says yes emphatically. Hazel says, 'No, it's the middle,' and goes on to explain a little obliquely, 'On the farm where I grew up there's a tree and that's in the middle of the Cheshire plain. We are in the middle of England, between the hills and the sea.' Then, when Dave's back is turned, she chuckles to me conspiratorially, 'It's the north really. I'm just saying that to wind him up,' implying that the subject is hotly debated every day in this cracking little chip shop.

Back on the Nantwich Road, I decide to test Dave's claim by counting all the takeaways. I give up at twenty-one, though, as my head is spinning with Bombay Gardens and Kebablands and Thai Palaces. My favourite, though, is Full Bellies, which has a kind of winning vulgarity, don't you think?

Armed with some directions to the town centre ('blink and you'll miss it'), I head off down Eddleston Road. According to local legend, Bedford Street is renowned for having the largest number of different house types in south Cheshire. The street (which was bombed during World War Two) features terraced houses, semis, detached houses, flats, three-storey houses and bungalows as well as a prominent church, a scout hut and scout shop as well as a chequered history of nefarious activity. Eddleston Road may have less of a flavour of the souk about it but it's an entertaining stroll up a classically northern street. There are back-to-backs as well as posh double fronteds. Plus there's an array of quirky entrepreneurial ventures: a sex shop coyly offering 'marital aids', Snakey Jakes (Custom Amplification Since 1971), Picnic Basket Quality Sandwiches and A1 Trophies, the sort of little shop selling tiny snooker cups and wooden shields that you often find in northern backstreets and whose continued existence is both mystifying and heartening. There are a number of hairdressers with the now compulsory punning titles, the best of which is Style Counsel, the worst Hair 2 Day Fade Tomorrow, which doesn't exactly sound like a ringing endorsement.

The unexpected appearance in the midst of all this of a Polish delicatessen reflects the town's large and fast-growing population of workers from Eastern Europe. Many have been here since World War Two, hence the long-established Polish Working Men's Club on West Street. But thousands more have come in search of work after Poland's accession to the European Community in 2004. Three thousand arrived in the first eighteen months and now Poles comprise six per cent of Crewe's population. According to a Polish proverb, 'Home is wherever you find your bread.' Well, you can find your bread at Grodziny's as well as your kielbasa and golabki, your poppy seed cake and borsch.

As warned, I don't blink so I find the town centre. Apparently this is due to be demolished and rebuilt soon. The locals I spoke to were very keen on this ('About bloody time too. Eyesore,' said an old man with a sticky bun in the bus station café), but I thought Crewe town centre had rather a pleasant 1930s air about it. There's an imposing clock tower in a vaguely modernist architectural style I can't name, although I have to say I am always a little disappointed when a bus station dominates a town centre. At night, though, it must be a great place to drink your own bodyweight in Smirnoff Ice.

Most days in the broadsheets, Hampstead-based cultural commentators can be found bemoaning the homogenisation of our towns. When they do, they always cite the prevalence of McDonald's, probably because it's a soft American target and the first thing to pop into their head. From my travels, there are two far more inescapable icons that are the ubiquitous emblems of modern Britain: Greggs and the high-visibility tabard.

Crewe has a Greggs and like every other Greggs in the UK it was rammed. Greggs' tasty home-baked fare has become synonymous with that other contemporary phenomenon, the chav, a tasteless, pallid, Burberry-wearing, jewellery-encrusted prole usually found as freakish exhibits on mid-morning TV after they have married their probation officer's mum or some such. While, like every other clear-headed Marxist analyst, I bemoan the fact that the working class has become enfeebled in this way, I do detect a pungent strain of good old-fashioned snobbery in the middle-class demonisation of the chav. Also, I quite like Greggs pasties. You wouldn't want to live off them but after a night on the Breezers, I'd certainly prefer one of their chicken and mushroom jobs to a rocket and shaved Parmesan salad.

Everyone knows about Greggs. The high-visibility tabard, though, now the unofficial uniform of all British working men and women, is something of a personal obsession. Once upon a time these luminescent lime-yellow plastic creations were only sported by AA men, railtrack maintenance men and lollipop ladies, people who genuinely had to a) stand in the pissing rain for hours and b) be quite visible. Now everyone wears them. Doctors, novelists, priests: they're like the leggings and baseball cap of the twenty-first century. And don't tell me that, strictly speaking, a lot of them are actually jackets rather than tabards. I can bang on about that for twenty minutes with a following wind.

Cheshire fantasy writer Alan Garner once described Crewe as 'the ultimate reality'. I'm not entirely sure what he meant by this but I don't think it's complimentary. But get this: Crewe has a crater named after it on Mars approximately 3 km in diameter located at 25° South, 10° West. Beat that, Hampstead. The sun comes out as I stroll by the Lyceum Theatre and I spot with some pleasure the library, a neat municipal building in that same thirties vernacular as the rest of Crewe's town centre.

I love libraries. As a kid I practically lived in Powell Street Library in Wigan, devouring everything from Norse myths to football reference books to Richmal Crompton's William stories to books about Romania, a country I was strangely fascinated by. Margaret Thatcher tried her best to bleed Britain's libraries to death (well, it stands to reason that if you want to read, you should buy a book – what do you think this is, the Soviet Union?) but they seem to be holding their own. Crewe's is the very model of a modern local library: bright, well laid out, festooned with posters of smiling multi-ethnic readers.

Public libraries in the afternoon attract a certain kind of melancholic misfit whom life, it seems, has somehow passed by. I don't know if this is a good description of me but I do like a nice public library of an afternoon. Crewe's was all quiet British busyness: fresh-faced students with reading lists and business-men returning their Andy McNabs and John Grishams as well as the more conventional, even caricatured daytime library clientele. For instance, the man sitting opposite me reading a doorstop-sized sci-fi tract that could stun an ox is wearing the wonkiest glasses I have ever seen. They have only one arm and that sticks out at a right angle like a wayward car radio aerial. Maybe he really is getting coded messages from an alien government beamed into his brain. Whatever, they must be staying on his face by sheer force of will. Now he is gently snorting to himself like a bull. In another corner are two men who clearly rendezvous here every day. One wears a seventies bobble hat; the other has an absurdly long beard, way beyond common sense, like those Indian blokes who are always trying to get into the *Guinness Book of Records*. They are discussing the raging toothache one is suffering from but this doesn't stop him eulogising, in a stage whisper, a new range of linseed bread in the local Tesco.

I stroll idly through the Local Studies section hoping to learn more about the town. Forgoing *All You Need To Know About H₂O: The Story of Crewe's Water Supply and Branch Lines,* I take down a red folder marked *Crewe: A Town of Lost Opportunities. Compiled by Harry Jones.* It's really just a collection of cuttings relating to the thwarted possibility of a transport museum in the town culled from fifty years of local papers. But it's also a sonata of quiet rage. Harry must have been so angry that he could hardly stop his hands from shaking. I bet there was glue everywhere. Having chronicled and lambasted the half-century-long short-sightedness of the local council, Harry seethes by way of conclusion: 'By contrast the photographs at the back of this folder show what one town with foresight and imagination can achieve ... Swindon.' This is surely the most glowing tribute that particular Wiltshire town has ever received. As is always the way when you look through old newspapers, I quickly lose interest in the stuff I'm supposed to be reading and am drawn to those incidental stories elsewhere on the page: 'Methodist Queen Yvonne Is Crowned' and the brilliant 'Baths Car Park Plan Total Lunacy'.

The nice librarian has a definite hint of Welsh in her accent, a reminder that on a clear day you can see the hills of Snowdonia from Cheshire. As I leave, Beard and Bobble Hat are discussing the opening hours of the new Morrisons and the massive robbery from the Securitas depot in Kent that's dominating the news pages, the biggest in British history. 'They got greedy, that was their downfall,' Bobble Hat explains sagely, with the great worldly wisdom of a man who spends all his afternoons in a public library in Crewe.

Back at the station, you can glimpse in their natural habitat another kind of British male often thought of as melancholic and misfitted to the world: the trainspotter. I try to engage one in conversation but clearly he is elsewhere, his rapt face shining with pleasure and concentration as he studies the distant platforms for his quarry. You can understand it. For devotees of trainspotting, Crewe station must be a kind of Mecca, their Valhalla, their Nirvana, their, well, Crewe, I suppose. If Jeremy Clarkson were here, he would doubtless be pointing out in that plonking way of his that these individuals are 'sad'. Well, how come? Trainspotting doesn't appeal to me one bit but then neither does Jeremy Clarkson. How come if you're tragically obsessed with vile, globe-destroying, penis substitutes you get the nickname petrolhead but if you like trains, you're an anorak? Petrolhead sounds way sexier, you have to admit. It says something about our world that if you are an enthusiast for anything, if you dare lose your ironic modern detachment and world-weariness, you become 'sad' or 'a loser'.

As the Pendolino swings gently out of Britain's rail cathedral, you can see that Cheshire, damp and flat and green, is a dairy county. Old sayings still survive, like, 'In wet weather a cow has five mouths.' Bizarre at first or indeed second hearing, it means that each of the cow's feet destroy the sodden grass and ruin it for other grazers. Remember that: it may well win you an admiring audience from older drinkers in Knutsford or Nantwich. As well as milk, Cheshire has salt in its veins. They've been mining it here since the vast beds were accidentally discovered in early Victorian times and still each year enough salt is extracted from the Winsford mines to fill Wembley Stadium to the brim, pitch, terraces and all. Glance at any map of the county and you'll find it dotted with 'wich'es, denoting brine springs. One of them is Northwich, home to Tim Burgess and the Charlatans and my favourite British football derby. Northwich is not a big place but it has two decent non-league football sides, Witton Albion and Northwich Victoria, and the rivalry between them is ridiculously intense. A half-decent gob would carry from Witton's ground to

the Drill Field where Northwich play and yet the rancorous
schism divides the town to the bafflement of outsiders.

Fifteen minutes' train journey across those flat dairy lands of
south Cheshire and soon comes along seven giant cooling towers
and a cluster of chimneys with plumes of white smoke. At nearby
Ellesmere Port stands the colossal Stanlow Refinery at the end of
a fifteen-mile pipeline from the Tranmere plant on the Mersey. At
the height of the eighties' 'industrial romanticism', local boys
Orchestral Manoeuvres In The Dark wrote a song about it called
'Stanlow', a dreamy ballad awash with synthetic strings and
harps. My mate John's dad, who had worked there, listened to it
with a suspicious look and said, 'It doesn't sound much like
bloody Stanlow to me.'

Disembarking at Bank Quay station, you can smell the 'pear
drops' tang in the dusk, just as you used to be hit by the earthy
scent of hops from the Boddingtons brewery when you pulled
into Manchester Victoria. The Lever plant looms over the platforms and the early-evening air seems to be full of ether and
sodium.

Warrington is notoriously hard to pin down. These days it's
the largest town in Cheshire, being absorbed by that county
in 1974 though traditionally it was in Lancashire. It certainly
feels Lancastrian, built on heavy industry from steel to beer to
wire-making. The town stands on the muddy banks of the
Manchester Ship Canal and they take their rugby league very
seriously around here.

The gap – no, make that a chasm – between the two codes of
rugby is one of the great north-south divides. On the one hand,
there's union, 'a game for ruffians played by gentlemen', and on
the other there's league, 'tough as teak ... as northern as hotpot
and Yorkshire pudding', as the absurd Eddie Waring once said. Or
to quote Michael Herd of the *Evening Standard*, 'a sport that

Londoners don't give a toss for ... a game for ape-like creatures watched by gloomy men in cloth caps'.

It was a very simple schism once. Rugby union was for toffs from the south, league was for working men from the north. As far as most northerners see it, union was invented when a public schoolboy too stupid and unskilled to play football properly picked up the ball and ran off with it like a girl. In fact, like a Blackpool barmaid, rugby union's roots are always showing through. Look at how many Joshes and Simons and Nigels and Robs – working-class people always abbreviate Robert to Bob – there are in the England union squad. They may allow professionalism now and not have to reach for the smelling salts whenever money is mentioned, but in essence it's still a game for the middle classes, the southern middle classes to boot.

I will readily admit to a whole panoply of prejudices against union – except that some of them aren't just class and regional bigotry, they are founded in solid scientific fact. My dad's theory, one instilled in me at an early age, is that thirty people is far too many to have on a pitch at one time and hope to produce anything remotely skilful or attractive. The reason there are fifteen players on each side in union is that you can keep a lot of unruly, spotty schoolboys occupied at one time on a Wednesday afternoon. I went to a Catholic grammar school in Wigan – arguably the rugby league capital of the world – and we played union rather than league in what was clearly a pathetic attempt to ape the mores of the public schools. This – alongside being hit with a strap by forty-year-old male virgins in frocks – is one of the many things that rankle about my alma mater.

League, I contend, is the vastly superior code: faster, harder, infinitely more skilful. The ball is actually passed at speed from one player to another rather than merely hoofed skyward and then bundled upon en masse on its snow-flecked return to earth.

Until relatively recently, union almost prided itself on its lack of application, fitness and rigour, on what it treasured as its amateur status. Indeed, as my old friend the comedy performer Neil Ashurst would say, 'The only good thing about rugby union is that it's always nice to see policemen and barristers getting knocked about a bit on their day off.'

Worryingly for those of us who like our prejudices intact, things are more complex now. Union has become professional and unarguably a better sport for it, though to these eyes it's still an ugly free-for-all. Rugby league doesn't really even exist any more. It's called Super League now, and Murdoch's Sky money – initially regarded as tainted but now grudgingly welcomed – has transformed the game, clubs and stadia. The most obvious and least edifying change has been in nomenclature. I will gladly take Murdoch's dosh if it means a great sport is kept alive and kicking, well, passing and running. But no one outside of the branding consultancies can have welcomed the coming of those stupid nicknames with their second-hand American football feel. The Keighley Cougars, The Oldham Bears, The Halifax Blue Sox; almost none have caught on with the public, with the possible exception of The Bradford Bulls. If anyone in Wigan said that they were going along to the JJB to watch 'The Warriors' you would know instantly that they were an impostor, like when Gordon Jackson speaks English to the sneaky SS man in *The Great Escape*.

Rugby league is a proud sport, proud of its working-class lineage, proud of its family values, a phrase which actually has some meaning here. If you ever went to a Wigan and Warrington game in the late seventies or a Good Friday Humberside derby, you'll have learned first-hand from the dodging of flying bricks that rugby league has not always been hooligan-free, despite what it cosily likes to think, but these were brief aberrations in what has generally been a game watched and played in the very best of spirits, a man's game where women and children have always been made welcome and secure on the terraces. In his book on rugby league, *To Jerusalem and Back*, Simon Kelner recounts a wonderful story of the 1982 Challenge Cup Final in Leeds where, in a crowd of 44,000 people, there was just one arrest, for drunkenness, and outside the ground. Kelner recalls how, on that day, the only minor incident he witnessed was a mild fracas when a Hull supporter, dressed in black and white kit and wearing a stripy top hat, tried to push into a taxi queue. He was insisting he was the Minister for Sport.

Warrington, or the Wires, are one of the stalwarts of the thirteen-a-side game. I always loved the name of their old ground, Wilderspool, more Tolkien than Eddie Waring. But for all this, Warrington seems different from the rest of Lancashire. There is something faintly Scouse about the people and their speech (Chris Evans and Kerry Katona are well-known Warringtonians of today and may still be by the time you read this). Also, right here in Labour's Lancastrian heartlands, Warrington has a place in political history for being the first place to field a candidate for the SDP-Liberal Alliance back in 1981, when 'Woy' Jenkins lost narrowly to Doug Hoyle.

Perhaps of more cultural import than its industrial past or its importance in the Civil War or its place in modern political history, Warrington was chosen as the site of Britain's first Ikea. I remember well it opening in 1987. My friend Geoff suggested we drive out from Wigan in search of some cheap furniture for college and we spent the afternoon chuckling at the sofas called Billy and bookshelves called Git. No one laughs now. In fact, some people think there's something rather sinister about those funny names. Joe Kerr, head of the Department of Critical and Historical Studies at the Royal College of Art, has argued that,

'They have subtle techniques for encouraging compliance. And in following them you become evangelists for Ikea. If you look at police interrogation techniques, for example, you see that one of the ways you break somebody's will is to get them to speak in your language. Once you've gone to a shop and asked for an Egg McMuffin, or a skinny grande latte, or a piece of Ikea furniture with a ludicrous name, you're putty in their hands.' Blimey. Come on, Joe, lighten up. Those tea lights are a real bargain.

As you leave Bank Quay station, one of the very first signs you see promises directions to 'The Cultural Quarter', not a particularly northern notion, certainly one that would be chortled at in the Chelsea Arts Club. Naturally I set off in the gathering dusk with a spring in my step.

When I soon encounter another sign pointing back the way I have come and also bearing the legend 'The Cultural Quarter', I realise I have walked through the quarter without noticing. Disappointing. Perhaps I am being unfair. Perhaps it was unrealistic to expect bearded bohemians setting up easels by the dry cleaners or men in berets playing atonal jazz saxophone on the town hall steps but I had expected something more. So I go back and have another look.

The Pyramid Arts Centre, focus of the cultural quarter, is closing as I arrive at 5 p.m., which must make it rather less than useful for Warringtonians with day jobs. And there are plenty. Warrington has one of Britain's lowest unemployment rates with a booming hi-tech sector. A pity: I would have liked to look at an exhibition or two or maybe caught Warrington's Improvised Music Collective 'back with their blend of Balinese and Javanese Gamelan for multiple Guitars, a celebration of the ancient Japanese form for electronics and an evocation of the inter-war serialism of Schoenberg and Webern with live electronics'. And you thought it was all brass bands, didn't you?

Warrington has mushroomed in modern times. Northern readers of an eighties vintage may well remember being constantly urged by excitable TV ads to 'ring Eileen Bilton' about relocating to Warrington Runcorn New Town. The projected Chapelford Urban Village is the largest brownfield redevelopment in the north-west. Thousands of new homes are scheduled on the site of World War Two's largest air base, Burtonwood, once home to all those US airmen who were 'over-sexed, overpaid and over here'.

In 1973, Warrington town centre was pretty much razed to the ground in an orgy of 'planning'. Said planners felt that only Palmyra Square and the town hall had any architectural merit and the rest was gone with the wave of a draughtsman's ruler. You can see why they spared Palmyra Square. It's rather grand with famous venue the Parr Hall on one side and the fine old houses of long-dead soap barons on the other. In between, they've laid out a long thin square – OK, geometrists, a rectangle – called Queens Gardens, and in it there's a plaque that reads: 'These Russian Guns, captured on the eighth day of September 1855 by the victorious arms of Her Majesty and her allies in the Fortress of Sebastopol, were presented to the Mayor and the Corporation of the Borough of Warrington by Her Majesty's Government as a memorial to the sufferings and the triumphs of the British Army in the Crimea.' Unfortunately there are no guns anywhere to be seen. Maybe the Russkis came and snatched them back in a dawn raid from St Helens.

The result of the planning fest of the seventies and beyond is a city centre that is positively crowded with a hotchpotch of development, huddling and looming everywhere, towering above you and blocking out the sky. It feels a bit like a central European market town circa 1500. But with a Greggs and a Superdrug, of course.

Peter Andre is appearing soon at the Chicago Rock Café (evidently Warrington Rock Café was thought too literal) and there are real ales at the Friar Penketh. A blackboard outside the Postengate pub reads 'Your fun starts and ends here', which is meant to sound alluring but actually comes across as faintly threatening. If you're peckish, you can eat at Cromwell's, just as Oliver Cromwell did himself when the town was much smaller and the site of a decisive Civil War encounter.

In among all this ersatz antiquity and twenty-first-century redbrick gothic, you turn a corner and come up against something genuinely 'getting on a bit' and really fabulous. Golden Square has given its name to a typically soulless modern shopping development but it's a real square with a covered piazza that could hold its own with Covent Garden's. The Barley Mow pub lounging attractively to one side is one of the oldest pubs in Britain and a building that wouldn't look out of place in Stratford-upon-Avon with its lovely, fussy Tudor frontage. A plaque tells you that the pub dates from 1561 and that it is reputed to be haunted. At lighting-up time on a chilly late winter dusk, it is haunted by a particular kind of drinker. Chefs on their way to other shifts at pubs, elderly men on barstools slowly turning the pages of racing papers as their cigarette smoulders in a nearby ashtray, indie kids comparing CD purchases. A resolutely unsmiling knot of regulars eye me suspiciously from the bar corner where they are in hushed conversation with a glacially cool barmaid. The Barley Mow promises more than it delivers though perhaps I just caught it on a bad day. I necked a warming Jamesons and left.

If these old northerners were taciturn, the new northerners I spotted having a crafty gasper in the doorway of the shopping precinct were much more warm and voluble: two dark-haired young women smoking furiously, waving their hands and flicking their raven tresses as they talked at staggering speed and volume in Italian. I wanted to ask what they were doing in Warrington but I was afraid I wouldn't get a word in edgeways. Less lively was Cockhedge Shopping Arcade which, maybe because of its fantastically unappealing name, was a ghostly alley of To Let signs and Closing Down Sale notices.

Bridge Street runs through the centre of town and plays host to a pretty rum selection of street sculpture. A sort of water trough dribbles onto a partly submerged cupola covered with little handprints. I couldn't see a name but I bet it was called 'Zeitgeist 5' or 'Resolution'. There are also some big sticks that light up for a purpose I couldn't fathom. At the very top of the street are ten outsize translucent green tent pegs. It turns out that these are the Ten Guardians of Warrington, representing the people of the town over 200 years. Representing them fairly obliquely, I'd say, but quite nice.

It's nearly dark as I head back down Bridge Street en route to the railway station but my eye is caught by a plaque in front of Boots. Right by the sign offering '1/3 Off Selected Fragrances' is a simple black marble oval set in granite. On it is a picture of a smiling young boy and a toddler and an inscription that reads 'In Remembrance of Jonathan Ball and Tim Parry 20th March 1993'.

I had forgotten that Warrington was one of the last British cities to be bombed by the IRA. It followed a bomb attack a few weeks earlier on a gas storage plant which caused major damage but no casualties. The second attack killed these two children and injured many other people. The bombs were hidden in cast-iron litter bins outside Boots and Argos and wreaked havoc among shoppers on a fine spring afternoon the day before Mother's Day. Three-year-old Jonathan Ball died while buying a card.

The attacks were the work of the Provisional IRA. A pointless, brutal assault on a northern working-class town; even those people who'd sometimes sympathised with the aims of the Republican movement were confused and despairing. As it turned out, it was one of the final and most horrifying and absurd acts of that whole Irish tragedy. Other fears, threats and bogeymen are alive in the British psyche in the late winter of 2006 as I walk through the chilly dusk back to the railway station. With newer anxieties to keep us busy, many of us may have forgotten the Warrington bombs. Warrington hasn't.

I pick up a discarded newspaper in the waiting room, having exhausted the news service offered by the graffiti on the wall (tonight they lead with 'Paul Burton is a child molester' and 'Robbie is shit scared of Wogle'). As opposed to the headlines of 20 March 1993, the news is comfortingly everyday and inconsequential. Local families are objecting to a planned mobile phone mast in a beauty spot and a man called Menzies Campbell who pronounces his name quite ridiculously has been elected leader of the Liberal Democrat Party. Ho hum. I can almost feel the grease of tomorrow's fish and chips forming on the pages as I read them.

So if for those heading west at least Crewe is the gateway to the north, and Warrington the first big proper indisputably northern town, then Cheshire is where the north begins: the Mild Frontier, complete with grazing cows and footballers' wives rather than buffalo and squaws. We may be 'up north' now but there are parts of Cheshire where the incomes and the wine bars and the 4X4s make Islington look like Ancoats. We'll be visiting there a little later in search of the posh north. But I've got a long, long overdue return visit somewhere else first. Home, soft lad.

Scally, Scally, Pride of Our Alley

For some people, going back to their place of birth must be really special. For instance, if you were born high atop a lofty Cairngorm peak or in a box at the Royal Albert Hall or, for some reason, in the penguin enclosure at Dudley Zoo. Or maybe like Tom Waits, who legend has it was born in the back of a New York taxi while stopped at some lights.

I was born in the big modern maternity unit of a big modern-ish hospital. For the purposes of this book I went back to see it, hoping for some epiphany, some flash of Proustian revelation. In fact all that happened is that I stood on a grass verge watching some out-patients being pushed about in wheelchairs, catering suppliers having a crafty fag and the odd ambulance come and go. Once upon a time, I might have been able to actually stroll into the hospital with impunity, maybe even ask a passing orderly or pretty nurse for the very ward I was born in and get a cheery patient in a head bandage to take a picture of me with thumbs aloft in front of the actual incubator I spent the first few hours of life in.

Not any more. Strangers in hospitals these days are seemingly only ever there to abduct babies or steal methadone or attack some overworked receptionist and this has made hospitals as security conscious as airports or nuclear power plants. Men in uniforms with badges and logos shouting 'ProtectoSquad Elite Team' prowl around constantly. One such began to take a keen interest in me. I wandered off just as a laundry van arrived full of sheets and towels.

The big modern hospital where I was born is called Whiston Hospital. The first recorded reference to the place is as Quitstan in 1245 and then Wystan, Quystan, Whystan, Whytstan, Whyghstan and Quistan, eventually reaching its present spelling of Whiston around 1355. Exciting, eh? The hospital is by far and away the most widely known building in the parish. The more aesthetically minded local often rails against the look of it. One correspondent to a local paper, voting it the ugliest building in the area, explains, 'I'm not against babies – or maternity per se – just crap architecture.'

But for me, the only really interesting thing about my place of birth is that it was not in Wigan. That's where I grew up, an almost comically northern town, and that's another story. But due to a thrilling quirk of fate that my mother has never adequately explained, I entered this life many miles away, over the border in a strange and foreign land. Though everything about me – my views on sport, my taste in food, my accent – marks me out as a dyed-in-the-wool Lancastrian, I am in truth something else entirely: a double agent, a spy, a foundling, a mystery man.

A Scouser.

Well, sort of. Whiston is located one and a half miles south of Prescot, three-quarters of a mile east of Huyton, four miles south-west of St Helens and one and a half miles west of Rainhill. In Wigan, the hospital is called, simply, Whiston Hospital. In Rainhill, though, it's 'Whissie Ossie', as in the characteristic linguistic trope of Scousers that also gives you 'footie', 'leckie' and 'Tarby' for football, electricity and cheeky sixties comic Jimmy Tarbuck.

Prescot, you see, lies in the hotly disputed, semi-legendary borderland between what Scousers see as the primitive rural wastes of Lancashire – a dully undulating hinterland of chimneys, whippets and flat caps – and the bracing, lively, dynamic metropolis of Liverpool with its irresistible humour, joie de vivre and catchy tunes.

Now all this talk of hospitals and identity must seem parochial to those readers who were born in taxis and penguin enclosures, but it is something that seems integral to the north. Most big towns have maternity uber-factories where nearly all the local babies are churned out. Nearly every Wiganer I know was hatched in the maternity unit at Billinge, a part of the town famed for a very negligible hill and a very particular kind of misty rain – 'that fine rain that soaks you through', as it was famously described by Peter Kay. If I'd been born those ten or so miles away from Wigan in another direction, over into Oldham, say, or Bolton or Burnley or even Manchester, it wouldn't really have mattered. But I was born in the Tijuana of Lancashire, the Kashmir, the Korean Demilitarised Zone where two mutually uncomprehending cultures clash and trade insults in their native tongues.

In the language of the Scouser, people from Wigan, and for that matter Bolton or Oldham or Bury, are woollybacks. In fact, I tend to think that woollyback is really just an imperious racial generalisation, like those ex-colonels who think it's all wogs after Calais or all non-Jews being gentiles be they the Dalai Lama, L. Ron Hubbard or King Haakon XIV of Norway. I think most Scousers secretly think of both the Milanese fashion designer and the Bantu tribesman as woollybacks, united in their tragic non-Scouseness.

If you want to be specific, though, 'woollyback' means those sooty Lancashire textile towns to the east and north of Liverpool. Wigan is the crucible of all things woollyback. As for the derivation of the term, well, if it ever crops up on *Mastermind* I'm sure the explanation given will be, as it often is in polite circles, that the term originated in the cotton industry, which once dominated the whole county when traders from the Lancashire towns used to carry the cotton on their back to sell in Liverpool. (The Scousers, it seems, mistook 'cotton' for 'wool'.) I have long suspected that the real reason is that Scousers believe that in their isolated rural state, without nightclubs or Tarby or impish tunesmiths, the average Lancastrian of an evening seeks solace in unnatural congress with his ovine flock. I could be wrong, though.

In Alan Bleasdale's *Boys from the Blackstuff*, a mild-mannered social security snooper finally rebels and in an act of defiance 'for a woollyback from Wigan' throws the keys to his DHSS car down a drain. When I first met legendary Liverpool band The Farm singer Peter Hooton, he was very excited that that night on *Brookside* ('Brookie', obviously) there was going to be a lesbian kiss between Anna Friel and 'that wool bird', i.e. the flame-haired actress from St Helens.

Most of the time this schism is acknowledged with good humour. For a few years I worked in a town called Skelmersdale while living in Wigan. It's a remarkable place worth returning to in a later chapter but for now let me just say that new Skem, as opposed to old Skem, a Lancastrian mining village with a Viking lineage, is a sprawling sixties new town in the Cumbernauld/East Kilbride mould populated almost exclusively by Scouse families moved out of Liverpool during the rapid development and population growth of the 1960s. Skem isn't far from Wigan but every day the bus felt like it was crossing some kind of border post when it went through Upholland. You could see the fashions change, hear the accent mutate so that it was a 'buzz' on one street corner and a 'bus' by the next. But I never got beaten up for being a 'wool', just gently teased by dope-smoking lads into Pink Floyd or cute girls in white fringed boots.

In other places, though, the tectonic plates of this very northern schism rub up against each other with a deal more edge and friction. Huyton and St Helens are five minutes' drive away from each other (in a hotwired Mondeo, Richard Littlejohn might add) but here the fault line between 'Scouser' and 'woollyback' is a crackling seam of animosity among the population, particularly the younger end. Essentially, they fucken' hate each other, la'.

It gets really complicated here because a new social group enters the already heady mix: the plastic Scouser. 'Plazzie' has been a term of abuse among Liverpudlians since the sixties, when local movers and shakers like Alan Williams (the manager who gave away The Beatles; see Really Stupid Scousers) used it to describe those people who talked up their Scouseness, laying on the 'fab gear wack' stuff with a trowel but who were off to Surrey at the first chance they got, such as Cilla Black or, let's face it, The Beatles themselves.

But then it starts to mean someone who lives on the Wirral peninsula, particularly Birkenhead or Wallasey, who sounds to us woollybacks like a Scouser but is in fact a softie fellow traveller. To be fair, the posh folk on the Dee bank of the Wirral are quite happy to distance themselves from the scallies over the Mersey and their burning cars and look instead towards leafy, affluent Cheshire and its Alfa Romeos. A friend of mine met an apparently Scouse couple on holiday, but when he asked what part of Liverpool they came from was met with the instantaneous, haughty reply, 'Oh no, we're not from Liverpool. We're from the Wirral. Do you know the Peninsula?'

And these days 'plazzie' has a third meaning, drenched in spittle and loathing. A plastic Scouser is what the real Scouser and the woollyback alike (there will be a handout and a chance to ask questions at the end) call one of the despised breed of chav scallies from those west Lancashire towns like Huyton and Rainhill. They are a distinctive tribe, identifiable for their penchant for Rockport, Henri Lloyd and Lacoste brands and for the stylistic quirk of wearing their tracksuit bottoms ('trackies') tucked into their socks. This looks just as cataclysmically shit as it sounds but hang around Huyton bus station and you will see scores of weasel-faced youths dressed like this, pallid from lack of vitamin C and generally looking for something to urinate on or set fire to. Plastic Scousers of this ilk have no interest in being witty, vital or revolutionising popular music but merely in being thought of as hard or criminal, not 'nesh' or soft. They are the sort of lads who seen from a distance or singly are kind of ridiculous, even pathetic, but who look very different when they converge in a quintet on your bus stop at half eleven at night and ask you the time. In 2005, a young black student called Anthony Walker found himself in the wrong part of Huyton with the wrong kind of Scousers and his murder appalled the country. Scousers hate 'plazzies' because they aren't real Scousers but cheap wannabes with no style. Woollybacks hate them because at some point they may have pinched your Plasma screen telly to buy smack. Sadly, there is no such thing as a plastic woollyback, i.e. a Scouser who says 'alreet cock' and ''ey up' and hopes to be taken for a Wiganer.

All of this geo-political analysis and ethnic labelling is simply to illustrate what all Merseysiders have known all along: that Scousers are different. They are the Basques of Lancashire, a race apart with a language and culture that seems to bear no relation to any of the people around them.

When I was planning this book (no, really, don't laugh) I always imagined Liverpool as a separate chapter. There was no sensible way it could be lumped in with Cheshire or Lancashire. The opening line of the city's current official glossy guidebook states: 'Liverpool is not really the north. Not quite Midlands. Closer to Wales and Ireland. And definitely Atlantic. Or is it just a state of mind?' Michael Swerdlow, an entrepreneur quoted in a *Guardian* piece, says, 'It's still an enigma... I don't think of myself as a northerner – what have I got in common with Newcastle or Yorkshire or the Lake District? What I am is a Liverpudlian.'

Despite all this, when J. B. Priestley undertook his famous tour of England in the 1930s for his book *English Journey*, he never thought for a second not to place Liverpool stolidly in Lancashire. Glance briefly at JB's chapter titles and at first you think he's missed the whole city out. In fact it's the very first place he visits at the beginning of the chapter 'In Lancashire', and he ends up, after a day mired in the city's then endemic poverty and squalor, dining alone and thoughtfully smoking a good cigar in the restaurant of the Adelphi Hotel. But never for a moment does he think that the city is anything other than Lancastrian.

That notion seems faintly bizarre now, not just because Scousers relish their outsider status but because we have become so comfortable with the idea of Merseyside. It may be the only one of those new-fangled seventies appellations that has actually caught hold and come to mean anything. The reason, as far as I can see, must be because rather than make a nonsense of local kinships and ties (like putting Wigan in some abstraction like Greater Manchester or the Old Man of Coniston in Cumbria or Hull in Cleveland), rather than putting local noses out of joint, it actually confirms what those locals have believed all the time; that they are different, separate, sovereign.

Merseyside was created, entirely seriously we should point out, on 1 April 1974 from bits annexed from the counties of Lancashire and Cheshire, along with the county boroughs of Birkenhead, Wallasey, Liverpool, Bootle and St Helens. Like much else about Scousers, the Tories were never very happy about the concept of Merseyside. It embodied everything they feared and distrusted about big Soviet-style seventies socialism in the region: men with northern accents sitting behind big desks in massive new civic centres drinking keg bitter and calling each other 'comrade'. In 1986 Thatcher abolished the county council (bet she had a whisky or two that night) although it still exists legally, and as a ceremonial county. But everyone still refers to it and still uses the term. It is that curiosity, a piece of governmental jargon and red tape, that ordinary people have taken to their heart, so much so that when Liverpool played Everton in the FA Cup Final of '86, the fans of these two fierce and historic rivals sang 'Merseyside, Merseyside' in unison. This was their chance, at the high point of the city's demonisation as Britain's capital of crime and corruption, to wave a cheery two fingers to London and the world.

Of course, others would see it as yet more evidence of the city's mawkish sentimentality. In October 2004, Boris Johnson, the likeable, buffoonish right-wing media personality, wrote a *Spectator* editorial in the wake of the horrific murder by beheading of Ken Bigley, a British hostage in Iraq. It was a fairly sober article in general, bemoaning the fact that since Princess Diana's death, we have become a nation of cry babies. But one thread of Johnson's argument provoked an outpouring of red, red rage.

'The extreme reaction to Mr Bigley's murder is fed by the fact that he was a Liverpudlian ... They see themselves whenever possible as victims, and resent their victim status; yet at the same time they wallow in it. Part of this flawed psychological state is that they cannot accept that they might have made any contribution to their misfortunes, but seek rather to blame someone else for it'.

He goes on to quote Captain Scott's last journals and bemoan the disappearance of the British buccaneer, etc., etc. But the hot stuff is right there in that paragraph above, a petrol bomb lobbed from the reading room of the Athenaeum Club and scoring a direct hit on the streets of Toxteth.

In the vernacular of the north, it all kicked off. Bigley's brother Paul denounced Johnson as a 'pompous twit' who should 'get out of public life'. The then Tory leader Michael Howard denounced the article as 'nonsense' and demanded that Johnson, up until then a rising star of the Tory Party, go round and apologise, like a schoolboy who's put his neighbour's window through with a football. Like that other blond Tory underachiever before him, Michael Heseltine, Johnson got a train to Lime Street and mooched about town looking sheepish and concerned, doubtless having health centres and renovated bus stops pointed out to him by local dignitaries.

Ken Bigley was held hostage for three weeks before he was killed, an agonising sentence for his family, who had to endure occasional videotaped messages from him in captivity and the almost certain expectation of a dreadful outcome. During this time, Billy Connolly had cracked a 'joke' on tour in London to the effect 'Ken Bigley – don't you just wish they'd just get on with it?' There was a brief cappuccino froth of disapproval but nothing more. No calls for an apology, no tearing up of contracts. Which is pretty amazing when you think about it. Silly old Boris makes a reasonable point about sentimentality and victimhood and is forced into the political wilderness in a sack-cloth demob suit; LA-based multimillionaire comedian Bill savours Bigley's imminent murder for a laugh and there's a mild tut. The difference is that though Connolly's remark was enormously more offensive, he had the good sense to leave Liverpool out of it.

For the phone-in shows and messageboards, Boris's broad-side was a godsend. The BBC received hundreds of messages like this one from Canada: 'Some people have a depressing need to demonise others to bolster their own pathetic self-image. Overt racism is no longer acceptable so people like Johnson must seek other ways to express their bitterness and hatred engendered by their own inadequacies. His use of the word "tribal" implies a sense of belonging that those who live in the commuter towns of the south-east can never experience. Very few Londoners are from London and can never truly feel at home there. I feel sorry for him. Ian Barry, Niagara Falls.' Sarah Dobie from Runcorn said: 'We should count our blessings Mr Johnson is not from Liverpool; if he were he would have been brought up to be a decent human being.' The city's good humour, compassion and resilience were conjured up again and again.

But the phone-ins, the saloon bars and the letters pages were also swamped with messages of support for the errant Boris. 'The article in *The Spectator* hit the nail on the head,' Jeff Martin in Bolton told the BBC news website. 'Liverpudlians all believe that they have the monopoly on grief. As for city of culture, they are having a laugh.' Ancient prejudices about thievery and work-shy dockers emerged from the recesses of the psyche. The most cherished parts of the city's self-image were challenged. 'Boris Johnson is about spot on this time. Liverpudlians also seem to think they are funny as well!' grumbled Melvyn Packham in Sittingbourne. 'The truth always hurts,' concluded James in Northampton.

It was as if, having held its tongue for generations, the rest of the country, the dull kids who'd been quietly getting on with their work, suddenly got a chance to say what they really thought about that cheeky, attention-seeking, class clown who'd been cracking jokes and showing off since, ohh, 1945 at least. The woollyback north and the benighted south, both fed up of being told (by Liverpudlians) that Liverpool was the greatest city in the world, was having its day in court. Liverpool, in character as ever, was The Accused.

I'd grown up hearing about Scousers and their fabled wit, though sometimes looking for evidence of it without success in the work of Jimmy Tarbuck, Arthur Askey and Stan Boardman. I grew up hearing Tarby and Cilla talk on every chat show about how great Scottie Road was, a kind of Scouse East End, where you could leave your back door open day and night and the worst that could happen was that a lovable Scouse neighbour would drop by returning a cup of sugar or trying out some new skiffle tunes on you or cracking a witticism. Whatever the Scotland Road once was, by the way, it's not much to write home about now. Not the bit I saw, anyway. Just kebab shops and boarded-up pubs and the feeling that Liverpool's undoubted renaissance is going on somewhere else and to someone else.

There was in fact nothing new about Johnson's article. Broadsheet journalists had been sneering and railing at the city, often much more vituperatively, for years. Days after the Hillsborough disaster, *The Times* printed a column by Edward Pearce arguing that 'the shrine in the Anfield goalmouth, the cursing of the police, all the theatricals, come sweetly to a city which is already the world capital of self-pity. There are soapy politicians to make a pet of Liverpool, and Liverpool itself is always standing by to make a pet of itself. "Why us? Why are we treated like animals?" To which the plain answer is that a good and sufficient minority of you behave like animals.'

Four years later in the same paper Walter Ellis, covering the James Bulger murder, said: 'Liverpool lives on emotion; fears and hatreds bubble constantly below the surface. The mob, as self-pitying as it is self-righteous, is a constant presence, whether on tour in the Heysel Stadium, Brussels, or at home among the social dereliction of Liverpool 8, or as this week in the back streets of Bootle.' Alan Bennett had once gently ruminated on the Liverpudlians' 'built-in air of grievance' and the 'cockiness that comes from being told too often that they and their city are special'. Even Sir David Henshaw, the chief executive of

Liverpool City Council, at a conference marketing Liverpool as the 2008 European City of Culture, complained that 'sometimes it can still be the most mind-bogglingly awful and whingeing place, where the glass is always half-empty'. With friends like that, who needs Boris?

I love Scousers and I love Liverpool. The years I worked among them in their Skelmersdale exile were some of the happiest of my life. Just like all those hoary old clichés have it, they are warm and funny and hugely entertaining, as well as, yes, devious, truculent and arrogant. Just like the rest of us, in fact. For me, it's entirely possible to read Boris Johnson's article as a snobbish, callous, inaccurate attack on a proud working-class city and also to think, 'You know, he may have a point.' On the morning after Liverpool's heroic comeback and victory over AC Milan in the 2005 European Cup Final in Istanbul (I won't call it the Champions League on the grounds that the teams aren't champions and it isn't a league), the aforementioned Peter Hooton of The Farm was being interviewed on BBC Radio Five Live. The presenter suggested that, this being Liverpool, we would never hear the last of it. Hooton's voice became thick and broken with emotion. 'I'm not going to answer that,' he trembled. 'Put it this way, John Peel would have loved it.'

I laughed out loud. Game over. Hooton slams down the sentimental card, evoking recently deceased national treasure, and defies anyone to have the temerity to take issue with him. The fact that his comment was fatuous and didn't actually mean anything was irrelevant. Like Inter's back four, the presenter was left silently sprawling, beaten but not sure how. It was a golden Scouse moment.

The problem in the end might be that, as someone said to me soon after Ken Bigley's murder, 'It's always Liverpool, isn't it?' From The Beatles to Bill Shankly, Ken Bigley to Jamie Bulger,

Hillsborough to Heysel, chirpy comics to inner-city riots, it's always Liverpool. The Icicle Works' Ian McNabb, one of the best songwriters the city has ever produced, got it just right in an anthemic track from the mid-1980s called 'Up Here In The North Of England': 'McDonald's finally found us and we're folk-lore in Turin/The southerners don't like us… Who can blame them? Seems we're always in the spotlight.'

Liverpool got its charter in 1207 from King John but was merely a sleepy fishing village until the fortuitous silting up of the Dee put Chester out of commission as a port. Liverpool grew rich on both Chester and Africa's misfortune. The first dock was built in 1705 to facilitate Liverpool's strategic importance in the slave trade, part of the triangle that linked Africa, the UK and America. That legacy is still contentious and difficult for sensitive Scousers; Liverpool's black community feel it partly as an open wound, part badge of identity. Some Liverpudlians feel it's a shameful episode to be hushed up, ammunition for those who criticise Liverpool's race relations (both Everton and Liverpool, for instance, were extremely slow to incorporate black players). Others are more rueful. Over a pint in the Philharmonic or 'Phil', one of the city's iconic boozers, a thoughtful middle-aged man from the Dingle explained to me, 'We never had slavery, no. We just made the money from it.'

Daniel Defoe came in the 1720s and loved it; 'a town so populous and rich that it may be called the Bristol of this part of England'. During the nineteenth century it was the embarkation point for waves of migrations. Between 1830 and 1930, a million people left via Liverpool for the 'New World', the USA and Australia. Many more would-be emigrants never got further than the Pier Head, staying in Liverpool to provide the cheap labour needed in the burgeoning port and giving it a vibrant multi-ethnic stew that few other British cities could match. Carl Jung called it the 'Pool Of Life', a gumbo of Irish refugees fleeing the potato famine, Caribbean families, Chinese sailors and laundrymen.

When The Cavern started to ring to the sound of Merseybeat, Liverpool was still a burly, broad-shouldered, bustling port. But as the sixties began to swing, the pendulum swung away from Liverpool. Mass air travel pretty much put paid to the luxury liner business, and the ports of Kent and the south-east prospered as trade with Europe became our national priority. Liverpool found itself facing in the wrong direction. In the seventies, Liverpool became a caricature: city of 'taches, perms, robbery and signing on. Sporadically, the city immolated itself in rioting, revelling in its own demise. 'They should build a fence around Liverpool and charge admission. For, sadly, it has become a showcase of everything that has gone wrong in Britain's big cities,' claimed a *Daily Mirror* editorial of 1982. Perhaps the blackest irony of all is that the city's one success story of the era, Liverpool FC's dominance of Europe, ended in tragedy at Heysel and Hillsborough.

The Rough Guide to England begins its section on Liverpool thus: 'If one city in England could be said to stand for a nation in decline it could be Liverpool.' That seems a bit strong to me, especially if, having 'detrained' at Lime Street station, you are taking in the view from the station's steps, the very steps where I once conducted an interview with New Order's Bernard Sumner dressed as Elvis after the 'World In Motion' video shoot in 1990. From here, even on a raw, filthy winter's morning, looking out across the pedestrian crossings to the St George's Hall, you get almost knocked down by a wave of sheer civic machismo from a century and a half ago.

It's a hell of a building. Imagine if the Parthenon had stopped fannying about sunbathing in Athens, done a day's work, got itself a manly patina of grime and then landed in the middle of Liverpool. The fact that it's the first thing you see when you exit Lime Street station is no accident. Back in the 1850s when it was built, this was Liverpool's swaggering announcement to the world that it had arrived; that a Lancastrian backwater was now the second city of the world's greatest empire. Once this is where you came to watch concerts or plays or exhibition snooker tournaments. These days its function has fossilised somewhat but it still opens to the public for craft fairs and the odd special exhibition and every August the famous floor with its 30,000 priceless Minton tiles is uncovered for general public consumption.

This misty morning (J. B. Priestley said that he had never seen the sun shine on Liverpool) a few late rush-hour stragglers are making their way across the wide, breezy piazza: a young woman with a briefcase anxiously checking her watch, a lad in a suit slightly too big for him with his funky hair plastered down into a more conventional style for a day's work in the bank or travel agents. It's eerily quiet this March morning but at different times this is where Liverpudlians have gathered in droves to celebrate and commiserate: the triumphant return of The Beatles from America, Liverpool and Everton's famous victories, the deaths of Gladstone and Queen Victoria, the stunned impromptu gathering after the murder of John Lennon.

Walk a little further along and you come to another prime piece of Liverpool real estate from the days of Victorian Imperial might: the Walker Art Gallery. I've been coming here since I was a teenager when I fell in love with art and, to be honest, with the idea of art and of wearing a second-hand overcoat and sipping frothy coffee in the café with a palely beautiful girl and talking about Rossetti or Stanley Spencer. Or maybe David Hockney's 'Peter Getting Out Of Nick's Pool', which you can see upstairs. I actually did this once or twice and am thinking of reliving those days but I'm a bit early for the 10.30 opening and the rumbling of the Gaggia suggests it'll be a while before it builds up a head of steam. I talk to some nice attendants instead who shower me with maps and advice and booklets, quietly radiating a touching pride in their city. For a time in the sixties, the psychedelic summer of The Beatles and the Liverpool Poets, McGough, Patten and Henry, a kind of gentle, wry artiness was what Liverpool was known for, as well as brashness and later the kind of bloke that Harry Enfield would have to tell to 'calm down, calm down'. Well, it lives on in the attendants at the Walker Art Gallery.

If the Walker Art Gallery is old-school, then the next imposing building along William Brown Street, the World Museum Liverpool (The Museum Formerly Known As Liverpool Museum) is defiantly cutting edge with its look-at-me atrium and brushed steel livery. I couldn't quite work out what the new theme of the place actually was, beyond a certain 'Gee whiz, isn't the world a richly diverse, multi-ethnic, scientifically mind-boggling free-for-all, eh, kids?' but that didn't seem to bother the junior school class from Fazakerley, who were busy 'interacting' with everything in sight with gusto and at impressive volume. 'Interactivity,' said a drained-looking teaching assistant as she passed by me. 'Basically it's hitting things, isn't it?' I skulked around the Fairtrade shop for a minute, feeling like the president of Rio Tinto Zinc or Rupert Murdoch for not buying anything, before heading back into the foyer to marvel at a spider crab the size of a Shetland pony and an enormous totem pole from somewhere called 'Something Terrible Happened House' in northwest America. From the sounds of screaming nine-year-olds behind me, something terrible was about to happen here as well.

I was en route to my favourite bit of Liverpool, surely everybody's favourite bit of Liverpool, and that way took me down via the offices of Liverpool Vision in The Observatory. I could see a scale model of a futuristic Liverpool city centre in there, and I'm a sucker for futuristic scale models, especially if they've got monorails and little stick people. This was surprisingly sober and realistic; in fact, the whole Liverpool Vision thing seemed remarkably clear-headed. The public were free to wander in and post little biro-ed notices with their feelings about the city's regeneration on the walls. They were amazingly sensible and perceptive. One commented on the 'decline of neo-liberal socialism', others made intelligent points about civic spaces. Frankly, I'd hoped for the odd puerile, blatantly untrue and inflammatory posting, like 'Steven Gerrard Is Gay' and was a little disappointed.

The freshening wind on my face told me I was heading in the right direction. Liverpool has a ton of stuff to be proud of but it has one undeniable 'dah-dah' moment, one bit of sleight of hand that never fails to impress. And that is the moment when the pedestrianised 'everytown' falls away behind you and the drag down from Derby Square and James Street suddenly, inexplicably, becomes the finest waterfront in Britain, the Liverpool Pier Head.

When I was in a band (floppy fringes, semi-acoustic guitars, bootlace ties; the full Aztec Camera obsession) I got so romantically taken by this stretch of the Mersey and those Pier Head buildings seen in the early morning after a wild party on the Wirral that I wrote a song about it. It was called 'That's Birkenhead', which is a bit literal and, unless I'd had a real skinful and was looking backwards, not strictly true. It sure is a pretty sight, though. Finer minds than I have been charmed by this bracing, beautiful part of town. Former Poet Laureate John Masefield said: 'The Thames is a wretched river after the Mersey and the ships are not like Liverpool ships and the docks are barren of beauty ... it is a beastly hole after Liverpool; for Liverpool is the town of my heart and I would rather sail a mudflat there than command a clipper out of London.'

The famed highlight of the Pier Head is the Three Graces, the trio of monumental buildings comprising the Royal Liver Building, the Cunard Building, and the Port of Liverpool Building. The official guide says that after Big Ben, the Liver Building is the most recognisable building in Britain. Now Westminster Abbey or Edinburgh Castle may have something to say about that but I wouldn't say anything to the Liver Building's face. A rugged, handsome face it is too, in a style and scale inspired by Chicago, a city itself on the dizzying rise at the same time as Liverpool. This morning, judging from the hordes of besuited Scousers stamping their feet on Canada Boulevard and taking the opportunity for a quick B&H, it seems to be in the throes of a fire alarm. The famous birds, by the way, are made of hammered copper and three times the size of a man, though possibly five times the size of Polly James. In case you didn't know or have somehow forgotten, Polly James and Nerys Hughes played the titular Liver Birds in Carla Lane's seventies comedy. Mingling with the fire-alarm evacuees and looking up at those funny haughty birds, it strikes me that Carla Lane's two best-known comedies reflect just how Liverpool's image changed between the seventies and eighties, from home of mini-skirted singletons with heads full of pop to home of curly-permed doleites on the make with no hilarious consequences.

In the early part of the twentieth century, the Cunard Building, the American eagles on each corner reflecting Samuel Cunard's nationality, was the hub of Britain's cruise ship industry, intended as a dry-land echo of the magnificence of the cruise liners. It's still an impressive edifice but imagine what it must have been like eighty years ago when film stars, comedians, hopeful migrants and well-heeled tourists took their papers and luggage down there in preparation for that choppy, churning 3,400-mile ocean crossing, then the only way to America. The

Scousers themselves worked here or on the liners in their hundreds, an army of painters, cleaners, plumbers, electricians and maids. In the 1900s there were approximately 300 laundries in the city simply to clean the tablecloths and bed linen for the big ships and when a liner docked for an overhaul it would take four weeks and 2,000 people to spruce it up.

If you're counting, the Port of Liverpool Building, an exercise in Edwardian opulence, formerly the Mersey Docks and Harbour Board Building, is the Third Grace. There was going to be a fourth but there isn't now. It's all been a bit of an embarrassment, really. There were certainly some strong opinions expressed back there on the walls of the Liverpool Vision offices. Essentially what happened is that Liverpool Vision ran a competition to design a Fourth Grace and something called 'The Cloud' by Nicholas Alsop was chosen. We will never see it as intended now but from the artist's impression I glanced at, it looked a bit like the rings of Saturn done in melting Lego. Anyway, what no one thought to take into account is that the Pier Head is a World Heritage Site and the mandarins of that scheme flatly refused permission for 'The Cloud' on the grounds that it was too big and not 'in keeping'. This has polarised the locals into traditionalists who are secretly quite pleased and a surprising number of modernists who have blamed 'Victorian theme-parking' and small-mindedness. As one critic has wailed in the magazine *Downtown Liverpool*, 'Why did we let height restrictions kill this project? Are we Milton Keynes or Manhattan?'

The answer is quite obviously Manhattan. As my friend the writer Andrew Harrison put it to me, 'Liverpool is the easternmost city of the United States. Think about it; a bustling Atlantic seaport full of off-duty sailors, Irish, Chinese, Catholics, black marketeers and the like, a huge diverse working-class population.'

After Liverpool, it's next stop New York, and the city's culture has always reflected that, from its markedly transatlantic street speech and slick slang to the young 'uns long-standing predilection for blues, black music, R&B and rock and roll, brought home by sailors ('the Cunard Yanks') as presents for siblings and sweethearts. Whereas London looks towards Europe, wants to be more stylish than Milan, Paris or Rome, Liverpool emulates the brash, wisecracking melting-pot mentality of the Big Apple.

If you want to see and feel just how American Liverpool is, though, you have to see it from the water. This is my intention: to take to the Mersey again. But the woman in the ferries office is looking doubtful. 'The midday's definitely not sailin', sweetheart, and I don't wanna sell yers a ticket that's no good so why not come back at half twelve and we'll see, alright, luv?' Outside, sheets of hail moved horizontally across spumes of icy water. I left her trying to explain the vagaries of Britain's weather to a couple from Somalia. It was the week the clocks went forward. British Summer Time.

I spent the tense intervening period in the Museum of Liverpool Life. Like the World Museum, this is very much a modern artefact, less about the grandeur of past civilisations than the experience of ordinary people. There's a soberingly critical exhibit on Liverpool's race relations, as well as a tableau almost-but-not-quite celebrating the city's long-standing enthusiasm for rioting, from the Dock Strikes of 1911 to petrol bombs in Toxteth in the eighties. There's a section of the old Kop terracing and the River Room is an evocative little space full of old home movies and reverberating to anachronistic pre-Beatle pop, devoted to memories of the days when nearby New Brighton was a bona fide tourist resort.

To my (and the Somalian couple's) delight, as well as a small knot of hardy and slightly damp would-be mariners, there is to be a one o'clock sailing, not from here, though, but from the Isle of Man steampacket landing a couple of hundred drenching yards along Canada Boulevard. The Boulevard is lined with tributes paid for by the governments of Canada, the Netherlands and America, an avenue of trees here, a sombre plinth there, reminding one of 'those who have no grave but the sea' and the city's importance during World War Two convoy missions.

It's impossible to set foot on the Mersey ferry without hearing the strains of Gerry and the Pacemakers' 'Ferry 'Cross The Mersey' in your head. Literally impossible. Because they play it at the start and finish of the trip. I've spoken to Scousers and woollybacks alike who find this appallingly cheesy. I think it's kind of cute, although surely they only play it on the hour-long cruise, not the direct crossings for the Birkenhead commuters. Otherwise Gerry Marsden would be the most hated man in the city. As it is, the movie *Ferry Cross the Mersey*, from whence the song came, seems to have disappeared from the popular consciousness (never on telly, no DVD) even though it's quite a neat little snapshot of Merseybeat, albeit via Cilla and Jimmy Savile rather than the Fab Four.

The taped commentary proclaims proudly: 'Welcome to the most famous ferry in the world.' It's a bold claim. If they have a taped commentary on the Statten Island ferry or the ferry across the Styx to the Underworld, then maybe that makes the same claim. I'm happy to go along with the Mersey one though. In the interests of research, I strain to hear the doubtless fascinating titbits of ferry-related information but it's hard to hear above the mournful howling of the wind and the clanking of doors and the shifting of tables. None of my fellow passengers seem to be interested. An over-boisterous grandad is encouraging his 'little smasher' in pink to sing and dance, pepped up by a family-sized bottle of Coke and some pick'n'mix. Two severe-looking

German men in bottle-green anoraks are both training their camcorders on the Cammell Laird shipyard across the river. Sixty or so years ago, when this waterway led out on to U-boat-infested ocean and when the heroism of the Atlantic convoys were all that stood between Britain and starvation, Germans in the Mersey making films of an important military/industrial installation would have been A Very Bad Thing Indeed. At this remove, though, I think a citizen's arrest will be unnecessary.

The ferry cruises downriver to avoid the passing cargo boats before heading straight across the Mersey to Seacombe. Amazingly, ferry boats have done this for 800 years, since 1150 when the monks of Birkenhead rowed passengers by hand across the river. Back then, the Mersey was far more treacherous and the crossing extremely hazardous, taking at least two hours. By the 1500s the ferries had acquired the very latest in modern technology, namely sails and rigging, and raced across in an hour and a half. After risking hypothermia on the promenade deck, I go to the café for a reviving Kenco. 'How long does the round trip take?' I ask the girl behind the counter. She frowns sweetly. 'Oh, I don't really know... I suppose I should, shouldn't I?' she giggles, as if I'd asked her the circumference of Neptune.

Twenty minutes of chilly, choppy river-going later, you're docking with maximum clanking and shouting at Seacombe, gateway to Birkenhead, which from here looks just like Trumpton. These days there are just three stops on the ferry. But in the Victorian steam heyday, boats buzzed between Birkenhead and Woodside, Tranmere, Rock Ferry, New Ferry, Bromborough, Eastham, Wallasey, Seacombe, Egremont and New Brighton. Individual boats became famous, like the *Royal Iris*, given the prefix Royal for seeing active service at Zeebrugge in World War One. Later, it was known as the *Fish and Chip Boat*, hosting evening entertainment cruises where Scouse talent from Gerry

And The Pacemakers and The Searchers to The Beatles and Elvis Costello played. It even got its own series on ITV in 1979, *The Mersey Pirate*, which I don't remember but was probably crap.

After Birkenhead, the ship heads up-river past the afore-mentioned Cammell Laird shipyards and out towards Eastham, where the Manchester Ship Canal begins (if you fancy a long day afloat, it's six hours to Salford and a bus brings you back to Liverpool) and the Tranmere Oil Refinery where the pipeline runs to Stanlow. Last time I came that way I took the train under the river to meet Half Man Half Biscuit, the world's leading pop satirists and Tranmere Rovers fans.

This time, though, I'm trying to get the circulation back in my hands and wishing that the café sold whisky to go in this Kenco. I remember the wry words of Liverpool striker John Aldridge, commenting on the intense heat in Florida for the '94 World Cup: 'It gets like this in Liverpool when you're on the ferry and the sun reflects off the Mersey.'

You could almost forget the cold that's now deep in your marrow, though, when the ferry swings around in a great loop and begins its return to the Pier Head. First the city's two cathedrals come into view through the grey murk; a Protestant one designed by a Catholic, and a Catholic one designed by a Protestant, a piece of sixties concrete psychedelia known as Paddy's Wigwam.

Then as you approach the Pier Head, Liverpool suddenly turns it on in a dazzling display that has everything to do with Manhattan and nothing to do with Milton Keynes. From here, you can see that though Liverpool is twinned with Odessa, Dublin, Cologne and others, its real twin is New York. You wonder if the Rough Guide writer could have been so slighting and pitying if they'd seen Liverpool from the prow of the ferry. There cannot be anywhere else like this in England.

The commentary draws our attention skywards to the top of the Liver Building and the two liver birds in their lofty and solitary splendour. 'They can never mate as they have their backs to each other; she looks out to sea for the returning sailor, he looks towards the city to see if the pubs are open.' The ancient legend (which stretches back a barely believable, erm, eighty years) states that if the birds should ever leave, then the city will crumble and disappear. I doubt very much that this will happen since, unlike the similarly significant ravens at the Tower of London, the liver birds are made of metal and nailed to the top of the building. I suppose it's possible a scally might rob them and sell them for scrap in Bootle.

Just as we're about to disembark and the crew start to do manly, maritime-ish things with chains and gangplanks, a fellow passenger sidles up to me, a middle-aged man in a trench coat and flamboyant trilby. I make the mistake of catching his eye and am treated to a verbal assault that is both quintessentially Scouse in its speed and prolixity and quite, quite mad; beginning as a kind of rhapsody of complaint against the Isle of Man steam-packet company and swelling impressively to a symphony of meaningless rage.

'You see, dey say that they let ar lads use their landing stage but if we had done this properly we could have finished our own landing stage and den we wouldn't be in this mess... See there, they lock ar lads out and won't let them get near the boat. Fucken ridiculous. You know how much these landing stages cost, ey, do yer...'

Erm , not really.

'...and then you see the amount that they spend on sculptures and, and, and... I mean I know it was a shame what happened to that lad Anthony Walker but last week a white lad was murdered and you know how much it got in the *Echo* (holds finger and thumb a centimetre apart)... That much. Now when I gerrof this ferry I'm going for a bevy with my mates in the town – black lads I used to work with on the boats. I'm not a racist and you know why... you know why... THERE'S NO SUCH WORD AS RACIST!'

I'm just about to say that I'm pretty sure there is, when I notice a wide-eyed look of pity in the eyes of the ferrymen. They have clearly been privy to this wide-ranging stream-of-consciousness tirade many times before. In defiance of the safety instructions, as soon as the gangplank is down, I leap for the jetty and am off the steep ramp en route to the Albert Dock.

The Albert Dock was an early jewel of Liverpool's civic regeneration. One of the world's first enclosed docks and with the highest density of Grade 1 listed buildings in England, you can only marvel that at one point in the 1980s, the council were going to drain it, flatten it and make it into a multi-storey car park. For many years, before their frankly treacherous sell-out to London, this was where Richard and Judy sipped elevenses and talked nut allergies and liposuction on *This Morning*. Behind them, the wearyingly high-spirited weatherman and local TV fixture Fred Talbot (a former biology teacher who taught The Fall's Mark E. Smith) would loon around uninformatively on a polystyrene raft in the shape of the British Isles; as he prepared to make the one-foot leap to Northern Ireland, all of Britain would hope he fell in.

Nowadays, the Albert Dock's a curious mix of tat and art. On the quality side, there's Tate Liverpool, impressive, ultra-modern, all Rothko poster books and carob cake in the café. There's the Maritime Museum (by the way, in place of the Fourth Grace, they're going to build a new museum on the Pier Head because evidently Liverpool thinks you can never have too many museums). There's Babycream, an offshoot of the city's hugely successful superclub Cream, where you can sip a Mai Tai on an uncomfortable tan leather pouffe and hope Robbie Fowler pops in. There is the splendid launch point of the Yellow Duckmarine, a canary-coloured amphibious vehicle that churns and circles about in the Dock for a while before – in an ooh-ahh *coup de théâtre* loved by kids of all ages – actually rising up out of the water in a sheet of spray and taking to the streets of Liverpool. The sheer fun of the enterprise is inversely proportional to the ferocious and very un-Scouse surliness of the girl in the ticket office, who seemed to be getting divorced over the phone and regarded me as an unwelcome interruption.

There's a ripe chunk of cheesiness, though: gift shops selling those souvenirs you might buy if very drunk or if you were a Shoreditch ironist – tea towels emblazoned with Scouse glossaries, ashtrays, posters and wristbands bearing insulting messages about whichever football team you don't support. I buy one for an Evertonian friend that reads 'Everton Are Scouse. We Are The People's Club. Liverpool People, Not The Ones Who Come Over On The Friday Night Flight From Oslo'. It takes me a while to unpack this enigmatic statement. Eventually I decode it as a sideswipe at the element in Liverpool's support, perceived or actual, who live in Scandinavia and jet in at the weekend for a spot of sexy Premiership action and a prawn sandwich rather than some gravadlax and a nil-nil draw between Bergen and Tromso. I marvel again at the unquenchable ability of football fans to make the best of anything, as Everton's long-overshadowed Bluenoses rebrand themselves the People's Club, proudly displaying community loyalty and pride where the trophies should be.

Tucked away at the far end of the Albert Dock from Tate Liverpool is an underground exhibition that celebrates Liverpool's real cultural contribution to the world. You wondered when I'd get round to it, didn't you? Yes, Salzburg has Mozart, Shakespeare has Stratford, Liverpool, well, it has Atomic Kitten, The Swinging Blue Jeans, Sonia, Frankie Goes To Hollywood and Echo And The Bunnymen, and one day they may name airports after them. Until then, though, as far as pop music goes, this city is very keen on reminding you that it's Liverpool 4, The Rest Of The World 0.

If your city had produced one of human civilisation's most important cultural forces ever; a group of individuals who in their global significance almost transcended the bounds of the human; who became demi-gods, responsible for changing not only the sound of a planet's music and the shape of its culture but the look and structure of its societies, then you could be forgiven for making a bit of a fuss about it. Yet you can't help thinking that Liverpool does go on a bit about The Beatles.

There are plenty of ordinary Scousers who find the cult of the Fabs embarrassing, hopelessly backward-looking and recherché. The City Fathers have no such reservations. If you arrive by plane ('Lucky you!' trills the City Guide), you 'deplane' at John Lennon International Airport, with its motto of 'Above us, only sky' taken from the glutinous anthem 'Imagine' by the airport's dedicatee. Frankly, I'd have preferred 'Nothing To Kill Or Die For … And No Religion Too … Now Visit Our Fabulous Duty Free Shopping Area!' There's a statue of Lennon in arrivals based on the Abbey Road cover. Taken out of context, it looks like he's storming out of somewhere in a huff. This is kind of appropriate, I feel, as rather than the sainted holy man that he's now absurdly regarded as, Lennon was actually a rather sour personality, short-tempered, sulky and often cruel. I wonder if he'd have turned up for the renaming ceremony. I think he would have. I can just see him now, pulling the little curtains to one side and doing his hilarious 'mong' face.

Liverpool's Beatle heritage industry embraces the tacky and the thoughtful simultaneously, sentimental and savvy as only Liverpool can be. Mathew Street, site of the famous Cavern Club, is now heart of the 'Cavern Quarter', and in the Cavern Walks shopping centre, incongruously alongside the Vivienne Westwood shop, you will find From Me To You: The Beatles Store (Store, not Shop – you can see who it's aimed at). Here, as you might think, you can find all manner of Beatle memorabilia from a Doug Millings Nehru jacket to a Yellow Submarine duvet cover. Alongside all this, though, is the kind of general rock tat you'd find in Carnaby Street's sundry emporia; Motorhead bullet belts, Led Zeppelin T-shirts. I couldn't for the life of me see why: surely there can't be any shortage of Hard Day's Nighties or We Can Work It Out calculators? The store is owned by Gary Blaine, who's run it for five years. He told me this having stopped me on the way out of Cavern Walks and asking me why I was making notes in his shop. Having assured Gary that I wasn't from the Department of Fair Trading or engaged in Beatle-related industrial espionage, he became extremely personable and gave me a free map.

Downstairs, you can have a baked potato (with choice of fillings £3.50) in a café claiming to be sited on the exact spot of the Cavern's stage, where The Beatles played 272 times between 1961 and 1963. When you consider that there are in the Beatle canon songs such as 'Savoy Truffle' and 'Honey Pie' actually named after food, or even some that sound a bit like greasy spoon proprietors, like 'Rocky Raccoon', 'Lady Madonna' or 'Polythene Pam', it's disappointing that the café is called Lucy In The Sky With Diamonds. They didn't really go that extra mile, did they? At least it wasn't called The Beatles Café, I suppose. Outside, there's an Abbey Road pub and another called the John Lennon, though for authenticity, you should sip a bottle of light ale in the Grapes just as the underage Beatles did before they discovered Scotch and Coke. On North John Street, there's the beginnings of the Hard Day's Night hotel, due to open in 2007, with every floor commemorating a different phase of The Beatles' career, from the Cavern Club in the basement to the roof modelled on that last Apple building concert.

But why shouldn't Liverpool boast about The Beatles? Without The Beatles, there are no pop groups; in fact, no pop music in the modern sense of the word. This, after all, isn't Stereophonics or Green Day. This isn't some bunch of lad-rockers going through the moves and the motions. No. These are the lads who invented the moves and the motions. These are the four lads that shook the world as Arthur Dooley's Mathew Street statue has it, a queasy thing with a halo-ed John cradled by 'Mother Liverpool'. Once a landmark, it now has competition from ton upon ton of city-centre Beatle statuary, from Tommy Steele's maudlin 'Eleanor Rigby' to the slightly too small John Lennon lounging on the Cavern wall to, of course, a Yellow Submarine or two.

If Stratford can have its As You Like It tearooms and Salzburg can have its Barber of Seville barbers, then let Liverpool celebrate its most famous sons. The Beatles Story – just follow the sound of the endless loop of Beatle songs from the south end of Albert Dock – tries hard to do this authoritatively and with some grated entertainment cheese liberally sprinkled on top. Again, I can't help wishing that they'd brainstormed a little longer at the slogans meeting. 'Let Me Take You Down' implies you're going to find it depressing – and to be truthful, the Lennon and Harrison tributes aren't chucklesome – and 'Getting Better All The Time' makes it sound as if it was rubbish when it started.

As of winter 2006, it's a very slick operation. You can get an audio guide and hear Epstein and Macca et al actually talking as you look at actual replicas of some clothes they might have worn and guitars they might have played. I'm a bit obsessed with the epochal first meeting at Woolton village fête on 6 July 1957 so I linger in front of the huge blow-up of that famous black and white picture of the Quarrymen. It's not the surly defiance of the young John Lennon that I find especially compelling – though it certainly is; he's the only one in the whole picture staring at the camera – as much as the minor players. There's a young girl smiling in an Easter bonnet and a bloke arranging a floral Union Jack. They go about their breezy business on a sunny suburban holiday afternoon in Liverpool, unaware that the history of the world will be changed today by the meeting of two teenagers a few feet away from them, in the little shed-cum-dressing room behind the stage.

Some exhibits work better than others; the recreation of the Cavern really gives you a feel for how cramped and exciting it must have been in 1962. Brian Epstein's NEMS record shop (now actually a branch of Ann Summers) is perfectly done. Something, though, has gone badly wrong with the First Beatles London Recording Session tableau. The suits are grotesquely outsized, and George's arm has come adrift and it hangs limp and twisted down to his knee. It looks more like Night Of The Living Dead than Birth Of An Era. I found the Through The Lenses Of Lennon mawkish and pointless; though, as you may have guessed, I've little appetite for the New Church Of St John.

The young staff in the gift shop are cheery and helpful. I buy a Revolver mug and am unnerved to see a punter loitering by the tea towels dressed exactly like 1975 vintage Lennon, the circular shades, centre-parted hair and New York City T-shirt. I find this very odd, as odd as seeing a chap dressed as Goebbels in the gift shop of the Imperial War Museum. ('What? This old thing? The jackboots? Oh, I'm just a big fan, I guess.')

You won't be short-changing The Beatles Story if you're in

and out in forty minutes. If you have a couple of hours, though, go on the Magical Mystery Tour, a trip on a coach straight from that misunderstood film which takes in most Beatle-related Liverpool landmarks. Beatles music plays throughout, naturally, sometimes slightly out of sync thanks to a recalcitrant cassette deck – they may have an iPod by the time you read this – and Japanese tourists sing along winningly all the way. The tour stops at all the places you'd expect – Penny Lane, Strawberry Fields, even the road where Lennon's mum Julia was knocked down and killed – but the latest attractions are the National Trust properties at 20 Forthlin Road and the Mendips, childhood homes of one Paul McCartney and John Lennon respectively.

There was a deal of sniggering about the National Trust buying what, in the case of Forthlin Road, amounts to a mass-produced council house, an 'Intermediate Type Standard Building 5' built in 1952 for little more than a grand. Under the layers of 'modernisation' introduced by well-meaning, house-proud tenants down the years, the Trust were excited about finding 'the original lino' in the young Paul's bedroom. At the time of purchase this prompted yet more sniggering from those who believe that the upkeep of ugly, ostentatious, stately homes in Surrey and Gloucester is the correct use of National Trust money, not council houses in Liverpool.

Mindful of the fact that my soapbox is never far away at moments like this, I'll just say that even if 20 Forthlin Road were merely an example of how upper-working-class families lived in the years after the war – modest, much-loved homes for ordinary people viewing the future with trepidation and hope – it would be worth preserving. But it isn't just that, of course. This is where Paul and John wrote the early Beatles classics 'eyeball to eyeball' on the sofa while Paul's dad was out at work, breaking off for fried egg sandwiches and crafty Woodbines. The grandiose country piles and family seats of our various Lord and Lady Mucks pale into insignificance next to this compact wee house. From this stolid, mildly frumpy little room, the north revolutionised the known world.

As an alternative to this chest-swelling proletarian pride, let me say that some of the town's Beatle industry is pretty unspeakable. The Mathew Street Gallery has original pieces by Lennon as well as Beatle associates Klaus Voorman and Astrid Kirschner but also houses pieces such as Alex Corina's 'Mona Lennon', which the city's official literature describes as 'unconventional' and 'marvellous' but which is in fact a ghastly piece of gimmicky tat. Why not stick Ringo Starr's head on 'The Scream' by Edward Munch? It would be just as meaningful and attractive... Oh no, let's not give them ideas.

When you're sated with The Beatles, and never want to see another Mona Lennon or hear another kitsch shopping centre version of 'Yesterday' again, remember that Liverpool, according to Paul Du Noyer's excellent book *Wondrous Place*, has always 'made more music than most cities, and made it more passionately, because it was in the personality of Liverpool to do so. And Liverpool has the personality it has because it is a seaport. Liverpool only exists because it is a seaport. Its virtues and its vices, its accent and attitude, its insularity and its open-mindedness, are all derived from that primary fact.' Interestingly, when Daniel Defoe was eulogising the Pool in the 1720s, he made reference to the ships that sailed from here 'to Norway, the Baltick and Hamburgh'. Three and a bit centuries later, it was the musical trade between Liverpool and Hamburg that made The Beatles a seaworthy crew, ready to conquer the world.

Liverpool music has always been joyous, skittish, heady and psychedelic while, say, Manchester's has usually been more dour, cool and narcotic. At the end of the seventies, the Cavern blossomed again, this time as Eric's, centre of a kaleidoscopic scene where The Teardrop Explodes, Echo And The Bunnymen, Wah! Heat, Pink Military, The Icicle Works and more fused punk attitude with hippy beatitudes to produce a new northern psychedelia. Ever since Macca went upstairs to have a smoke and then off into a dream in 'A Day in the Life', Scousers have loved a bit of blow. In the eighties, the city's lads created their own version of the football casual, the 'scally': a roguish, whippet-thin chancer dressed in Tacchini and Lacoste. Add a mellowing joint or ten, and he becomes the retro-scally or cosmic Scouser.

I first came across this strange, engaging sect when I was working in Skem. While the girls dressed as only Scouse girls can – flamboyantly and defiantly glamorous and skimpy even in the depths of winter – the lads would sport leather bomber jackets, frayed, flared jeans or 'keks', implausible fringes or straggly manes. Trainers were ubiquitous and sometimes beanie hats. While the *NME* would tell them on a weekly basis that they ought to be listening to Public Enemy, Pop Will Eat Itself or Einstürzende Neubauten, they existed in an aromatic world of their own making, built on their older brother's record collection, escaping from the privations of Thatcher's Britain not through officially sanctioned 'indie' music or American hip-hop but through the Floyd, Genesis, Frank Zappa and late-period Beatles. I would spend lunchtimes in the pub with them, arguing the relative merits of Atom Heart Mother and The Lamb Lies Down On Broadway and haggling to buy the college's video player back via the town's black market after its weekly theft.

In case that sounds like I'm condoning criminality, let's just say that a certain low level of nefarious activity was regarded as normal. After all, if crooks in good suits in London could line their pockets flogging off gas, water and railways that actually belonged to me, why shouldn't a scally make the odd tenner selling me my own video back from time to time? The way I felt about it is summed up perfectly in a song by The Beautiful South in which a scally thief turns up at a posh London bash celebrating 'enterprise' and rewarding the kind of entrepreneur beloved of the eighties Conservatives. The scally takes the stage and points out that he has followed their credo to the letter, working hard, living on his wits, getting to the top of his profession by being the best and to hell with those he had to step on. He is, he claims, the ultimate Thatcherite. The song is called, brilliantly, 'I've Come For My Award'.

All that said, though, Liverpool isn't red the way Manchester is red. The socialism that created the Labour Party has no history here as it does in Manchester or, for that matter, Sheffield. Liverpool was never that kind of industrial city with a stable, unionised workforce. Dock labour was casualised until the sixties, and was not regarded as a job for life, complete with a pension and rights. The kind of socialism that grows out of religious non-conformism barely existed in this city with a large Catholic population.

I doubt very much if in Manchester or Sheffield, with their strong, moralistic, conventional socialism, something as mad as the Militant Tendency could ever have taken over as they did here; a mafiosi who talked Marx but looked like a cabal of wide boys in flash suits on the make, the ultimate Thatcherites. Persistent rumour has it that as the tide turned and Kinnock began to gain the upper hand over Militant, many a member of Derek Hatton's notorious security squad, a private army in all but name, moved effortlessly into the city's newly burgeoning dance music scene.

Once I became a music writer, I spent a lot of time in Liverpool in the late eighties, encouraged by charming proselytisers such as The Farm's Peter Hooton, who would tell me the town was buzzing again and talk up the city's new bands, then The La's, Rain and The Hoovers. The former are still legendary, the middle a big influence on early Oasis, the latter a band of delightful hairy misfits who sounded like Captain Beefheart and lived on a section of Cantrill Farm estate that looked like an East German military installation. In 2006, the Scousers are still cosmic, by the way, be it The Coral, The Stands or The Zutons.

Liverpool was slow to pick up on house and dance music in the nineties, being, as Andrew Harrison puts it, 'suspicious of any trend they hadn't started themselves'. But when they did embrace it they did so with gusto and a superhuman appetite for excess. Liverpool invented the superclub and the city's club scene is still riotously fertile and very different from the southern version. The accent in Liverpool is not on untouchable cool but on irrepressible fun. If you'll let me point you in the direction of another Ian McNabb song, listen to 'Liverpool Girl' for a lovely, cheeky, affectionate portrait of the city's young womanhood who 'looks exactly like her mother, though strangely nothing like her mother' and 'wears her silver jeans, going out to Cream, dancing under laser beams'.

But is that Liverpool girl northern? I think so. But then, Whiston Hospital notwithstanding, I'm not really a Scouser. I ask a real one, a craggy, middle-aged chap with a firm handshake who's shifting barrels outside one of the Beatle theme pubs on Mathew Street. 'I'm a northerner, definitely, and Liverpool is the north. But a lot of Scousers don't reckon it is. You see, the thing is, for all that stuff about being outgoing and that, Scousers are very insular, very inward-looking. It got a bit too much for me. So I moved to Southport.'

We, though, are moving somewhere else. When Liverpool does deign to call itself 'northern', it assumes, by natural right, that it is the capital of the north. But it has a rival. There is

another power in the north-west, Moscow to Liverpool's New
York, Pyongyang to its Seoul, Minas Morgul to its Minas Tirith;
a mortal enemy glowering from across the Lancashire plain,
along the asphalt ribbon of the M62. It rises in the east,
curtained with rain, swearing, walking like a monkey and wearing
a beanie hat.

So Much To Answer For...

It's late in the evening of Good Friday 2006 and I am staring at the television slack-jawed in disbelief. BBC3 is showing, as their trails and teasers have been promising for days, an updated, modern-dress version of the Passion, the story of the final days of Jesus. There's something reassuringly old-fashioned about all this. Ever since I was a wee lad, well-meaning religious teachers with halitosis, ginger beards and sandals have been singing Simon and Garfunkel ballads or 'Nowhere Man' to us 'kids', desperately keen to make Christianity sexy and telling us that, hey, I suppose Jesus was a kind of rock and roll rebel himself when you think about it, right! Evidently, the Church is still gamely engaged in this endeavour. Why not? Mitres off to them, I say.

But that's not why I'm so thoroughly gobsmacked by this particular trendy update of the New Testament. That's not why my tumbler of Scotch is untouched on the table next to me, ice slowly melting. That's not why I'm shaking my head and telling anyone who'll listen that 'this is just incredible'. No. What is so gloriously, brazenly outrageous about this spectacle is that it is the Manchester Passion. The momentous events of the Holy Land two thousand odd years ago have been, yes, resurrected and relocated to Piccadilly Gardens on this freezing Friday night. In the audience, Manc revellers clutch Bacardi Breezers and, gurning at the cameras, mingle with well-scrubbed God botherers from around the world sporting the sweatshirts of their various parishes and groups. Tim Booth, the former singer with James, always a man with thespian tendencies, is giving us his comically intense Judas: 'How does it feel to treat me like you do?' he sings accusingly at Jesus, cast as a sort of a heartthrob brickie. Wait a minute. 'How does it feel to treat me like you do?' That's…

Yes, it's New Order's 'Blue Monday'. For this Manchester Passion is not just set in the north-west's most self-aggrandising city. Oh no. It is also a celebration of that city's music, shoe-horned, arc-welded, crowbarred, Superglued, if you will, onto the trifling matter of the last agonising hours of the saviour of humanity and his subsequent resurrection from the dead. But we're getting ahead of ourselves. Jesus isn't dead yet. It's still the Last Supper and he's still got something to say/sing to those unshaven disciples in their fatigues and parkas. 'When routine bites hard, and ambitions run low…' He is now giving them the Gospel According To Ian Curtis taken from Joy Division's 'Love Will Tear Us Apart'.

Later, in a moment of understandable glumness after consigning the only son of God to a brutal death, Tim Booth/ Judas sings 'Heaven Knows I'm Miserable Now' accompanied by some meaningful sighing. Jesus in the Garden of Gethsemane sings James's very own 'Sit Down' to his sheepish apostles, presumably because there isn't a Happy Mondays song called 'Thanks A Bunch. I'm Going To Be Nailed To A Cross Because One Of You Bastards Snitched'. Eventually, Jesus rises from the dead atop the town hall to the strains of The Stone Roses' 'I Am The Resurrection', the one Manc song you might legitimately include in your biblical Easter pageant without fear of ridicule.

It was simultaneously both breathtakingly awful and kind of admirable. You had to chuckle at the sheer Mancunian chutzpah of it all (yes, chutzpah; Manchester has a strong, long-established Jewish community though, come to think of it, they probably didn't have much to do with this particular bit of street theatre). Forget what has been said about the Scousers. In its own brassy, hard-faced way, Manchester is far more sentimental than Liverpool. Can you imagine the Wolverhampton Passion, the Ipswich Passion, the Luton Passion? No. No other city in Britain would have had the inflated sense of self-regard to do this, namely to restage the crucifixion as an out-take from *24 Hour Party People*. No story, it seems, is so sacred that Manchester can't use it as a promotional tourist video. Nice one, our kid.

Where does it come from, this monumental, hubristic vanity, this 'cock of the walk' self-assurance, this civic, city-wide swagger pimp-rolling its way from Ancoats to Harpurhey, from Crumpsall to Chorlton, from Didsbury to Whalley Range? Not from the Gallagher brothers or Shaun Ryder or from the heady chemical euphoria of Madchester. It predates all that, just as it predates the swelled chests and heads of Cantona or George Best or the quieter glories of the Busby Babes. Basically, Manchester has fancied itself rotten for as long as anyone can remember.

Its mouthy arrogance rankles with a lot of people, many southerners in particular. But nowhere more than on Merseyside. The rivalry between Liverpool and Manchester is not like the rivalry between, say, Edinburgh and Glasgow, based on a philosophic and cultural gap between two proud cities whose very difference and diversity is somehow useful and fruitful. It doesn't actually make sense to think of what goes down between the Scousers and the Mancs as a rivalry at all; it's a vendetta, a blood feud that's Sicilian in intensity, contemptuous at best, raw, visceral hatred at worst, each always out for vengeance and reparation like the Hatfields and McCoys or the Campbells and MacGregors. No player has been transferred between the two teams since Phil Chisnall moved from United to Liverpool in 1964. Also, the malice and ill-will borne by fans of Liverpool and

Manchester United's football teams outweighs by far that felt by either team for their traditional rivals across the city, Everton or Man City. Just check the priorities evident in this charming ditty sung by Manchester United's Stretford End supporters to the tune of 'Oh My Darling Clementine'.

Build a bonfire, build a bonfire
Put the Scousers on the top
Put City in the middle
And we'll burn the fucking lot

On 19 April 1992, Manchester United were beaten at Anfield in one of the last games of the season and thus, right at the death, forfeited the league title. Stunned and distraught, United manager Alex Ferguson and his players scuttled to their bus, pausing politely to sign autographs for some waiting Liverpool scallies. After Lee Sharpe, Paul Ince and Ryan Giggs had scrawled their names on the proffered scraps of paper, the Liverpool fans jeered, tore them up and threw the pieces back at them, crowing derisively. As they left Liverpool, a trembling, angered Alex Ferguson told the silent coach, 'Remember this day. What has just happened should tell you all how much people envy you.' By people, he really meant Scousers. And remember they did. United won eight championships in the next eleven years, succeeding and usurping Liverpool as the country's dominant football power.

The balance of power is much more even these days and so hostilities have, if anything, become even more fractious and intense. As tensions built in 2002, before the Second Iraq War, a huge banner was unfurled at the Millennium Stadium at the Liverpool/Man Utd Carling Cup Final. It read 'Don't Bomb Iraq, Nuke Manchester'. During a superheated FA Cup tie between the two in February 2006, United's Alan Smith slid in to block a shot by Liverpool's John Arne Riise and snapped his leg in gruesome fashion. Team mates running over to assist turned away, covering their eyes in horror. Neutrals were shocked. Among sections of the Liverpool fans, though, a chant soon rang out to the tune of cheesy Euro-hit 'Hey Baby'. It went 'John Arne Riise, we wanna know-oh-oh-oh, how you broke his leg'. Objects were even thrown at the stretcher as Smith was carried off.

It gets much, much worse than even this. The sickest, thickest sections of both sets of supporters take pleasure in rubbing salt in either city's rawest wounds: the 1989 Hillsborough tragedy and the Munich air crash of 1958. Some Liverpool fans sing 'Always check on the runway for ice' to the horribly jaunty tune of 'Always Look On The Bright Side Of Life' while doing childish airplane impressions. United's idiot rump chant 'You should have all died at Hillsborough' to the lilting melody of 'Guantanamera' and 'If it wasn't for the Scousers we could stand'. I've been among otherwise reasonable people who, after a drink or two and in the red fog of the moment, have sung these songs. That tells you a lot about just how crazy some people can get around football and even about how deep the rifts and the old scores go between the Scousers and the Mancs.

They go right back to what ex Man Utd boss Ron Atkinson used to call 'early doors'; the kick-off of British economic might, the Industrial Revolution. As smoke and noise and seismic change shook the whole of northern England, Manchester and Liverpool were already stoking the fires of their vituperative feud from a mere thirty-five miles' distance. Liverpool became resentful of Manchester's staggeringly swift civic rise; it mushroomed in size from what Defoe patronisingly called 'the greatest mere village' in the 1700s to a metropolis of 100,000 people by 1812 and the world's first industrial city. Its wealth was based largely on cotton, the raw materials of Manchester's booming textile mills. As you'll know if you've spent any time around these parts, cotton fields are at a premium in Chorley and you've always been hard pushed to get a decent Mint Julep in Ramsbottom. Manchester's cotton therefore had to be imported from the plantations and the slave estates of America's Deep South. And after its journey across the Atlantic, how did it get to Manchester, resolutely and distantly inland? Via Liverpool, of course, which, as we've seen, opens its blousy arms wide to transatlantic travellers of every kind.

Thus Liverpool spied a chance to get its own back on uppity Manchester. Holding the trump card of that sea access, it imposed a tax on US cotton imports. But Manchester retaliated in audacious and spectacular style by constructing a broad, artificial waterway pretty much parallel to the Mersey on the Wirral bank of the river and carrying traffic from the ocean. This grandiose gesture was the Manchester Ship Canal, the civil engineering equivalent of Gary Neville running the length of the pitch to kiss his United badge in front of enraged Liverpool fans. The canal was opened in 1894, rendered Liverpool's levy redundant, and for a century made a thriving port of a landlocked city. No mean feat. The glory days of the Ship Canal have gone but the waterway still has a shining place in the city's history and culture. Just as Bethnal Green market traders and city wide boys will boast to you of being born within the sound of Bow Bells and therefore 'pukka Cockney', so you may be collared by a nasal, drawling man in a Burnage boozer who will tell you that he is a 'proper Manc' by virtue of having a grandad who 'worked on the canal'.

In 1830, when the world's first passenger railway was built between the two cities, not even Stephenson's Rocket could bring those hearts and minds together. The opening day was somewhat marred in any case by the fact that William Huskisson MP got hit by a train and killed, but even before this, many people were hostile to the enterprise and wanted it to fail. Some Liverpudlians felt that passenger traffic with Manchester, a grubby, sooty inland town with ideas above its station, railway or otherwise, would bring the wrong sort to Liverpool.

'The Liverpool gentleman and the Manchester man' is a nineteenth-century distinction still preserved by some old-school Liverpudlians, meaning that the inland city grew prosperous on oily, blue-collar industry and manufacture, while Liverpool was a city of commerce: shipping, insurance, trade, customs and excise.

My agent, a delightful woman called Kate, not known for misanthropy but nevertheless a Scouser, claims that she 'even hates the Manchester one-way system. I always get lost on it. It's nasty and unhelpful. Typical.' Bernard Manning, a comedian who has done much to help prove the Merseyside assertion that Mancs aren't funny, says, 'I like Liverpool. I go there to visit my hubcaps.' When I worked among Scousers, my Mancunian mates found this both baffling and humorous. 'Watch your wallet,' they'd caution before telling me the de rigueur Mancunian joke of the late eighties: Q. What do you call a Scouser in a suit and tie? A. The Accused.

At their most caricatured and embattled, the citizens' attitudes towards each other might be summarised thus. Mancs think Scousers are lazy, sentimental, smackhead thieves in tracksuits; Scousers think Mancs are dour, gun-obsessed wannabe gangsters with no sense of style or humour. Guildford probably thinks both are pretty much right.

As a kid, Manchester seemed to me the very acme of big city allure. Growing up in a cotton town loosely in its orbit, Manchester was rich, sexy, glamorous, cool, near enough to be kindred but far enough away to be exotic. The buildings were bigger, the people brasher, the accent racier. Manchester was nightclubs, steakhouses and pizza parlours, the floodlit fairgrounds of Belle Vue, Denis Law and George Best with their shirts untucked and sleeves worn long like Bash Street Kid superstars, or Colin Bell, balletic elegance in that fabulous seventies red and black striped City kit.

I had family in Swinton, a suburb of Manchester, and my cousins Eileen and Elizabeth were archetypal Manchester girls of the period: mini-skirts, crocheted tops, white PVC boots, hotpants, cobalt eye shadow. They had boxes full of seven-inch singles: Decca, Deram, Regal Zonophone, Major Minor. From being a toddler, Manchester was girls and pop music, an escape from routine, the liberating thrill of the city. How could I not love it?

In my teens, I would go there under my own volition with mates to see gigs at the Free Trade Hall: Tangerine Dream, Martha Reeves, Gentle Giant, Linda Ronstadt (I had absurdly catholic taste, it would appear). It was always an adventure. Pulling your trenchcoat up around your bumfluffed cheeks and sneaking past the bouncers for a crafty pint of Best on Deansgate. Later on, the rattling train home through eerily deserted late-night stations like Hindley and Westhoughton, sharing a can of Colt 45 or, if you were very lucky, snogging a girl in a cheese-cloth shirt and faded Levi's, missing your stop and ending up in Maghull.

In my late teens, I started going out with a girl from Manchester. Actually, she was from Boothstown, a rough suburb straddling the arterial East Lancs Road and later famous as the bit of town where the legendary Eric Cantona made his home in a typically maverick gesture. Boothstown's distance from the bright lights of Piccadilly Gardens didn't matter to me, though. As far as I was concerned I was going out with a girl from Manchester, which conferred upon me the same worldly sophis-tication as Mick and Bianca or Rod and Britt, those other famous pan-global couples. The fact that she really liked Rush only slightly spoiled her metropolitan chic.

Greater Manchester buses of the eighties were famous for their 'fried egg' orange and white livery. Twice a week I would get the number 32, which would crawl slowly to her house through a succession of neglected and forlorn former pit villages like Atherton and Tyldesley, known for some bizarre reason locally as 'Bent' and 'Bongs'. I never passed through Tyldesley without a shudder; right there in the grand Victorian baths hall was where my Uncle Brian had taught me to swim by hurling me in from the side and then making encouraging noises as I spluttered and thrashed. Gin Pit, Astley, Mosley Common; the names as ringingly northern as clogs on cobbles, the route still etched in the memory.

This spring morning, though, I step down from the Pendolino high-speed train into a dazzling steel and glass piazza, the concourse of the newly refurbished Piccadilly station. For years, Piccadilly was a grim entrée to the delights of the city, windswept and soulless, with its one real advantage being that as it lay at the end of the line, you could fall asleep with an easy conscience and that way you passed through Stoke oblivious, always a bonus. Then for years it was a building site. But it appears to have all been worth it. Now when your train is delayed due to failure of lineside equipment in Congleton, Piccadilly is a diverting place to kill some time. You can buy a Coldplay CD or a caramel macchiato or *Heat* magazine or any of the other things that twenty-first-century Britons do.

It's a glorious day, and that's not natural, of course. According to myth, it always rains in Manchester. Rainy City was Manchester's CB radio handle during that brief fad and, in the days before sunbeds, it was said that if you saw a Mancunian with a tan they'd gone rusty. Adrian Mitchell wrote a poem about Manchester's moistness called 'Watch Your Step – I'm Drenched', in which he talks of the city's 'thousand puddles' 'poised on slanting paving stones' that 'lurk in the murk of the north-western evening'.

Manchester's damp climate has been mooted as responsible for everything from its textile mills (water and coal make good factories) to the gloomy sound of Joy Division. In fact, it's the ninth wettest city in Britain and positively arid compared to Swansea, Glasgow and Plymouth. Sheltered by the Pennines, it hardly ever snows here. Today it's just beautiful; blue skies and fluffy clouds above the endlessly evolving cityscape.

Every time you come to Manchester these days, the skyline has changed. It's the Shanghai of the north-west, construction crazy, in a state of permanent restless revolution, a frenzy of hard hats and scaffolding. In 1962, Frank Kermode wrote, 'The worst thing about Manchester is that it's unstoppable, like spilt beer.' And it's still spreading. The Beetham Hilton Tower is the latest vaunting gesture of architectural ambition to thrust its way skyward. On the very morning I emerge from Piccadilly station, the *Daily Mirror* carries an amazing picture of a construction worker (in high-visibility tabard, of course) catching forty winks stretched out on a girder hundreds of dizzying metres above Manchester's pavements. It will be the tallest residential tower in the UK and from the top there are views of the Pennines, the Welsh mountains, Blackpool Tower and Liverpool's cathedrals. Which it dwarfs, much to the locals' delight of course. This new tower is more than just a very tall partly constructed building; it's regarded by mooching Oasis wannabe and besuited branding consultant alike as a symbol of the city's resurgent virility and regional dominance.

If you think those cocky Mancs have only got this way in the last couple of years, think again. A century ago, folks round here were saying, puffed up with aldermanly pride, 'What Manchester does today, the world does tomorrow.' In the late sixties, in his wonderful book *The North Country*, Graham Wilson chided them on their 'ridiculous self-congratulation'. Filmmaker Chris Lethbridge probably came closest to how I feel about the place when he wrote in 1994, 'It has a compulsion to preen and show off; it is narcissistic, contrary and wayward, and yet you cannot help but love it. It is both admirable and maddening.' Nowhere is this galling, charming, maddening, admirable self-belief better seen than in the city's musical culture and, in particular, in the gloriously Mancunian tale of Factory Records.

Musically Manchester skulked in Liverpool's shadow in the 1960s. They did have the wonderful Hollies (Britain's unsung pop treasure, as I will expound on at length if you're buying). They also had in Graham Gouldman one of Britain's most gifted song-writers, who actually coaxed a clutch of brilliant singles from the irredeemably goofy Herman's Hermits. Manchester bands were ubiquitous in the charts here and in the States. But there was a sneaking feeling of inferiority; while The Beatles were experiment-ing with Indian music, blowing their minds and inventing rock culture, Manchester's Freddie And The Dreamers were jumping in the air, kicking their legs and singing 'We wear short shorts'. It was no contest, really; Manchester knew it and it rankled.

That said, Manchester did have the legendary Twisted Wheel soul club and later played host to what writer Richard Williams has called 'the most electrifying single event in post-war culture': the appearance of Bob Dylan and band powered by electricity at the Free Trade Hall in 1966. As Dylan cranked up the amps, the crowd instantly polarised into proto-hippies who'd never heard anything so loud in their lives and loved it and oddly puritanical young Mancunian folkies in bottle-bottom glasses, jeering, shouting 'Judas' and rending their tweed jackets in despair.

If the Dylan gig did electrify Manchester, it took a while for the city to feel the aftershock. 10CC aside – who admirably decided to build a state-of-the-art studio in a backstreet in Stockport – Manchester had a somnolent early seventies. Journalist and local boy Paul Morley remembers that 'Manchester was a very boring place to be. It had no identity, no common spirit or motive.' But then another bunch of noisy mavericks came to the Free Trade Hall (or its upstairs parlour, at least, the Lesser Free Trade Hall) and this time Manchester reacted as if the city had stuck its finger in the mains.

When the Sex Pistols played Manchester on 20 July 1976, there were more people there to see them than the first time a month earlier ('The audience was very slim,' according to one Steven Patrick Morrissey, who was present) but it was still an intimate affair. Brian Eno says that hardly anyone bought the first Velvet Underground album but everyone who did formed a band. So every one of the undernourished throng who saw the Pistols that summer night was empowered into action.

Bernard Sumner and Peter Hook of Joy Division and later New Order were there. So was Morrissey again. The gig itself was promoted by two students from Bolton, Howard Devoto and Pete Shelley, whose fledgling band Buzzcocks played that night. A young docks clerk called Mark Smith saw Buzzcocks, thought he could do better and formed The Fall, one of Britain's most subversive, unique and influential acts ever. Mick Hucknall was there and so energised was he by events that, well, a decade later he made some horribly dull plastic soul records. Or something. But you get the picture. If not, you can actually go and see the picture: Michael Winterbottom's terrific film *24 Hour Party People* recreates the gig and the rolling aftermath for Manchester's music scene.

A local TV reporter called Tony Wilson was so impressed that

he invited the Pistols onto his Granada TV show where, leering
and radiating menace and glamour, they played 'Anarchy In The
UK' to a generation of stunned northern teenagers. Watching in
Wigan, I could feel the tectonic plates rumble as the earth
shifted. Wilson himself was a man possessed. Formerly a
Cambridge-educated Leonard Cohen fan who'd come back to
his home town to present the local news show, he found himself
at the centre of the greatest youth cultural foment in a decade.

After promoting new-wave bands tirelessly and much to the
chagrin of dads across the north-west on Granada slots such as
What's On and *Granada Reports* (more used to items on inade-
quate drainage provision in Levenshulme), Wilson took the step
into independent gig promotion. In May 1978, in partnership
with his mate and sometime actor Alan Erasmus, he began putting
on bands at the distinctly insalubrious Russell Club in Hulme
under the name The Factory (nights recreated for *24 Hour Party
People* at sticky-carpeted city-centre rival Fagins, ironically). Those
early nights have become legendary: Joy Division, Cabaret
Voltaire, The Durutti Column, The Stockholm Monsters,
Orchestral Manoeuvres In The Dark, who were Scousers 'who
looked like Leo Sayer'. Factory may have been very Mancunian
but they were never parochial.

The club's distinctive advertising – Russian constructivism
relocated to Lancashire – was designed by Peter Saville. The first
poster became the now legendary and elusive Fac 1, the first
Factory artefact. Fac 2 was 'A Factory Sample', an EP of music
by acts who had played at the club: The Durutti Column, Joy
Division, Cabaret Voltaire and comedian John Dowie. Local
journalist Paul Morley wrote enthusiastically about the new
venture in the *NME* of 2 December: 'Send Factory Records your
cassette: The Factory, Hulme, Manchester. Let's all take risks this
Christmas!' It was a kind of backstreet nativity. Factory Records

was born under a grimy star overseen by four wise men, Wilson, Erasmus, Saville and producer Martin Hannett, partners in what would become Britain's coolest ever record label.

There's not space here to tell you the whole Factory story. You can read about that elsewhere. But it is a wonderfully Mancunian story, full of vanity, lunacy, obstinacy and grand gestures. There were no contracts; Factory preferred gentleman's agreements, and as many of the bands on Factory were far from gentlemanly, they never made the money they should have. They put out the biggest-selling, most influential twelve-inch single of all time, New Order's 'Blue Monday', but because Factory wouldn't join anything as prosaic as the British Phonographic Institute, there are no platinum discs around. If there were, maybe they could have hung them in the forbiddingly severe offices they built behind the BBC on Charles Street, and which they eventually had to sell for just half a million quid when Factory collapsed (just two-thirds of the cost of Ben Kelly's interior design alone).

I loved it, though. I've lost many an afternoon lounging in its weirdly uncomfortable chairs or around the boardroom table not interviewing the Happy Mondays, getting lost on my way to the toilet through a stone warren of corridors and high forbidding doors straight out of Mordor. If Sauron had a city-centre office, it would have looked liked this.

Kelly's masterpiece, though, was The Haçienda, a nightclub built in an old yacht showroom, maybe because a yacht showroom in a landlocked city is, in itself, a quintessentially Factory notion. It was a dreamer's gesture that for a time came true, part folly, part Folies Bergère, paid for by New Order's money, as they would regularly remind you with mordant Manc humour; a kind of temple to Factory's crackpot, intoxicating ideals. The Haçienda took brutalism and artiness to comic extremes. Here was a club that was named after an obscure Situationist tract, that was dauntingly laid out for the newcomer with *Cabinet of Dr Caligari* angles and corners, had decor based around police accident tape and industrial warning signs, had a bar downstairs called the Gay Traitor as a tribute to Guy Burgess and which even in mid-summer and mid-Madchester mania could feel oddly cool and inhuman. It was a club that celebrated and mocked elitism in its very girders and concrete stairways and on its night, it was the greatest place to be in the world. For a time, I practically lived there and I don't think I ever passed through the doors in those glory years of the late eighties and early nineties without a thrilling, almost sickly feeling that anything might happen. Often it did.

In the end, it failed; the new dawn faded. The Haçienda had always been built on cavalier fiscal foundations. As Peter Hook once said, 'New Order would have been better off if they'd given ten pounds to everyone who ever came to The Haçienda, sent them home, and not bothered with the club at all.' Later organised crime and firearms wormed their way into the club's engagingly disorganised body politic. ('Ah, Manchester... Cotton and guns!' as Steve Coogan's Alan Partridge once exclaimed.) It's a very expensive, very desirable apartment block now.

Factory Records were not just made in the north. They were entirely, fundamentally, immanently of the north. They sounded like the north, and Manchester in particular, made into sound. *Unknown Pleasures*, the astonishing first Joy Division album, actually sounds like the places where it was made. Thanks to Hannett's extraordinary production, it's haunted throughout by splintering glass, industrial hums, by whooshing and clanking that sounds like traffic passing by in the rain on the Mancunian Way or lifts ascending desolate Hulme tower blocks. Writer Jon Savage has talked of how the record is 'a perfect reflection of

Manchester's dark spaces and empty places: endless sodium lights and semis seen from a speeding car, vacant industrial sites – the endless detritus of the nineteenth century – seen gaping like teeth from an orange bus.' But there's more than that. Before moving to the tower blocks of the inner city, Ian Curtis had lived near Macclesfield and Savage is right when he talks of the 'witchy emptiness' of the Pennines weighing heavy upon them, making 'the definitive northern gothic statement'. According to Paul Morley, 'They transmuted what the Manchester damp and the shadows and omen called into dread being by the hills and moors that lurked at the edge of their vision.'

Later, Factory's music would come to enshrine and embody another and entirely different facet of Manchester's culture – not long overcoats and expressionist angst but baggy Day-Glo tops, flares and unbridled hedonism. Factory Records were crucial in the development of Madchester too, in providing it with a creative crucible in the chemical temple of The Haçienda and in giving a home to the Happy Mondays, a group of street urchins and footpads from the benighted suburb of Little Hulton. Streetwise, charismatic, dangerous, psychedelic, utterly unpredictable, most record labels would have been terrified of them. Wilson and Factory embraced them, even indulged them. It couldn't last but while it did, it made Manchester the most exciting city in Britain.

Maybe even the world. At The Haçienda and elsewhere, Mancunians were dancing to the new sounds of acid and Chicago house while most of Chicago was ignoring it and also using it as the basis of an alchemical new sound where rock and dance met on a nightclub floor beneath a strobing light. Wilson organised a panel at the deathly New York junket the New Music Seminar, called it 'Wake Up America, You're Dead' and, according to the *NME*, began it thus: 'Good morning, ladies and gentlemen.

Welcome to the New Music Seminar. The rest of the shit going on in the rest of this building is the Old Music Seminar. This is the New Music Seminar… There is a new music now, however it is probably only reflected in this particular room in the course of this week…' The Americans were outraged, stung into walkouts, threats and patriotic blather. It nearly turned into a brawl, there in the conference suite of a posh Manhattan Marriott hotel.

That was Factory for you. Excessive humility was never one of their failings. Peter Saville says, 'When I was working at Factory we didn't think we were the best, we knew we were.' He was probably right but in the mix was a great deal of Mancunian bluster. Factory could cock up for England. For instance, they signed and spent money they didn't have on the useless Northside but missed the greatest group ever to emerge from the city. And they had them on a plate. One day in the early eighties, Tony Wilson was invited round to tea by a well-known local character, one Steven Patrick Morrissey. 'So I went down to his mum's house in Stretford and he says, "I've decided to be a pop star." And I had to muffle myself. I thought, "Never in a million light years, Steven."'

It took a lot less than that. Steven did get himself involved with a group called The Smiths, who became the Manchester band incarnate. Oasis may talk the talk but The Smiths walked the walk. Like the city at its best, they had glamour and gloom, winsomeness and wit, they were magical and proletarian all at once. Morrissey had been raised on the film and stage play of Salford teen prodigy Shelagh Delaney's *A Taste of Honey*, fabulously evocative of post-war Salford whether it be kids playing in the bombsites that scarred the city for years or Dora Bryan dancing at the legendary Ritz nightclub. Twenty years later, The Smiths played their debut gig there, performing songs that often quoted liberally from Delaney's writings. She was the Morrissey of her day; striking, precocious, working-class. After leaving school she held a variety of jobs in Salford – shop assistant, clerk in a milk depot, usherette – but she burned with the zeal to write. When she was seventeen, she saw a Terence Rattigan play she thought drippy and banal and so took two weeks off work and wrote *A Taste of Honey*. Produced at the Royal Court, it was a sensation. Like Moz, she gave good quote, telling an interviewer in 1959 that 'north county people are shown as gormless, whereas in actual fact they are very alive and cynical'.

The Smiths' songs drip, like an evening drizzle off the Moors, with references to Manchester and its environs. Rusholme, Strangeways, Southern Cemetery, Whalley Range, the Holy Name Church. Morrissey has a video called *Hulmerist*, a wry reference to his childhood home. In an early interview, he said of his artistic self, 'I am forever chained to a disused railway line in Wigan.' While Thatcher, witchlike, cast the north into the outer darkness, The Smiths' songs illuminated it anew with northern lights and fireworks. We loved them for it.

Two decades on, our preciously, jealously guarded passion is an industry. In the tourist information centre, right alongside '100 Hillwalks Around Manchester' and 'Manchester United The Religion', you can pick up a copy of 'Morrissey's Manchester: The Essential Smiths Tour by Phill Gatenby'. Clutching it, you can embark on your own pilgrimage, taking in a disused French restaurant that was once Crazy Face, the clothes shop where Johnny Marr worked, or the very iron bridge on Kings Road, Morrissey's old street, under which he kissed and 'ended up with sore lips' ('Still III'). Gatenby's slim, cheery volume makes official the Smiths tourism that's actually been going on for some years now and has made some very unlikely spots into sightseeing opportunities. Like Salford Lads Club, for instance. It's a fine Edwardian building opened by Baden-Powell in 1904, where generations of Ordsall youths have learned how to box (including Graham Nash and Albert Finney), but is most famous for appearing on the sleeve of The Smiths' *The Queen is Dead* album. Today, like most days, I can find a clutch of nervously giggling Japanese teenagers posing for pictures outside, its barred gates watched by scowling, acned Salfordian counterparts. Gatenby is not the most reassuring of guides at times like these. An early section of his little book is titled 'Surviving In Manchester' and reads, 'Book your accommodation before arriving in Manchester and go straight to your hotel. Do not walk around the centre looking for banks and shops while carrying your bags. Blend in and look local... Plan your route before leaving your room... Do not travel alone but do not travel in too large numbers. Remember in the winter it starts to go dark around 4 p.m.' I would hate to see Phill's book about downtown Kabul. As it is, the Japanese tourists and I return unmolested to the town centre.

I take a walk around a few more old haunts for old time's sake. I walk past the new Haçienda apartments (you can have the penthouse for a few million and put your Bang & Olufsen telly where Bez and Shaun used to 'take a comfort break') down to the Boardwalk, where various bands of mine used to play and where Oasis used to rehearse. I never met them and I'm sure I would have noticed a man with one enormous eyebrow wearing a white leather snorkel parka in June. I stroll via Dry Bar, another uber-cool Factory enterprise, down to what is now depressingly branded the Northern Quarter, and then to lovely Afflecks Palace, an old department store converted into three floors of alternative retail outlets. On Saturdays in summer we would hang out here for hours, hoping for some kind of bohemian cool to rub off on us or to meet up with pale, interesting girls. If you were prepared to plough through the stuffed bears and ex-East German Air Force binocular cases, you could get some great stuff here; on the same afternoon in 1986 I once bought Prince's '1999', an import Woody Allen album, some oxblood Doc Martens and a vintage fifties Hawaiian shirt. And yes, I did still have change for chips and gravy.

Outside Afflecks, there's a fancy mosaic that reads 'And on the Sixth Day God Created Manchester'. This almost entirely meaningless phrase has echoed around the city since the Ecstasy-popping heyday of Madchester and reflects yet again that famous Manchester attitude. Like the accent, it can grate on some. Now that it's cleaner and safer and the IRA have stopped bombing it, the city's worst fault may be that boundless capacity for self-congratulation, for tacky self-mythologising rhetoric like the Manchester Passion, for laddish bluster that manifests itself biliously in a teary Noel Gallagher telling an interviewer, 'The thing about Manchester is ... it all comes from here,' and jabbing at his heart. At least Ian Brown was being funny when he said 'Manchester's got everything except a beach'. It was said of Humphrey Bogart that he was a hell of a nice bloke until 11 p.m. After that he thought he was Humphrey Bogart. Manchester is at its most unattractive when it thinks it's Manchester.

Pop into the city's fine art gallery on Mosley Street and make your way through the Pre-Raphaelites and the Pissarros and Canalettos and replica Elgin Marbles – architect Charles Berry was a devoted Hellenophile – and you'll even find a section devoted to 'Manchester attitude', billed as 'the first psychological profile of a city in an art gallery'. This probably seemed like a great idea when some enthusiastic young curator in rimless Issey Miyake specs first mooted it at the departmental meeting but it boils down to a couple of Happy Mondays sleeves, some oft-quoted Morrissey and a general sense of empty boasting. And in fact, if it stopped banging on about its football teams and its bands and its shops and its attitude, Manchester has something that it can be genuinely, enormously proud of, something that it should shout from the gallery's porticoed rooftops. Manchester changed the world's politics: from vegetarianism to feminism to trade union-ism to communism, every upstart notion that ever got ideas above its station, every snotty street-fighter of a radical philosophy, was fostered brawling in Manchester's streets, mills, pubs, churches and debating halls. Before it fled to London in the 1960s and became 'Islingtonised', the *Manchester Guardian* was Britain's most radical and liberal newspaper. (En passant, thirty years ago, as Nick Cohen records in *Cruel Britannia*, one third of journal-ists were based outside London. Now ninety per cent of reporters work in the capital.) Lydia Becker, the daughter of a Chadderton chemical works owner, pioneered the notion of votes for women with her National Society for Women's Suffrage, a movement later radicalised and turned into a potent political agency by another Manchester family, the Pankhursts. The TUC first met here in 1968. Vegetarianism in the western world began in Salford in 1809 when the Reverend William Cowherd persuaded his congre-gation to give up meat and the concept swept Manchester; there were more vegetarian restaurants in the 1880s than today. The greatest military and economic super-power the world has ever known spent half a century sweating nervously, armed to the teeth and generally terrified of an idea born in Manchester, namely communism. Now that's attitude.

Even the football team has a legacy as red as their shirts. An image of Manchester United as pampered aristocrats still clings to them even though the mantle of rich dilettantism has now largely passed to Chelsea. But United began, like many northern clubs, as a works team: Newton Heath LYR (Lancashire and Yorkshire Railway) in 1878. Ten years later, at the Royal Hotel in Manchester, the first professional football league ever was insti-tuted. Those Corinthians and Royal Engineers may have enjoyed their jolly afternoons of 'clogging' but football as we know it is a northern invention. Of the twelve founder members of the league, six were from the north and none of the remainder came from anywhere south of Birmingham. Northern teams dominated the league for the first forty-odd years of its existence; Blackpool, Preston, Burnley, Blackburn, Sunderland, Sheffield, Newcastle and Huddersfield were the prized names, the glamour clubs, the Barcas and Reals of the day, except these *galácticos* had waxed moustaches and allotments, and if *Hello!* had ever been welcomed into their lovely homes they would have found coal in the bath. A southern team didn't come close to winning the league until Arsenal in the early 1930s.

In contrast, by 1909 Manchester United had already won both the League Championship and FA Cup. Then they did what any good headstrong lot of northern workers would do: they went on strike. Manchester United's players were members of the Professional Footballers Union, which the FA refused to recognise. The players' union had been trying to affiliate to the Federation of Trade Unions, but the football authorities were worried that the players might get involved in other unions' strikes. In fact, they regarded the act of unionising as such utter impertinence that they decided to suspend any member of the union, stop his wages and ban him from playing. The clubs cravenly went along with all this, sacked their unionists and brought in amateurs.

Justifiably incensed and led by star striker Billy Meredith, most of the Manchester United players refused to leave the union and were suspended. They started training independently as 'The Outcasts' while the 'proper' United struggled to find enough amateurs to play. The day before the season began, the FA gave in. Back pay was forthcoming, The Outcasts returned to the fold and unionism in football was recognised. Manchester Eleven, Pompous Mandarins Nil, I make that.

I'm walking through Manchester's Gay Village unfolding a page torn from last week's *Guardian* from my soft leather 'manbag'. Frankly, could I get any more metrosexual? Obviously I could or I wouldn't be chuckling schoolboy-fashion as I do every time I turn into Canal Street and see the judiciously altered road sign that now reads 'anal trect'.

At 11 a.m. the street, whatever you may call it, is just a genteel cobbled thoroughfare running alongside the sluggish Rochdale Canal. But at 11 p.m., it is a very different sexy beast, part Grand Guignol, part fashion parade, part *Satyricon*. Manchester's Gay Village is the biggest and maybe the most welcoming in Europe. In the bad, frightened days of the mid-1980s when some of the north's nightclubs might as well have offered 'Free Glassings With Every Third Pint Of Löwenbräu', the Gay Village had great bars, played great music and tolerated women and straights wanting a fun, lively alternative to the grim subterranean city-centre cellars with their half-price Midori and T'Pau and sweating sales managers with their hands up their secretaries' pencil skirts. When Manto, the first gay bar, opened, it did it with a flourish: huge display windows, balconies, open terraces. Come and have a go if you think you're hard enough, it seemed to say, on several levels.

As I stroll along, I ponder whether I could guess merely from the names of the bars whether I was in the gay quarter. AXM has a policy of 'no tracksuits or football shirts', which seems an unnecessary fashion edict for a gay bar. I mean, really. But what does AXM mean? Possibly something far too sinful and exotic for someone as 'vanilla' as me. Hey, here's one called Vanilla! (I later find out it's 'the Lesbian mecca of the north', although I imagine Mecca itself is fairly uninviting for lesbians.) Taurus? I like it. Masculine but not too obvious. And what's this one? Queers. Oh well.

In the demure hour before lunch, none are offering anything more sinful or exotic than tapas and latte and bruschetta, which all sound very nice. But I'm just passing through. Guided by the *Guardian* article I'm clutching, I'm in search of Manchester's blood-red, fiercely leftist past. The article describes a tour of Manchester in the company of local radical historian Jonathan Schofield. There's no doubt where Schofield's sympathies lie. For instance, he's reverential about a table in the cloistered Chetham's Library. 'Parts of the Communist Manifesto were written right here... Marx would sit on one side of the table and Engels on the other. Whenever I bring people from the Chinese consulate here and get out the old books that Marx and Engels touched, they weep.'

I suppose communism did cause a great deal of tears what with one thing or another. In the Gulags and the Killing Fields, in Berlin and Budapest and the rice fields of China. And if communism began in Manchester then maybe Morrissey was right. Manchester has so much to answer for. But is that fair? When Manchester and Mancunian citizens had those bold new ideas, they were the underdog not the tyrant. Maybe another Smiths line, from 'This Charming Man', makes more sense here, one Moz borrowed from Peter Schaffer's *Sleuth*: Manchester has always been 'a jumped-up pantry boy/who never knew his place'.

Historian Asa Briggs remarked, 'If Engels had lived not in Manchester but in Birmingham, his conception of "class" and his theories of the role of class in history might have been very different. The fact that Manchester was taken to be the symbol of the age in the 1840s ... was of central political importance in modern world history.' Schofield is even more direct. 'Without Manchester there would have been no Soviet Union... The history of the twentieth century would have been very different.'

At the beginning of the nineteenth century, Manchester was

on its way, at breakneck speed, to becoming the world's first major industrial city. Its wealth came from cotton and from the crushing labour and the desperate hardship endured by the city's workers. Lake poet Southey talked of the 'narrow streets and lanes, blocked up from light and air, crowded together because every inch of land is of such value that room for light and air cannot be afforded them. Here in Manchester, a great proportion of the poor lodge in cellars, damp and dark, where every kind of filth is suffered to accumulate because no exertions of domestic care can ever make such homes decent.' But it was rich, and de Tocqueville put it succinctly when he said, 'From this filthy sewer, pure gold flows.' It had booming factories, grand hotels and fine parks. It also had 300 brothels and 700 prostitutes. So much for the good old days.

They called it Cottonopolis; a behemoth of wealth and power and prestige built around city-centre slums like Little Ireland. An excellent road system meant that the liberal factory owners could get in and out of the city without seeing the degradation suffered by their workers and thus pronounced that they were 'doing famously' before sleeping easy at night on feather beds in Cheshire or in the rolling hills of the Pennines. Dickens knew this; in *Hard Times*, his factory owners live on the moor in the fictitious town of Stone Lodge where they can escape the smoke and soot and sewers of Coketown. Coketown was Manchester.

Manchester's factories throbbed and roared day and night and as a result the city itself became a giant turbine for radical ideas. The Chartists rioted regularly in the streets. And whatever James Anderton and the city's mandarins thought of the Sex Pistols playing the Free Trade Hall, it was actually quite in keeping with the building's history. For this is the only building in Britain named after a revolutionary principle. The restrictive Corn Laws of the eighteenth century guaranteed good prices for landowners while putting bread beyond the reach of the working class until they were repealed, thanks to an alliance between radical middle- and working-class activists like Richard Cobden and John Bright, the Rochdale orator who said, 'We were not born with saddles on our backs nor were the gentry born with spurs.' Ironically, today the hall is a five-star hotel with suites that can cost you a grand a night before you even think about having that Toblerone from the minibar. But maybe that's just free trade in excelsis.

Cottonopolis horrified and charmed Friedrich Engels when he came here in 1842 to work as a partner in a textile company. In the company of his girlfriend, a local lass called Mary Burns, he toured the worst areas, found a wretched people 'who must have reached the lowest stage of humanity' and used them as the basis for his book *The Condition of The English Working Class*, a landmark text and a passionate call to arms. He sounds like a top bloke, actually, old Fred, even if he did ride with the Cheshire Hunt. According to Eleanor Marx, his favourite virtue was 'jollity' and his favourite vice was 'excess'. She also said that his motto should have been 'Take It Easy'. Eleanor was married to Karl, of course, who by contrast was a bit of a lardarse with rubbish hair who nicked all Friedrich's ideas.

Most of the mills that stretch for half a mile along the Rochdale Canal down Redhill Street and Jersey Street are now derelict; 'buildings seven to eight storeys high, as high and as big as the Royal Palace in Berlin,' said German architect Karl Schinkel in 1825. There are plans to turn them into a World Heritage Site. The slums that appalled Engels, Southey and de Tocqueville are long gone in the vast clearances of the sixties, but the more handsome face of Cottonopolis can still be seen when you turn from the Gay Village into Sackville Street. There's something typically Mancunian and blustering, something very Elsie Tanner about how these commonplace industrial warehouses and offices have put on their glad rags and slap and turned their best features to the town; a Friday night array of come-hither windows, fabulous frontages and spectacular décolletages and cleavages of brick and masonry.

In case any younger readers are confused about this apparent reference to leather workers, we'll come back to Elsie Tanner in a moment. Manchester is a scarlet woman who hasn't forgotten its blood-red past. Spinningfields is yet another 'landmark development' in the city centre, a giant Meccano riot of girders and cranes that according to the promotional literature will provide 'a natural expansion of Manchester's rapidly growing commercial domain ... to help the city achieve its best economic and social potential, home to world-class financial services, professional services and corporate business'.

By the way, there are two 'services' in there, guys. Maybe you had a long lunch. But let it pass. 'Spinningfields,' concludes the blurb, 'offers a real sense of place.' If you're not convinced that world-class financial services or corporate business can ever give that, then tucked away behind the clamour of Spinningfields is the People's History Museum. Located in an old pumphouse behind another putative apartment block, it prides itself on being 'the only museum dedicated to the working people of Britain and the story of how they organised to change society, improving life for future generations'.

I liked the museum a lot. The chap on the door looked like he might have been a former bus driver struggling manfully with the new demands of customer service, bless him. Perhaps mindful that the class struggle and dialectical materialism are not as immediately attractive to an eight-year-old as, say, a stegosaurus or Saturn V rocket, every effort has been made to make the museum all singing and dancing. You can 'have fun making your own badge, or shop at a 1930s Co-Op'. I think they should take this a lot further. Some games, for instance, commemorating the Miners' Strike: 'Hey kids! Can you get your flying pickets down the M62 from Leigh Colliery to Orgreave without being stopped by the uniformed bullyboys of the capitalist state?' Or maybe a coconut shy where you can win a goldfish for hitting Oswald Mosley or Norman Lamont.

I loved the sign that awaits you as you climb to the exhibitions on the first level. It's a period sign from an earlier, presumably 1930s, exhibition, featuring the classic rotund capitalist greeting you with, 'I don't approve of this exhibition at all. If I could stop you going in, I would. But I can't!' This really tickled Joyce, a large, genial lady who was here with a Trinidadian Trade Union delegation. 'Look at this little fella!' she cried delightedly before going off to make a badge. Who says the proletarian struggle can't be fun!

A little way away in Salford Crescent, opposite the Peel Park campus of the university, a handsome former nurses' home houses the Working Class Movement Library, set up in the fifties by two voracious book collectors and activists called Eddie and Ruth Frow. There's nothing to push or press here, it's not a theme park, nothing lights up or rotates. But if you want to know how the industrial north and particularly Manchester and Salford shaped modern Britain, then pop in. A year's subs are only a fiver. There's always a cup of tea on offer and, as well as a staggering book collection including a first edition of Thomas Paine's *Right of Man*, you can see the flyer actually signed by Henry Hunt announcing the meeting which led to the Peterloo Massacre.

I'm on my way across town to the site of that very incident, the most significant and emotionally charged spot in Manchester's political history. To get there I leave Sackville Street, which the Inspiral Carpets once wrote a song about, and wander through Chinatown. If you want Indian food in

Manchester, head for Rusholme. But the best dim sum in the north is here, within a lobbed spring roll of the Chinese Arch. Here I once saw a man demolish a full set menu banquet and then, having smoked a post-prandial fag, order and consume it all again. Having discussed this at length, my companion and I came to the conclusion that he had to be straight out of prison and this was the treat he had promised himself during the long nights in Strangeways.

I've written about the Britannia Hotel in another book (still some copies available, actually) so I won't repeat myself here. Suffice to say that for several years of my life I seemed to stay here at least once a week with a selection of bands and comedians and media people, usually getting back to my own room just as the chambermaid came to hoover in the morning. I never pass it now without a little shudder that's part horror and part wistfulness.

I take a meandering route by the rather nicer Palace Hotel and the Corner House – where in the eighties you couldn't get in unless you had a black zip-up top, a copy of *Marxism Today* and a packet of Gitanes – past the afternoon Special Brew drinkers on Oxford Road and, avoiding the temptation to double back into the Lass O'Gowrie for a quick one, down towards Deansgate via Peter Street. Eventually I find the spot I'm looking for. In the warm afternoon sunshine it doesn't look particularly horrifying or grisly; a sunny piazza between the G-Mex Centre and the new Convention Centre. The steps are crowded with delegates in name tags, puffing on inter-session fags, sipping smoothies, picking up their messages, utterly oblivious to the bloody legacy of the site where they stand, Britain's Tiananmen Square: Peterloo.

What happened here on 16 August 1819 should perhaps remind we English, maybe next time we're bombing a television station in Belgrade or a hospital in Iraq, of how sordid and uncivilised our own past can be. Not millennia back either, not in the ages of Celts and Picts running around in pelts and woad, but a few short generations ago. On my mum's side, I come from a line of Lancastrian weavers so it's not unthinkable that my great-great-grandad or some of his mates might have been murdered here, by British soldiers, on a summer's afternoon in Manchester.

A crowd of around 80,000 from across Lancashire had come to hear rousing orator Henry Hunt and others speak. It was a time of desperate poverty and of growing radicalism and the meeting was called to espouse various popular causes: universal suffrage, secret ballots, an end to unfair legislation. Henry Hunt, fearing that the magistrates would look for an excuse to over-react, asked people to come 'armed with no other weapon but that of a self-approving conscience; determined not to be irritated or excited'. Everyone really expected a peaceful meeting, though, and many turned up wearing their Sunday clothes.

However, at 1:31 p.m. the magistrates decided to stop the meeting and gave orders for the arrest of the leaders. Captain Joseph Nadin, Deputy Constable of Manchester, sent for the Manchester and Salford Yeomanry. These were a volunteer force largely comprising businessmen and landowners unlikely to be sympathetic to the rally's ideals.

Sixty yeomanry cavalrymen, possibly drunk, entered the field brandishing their sabres and charged towards the cart that served as the speakers' stand. When some demonstrators tried to stop them by linking their hands, they set about them viciously with their sabres. The yeomanry then began to strike down the flags and banners of the crowd with their sabres, until the Hussars arrived, who cleared the field in minutes and pacified them.

Eleven people were killed then and there, including a woman and a child another woman was carrying. About 400 were injured, 100 of them women, many of whom were trampled by horses. One man had his nose severed; others were carried from the field bleeding from numerous sabre cuts. Five died later of their injuries.

Many participants on both sides had fought at Waterloo, including one of the dead. This led James Wroe of the *Manchester Observer* to describe the events with bitter humour as the 'Peterloo Massacre'. He was later arrested for having the temerity to report the events, another echo of Tiananmen. But there were many journalists present and the events immediately found their way into the press. Shelley wrote the impassioned and angry poem 'The Masque Of Anarchy' as a response. Though there was widespread outrage, the government of the day supported the action of the army and magistrates. The Home Secretary, Lord Sidmouth, even congratulated the murderers on their work. By the end of the year, he'd introduced legislation to suppress radical meetings and publications.

But Peterloo had awoken something in the nation as a whole and the north in particular. The widespread public anger at the massacre swelled the support of the reform movement from which the Chartists would eventually emerge. Red with blood that day, some say Manchester and the north has been red ever since. My theory is that the north has never really trusted Westminster, king or country since. Historian A. J. P. Taylor was right on the money when he said, 'Manchester cares no more for the royal family or the landed gentry than Venice did for the Pope or the Italian aristocracy... It is the only place in England which escapes our characteristic vice of snobbery.' Let's hear it for Manchester then, The Red Venice Of The North.

No bloodshed in St Peter's Fields this afternoon, no screaming, whinnying or clashing of sabres. Just the quiet hum of polyglot conversation from the delegates at the 10th Annual International Conference on Research in Computational

Molecular Biology's Genomes to Systems Conference. They start to file back in after their break and on a whim, I join them. Straight up the escalators and in. Security guy even nods at me. They seem a nice bunch and the free Danish pastries and coffee are great. I'm idly looking at a leaflet for the forthcoming 11th Human Genome Meeting in Helsinki when a very pleasant blonde lady with designer specs and a smart grey suit catches my eye. 'Ah, Helsinki. That's my city. Are you going to that one?' Fortunately, before I have to say, 'Well, probably not since I just came in off the street in search of free Danish pastries,' the bell goes for the next lecture. Lightheaded with my new devil-may-care attitude, I almost accompany Johanna (she had a badge on) into the auditorium for the talk but decide that it will probably be slightly too advanced for me, what with a disastrously poor showing in my biology mock 'O' levels of 1977 being my last recorded venture into the subject.

Leaving Johanna from Helsinki behind and going back to A. J. P. Taylor, he also said, 'Manchester has everything but good looks.' This used to be a common refrain. In the late eighties, author Charles Jennings called it 'belligerently ugly' in his cheerless anti-northern polemic *Up North*. Even proudly northern writer Hunter Davies described it in 2000 as 'a building site ... full of gaping holes', claiming 'St Ann's Square is the only attractive part of town'. I like Hunter Davies but I have to disagree here. Building sites don't stay building sites for ever. Like caterpillars, they emerge from their cocoons of steel and wire as butterflies hopefully. This one certainly did, I think, as I stand on the walkway over the Manchester Ship Canal and gaze at Salford Quays.

Salford isn't really Manchester. It's a separate city; to reach it you go west, young man, across the Irwell, the 'river the colour of lead' immortalised by Shelagh Delaney in *A Taste of Honey* and Morrissey in The Smiths' 'This Night Has Opened

My Eyes'. Manchester sees itself as the new Barcelona, a cool, classless, cosmopolitan twenty-four-hour party capital with style. But it has its own class divisions too, even its own north/south divide. The south has better wages, bigger houses, posher suburbs, smarter eateries, while north Manchester has the poverty, the sink estates and the appalling health statistics. But the biggest divide in town lies across the Irwell. You can walk from Salford to Manchester in about five minutes. Most southerners think Salford's a district of Manchester. But real Salfordians get very upset at this. Salford, they will tell you, has its own cathedral and university and charter. They think Manchester is soft and conceited, shallow and flashy compared to Salford's older and often darker lineage. The two are inextricably linked, though, as the local writer Paul Gent put it: 'Like Siamese twins, joined at the chest and sharing several vital organs; but one is permanently aggrieved at the strength and health of the other. They grew up together, they depend on each other, but it doesn't mean they have to like each other.'

All of Britain and great swathes of the world know Salford; its streets and chimneys and two-up two-downs. They gaze on it in their millions night after night, with an omnibus edition at weekends. In the early 1960s, a young man from Salford called Tony Warren wrote a drama about the lives and loves and trials of working-class folk based on the people and places he'd grown up with. He called the town Weatherfield and he called his drama *Florizel Street*. Then a Granada producer said that Florizel sounded like a disinfectant and the name *Coronation Street* was chosen. At first, the show was dismissed by London critics as yet another piece of tiresome kitchen-sink drama from the desolate north. Ken Irwin of the *Daily Mirror* opined, 'The programme is doomed from the outset with its dreary signature tune and grim scene of terraced houses and smoking chimneys.'

Like Decca Records' rejection of The Beatles on the grounds that 'groups of guitars are on the way out', this must rank as one of the most myopic assessments in the chequered history of criticism. *Corrie* went on to become one of the best-loved, most iconic television programmes ever. Over twelve million people tuned in to watch Ken Barlow and Deirdre Rachid get married in 2005 compared to only 9.7 million who watched Prince Charles marry Camilla. For many years, till telly became an orgiastic riot of multi-channel madness, the most expensive advertising slot on British TV was 7.45 on Mondays and Wednesdays, smack in the middle of *Coronation Street*.

There's quite a lot of smack in the middle of *Coronation Street* now. And kidnappings, internet child abuse, sex changes, the usual stuff of Salford life, or so the producers must think. It retains its lightly camp humour and its huge audiences but I find it much harder to love than I once did. Its humour comes from a legacy bequeathed by Warren, a gay northerner who gave the show its characteristic tone as seen in the vivid portrayals of strong women like the aforementioned Elsie Tanner, Annie Walker and Ena Sharples. Warren loved a good catfight, a sexy, brassy femme fatale or formidable matriarch. I could be wrong but whenever I see the show now, the women – indeed all the characters – seem to be simpering fools or freaks. The one educated man, Ken Barlow, is a tragic bore who has careened from doomed relationship to failed employment opportunity. The one successful entrepreneur was a Cockney. In fact, as of 2006, half the cast seem to be Cockneys. Perhaps this is to snare the *EastEnders* vote. It certainly isn't snaring me.

This could just be me being po-faced, of course. If so, it seems I have a soulmate in Professor Michael Harloe, Vice Chancellor of Salford University. He told the local paper in 2006 that the show was doing 'untold damage to Salford's reputation… We are very closely tied to the image of the area, which is constantly reinforced in the media. If we could remove *Coronation Street* from the TV I would cheer; it does more bad for the reputation of Salford than anything else. It's a completely romanticised picture, and wrong. If people really want to know what it was like to live in Salford's slums in the 1930s they should go down to The Lowry and look at the pictures.'

And that's what I've come to do. With all due respect to Delaney, Warren, Graham Nash, Emmeline Pankhurst, Walter Greenwood, Albert Finney, Sir Peter Maxwell Davies, John Cooper Clarke, Alistair Cooke, Christopher Eccleston and all the rest, Laurence Stephen Lowry is the most famous son of the city. When Hunter Davies came here, 'The Lowry' may have been just a building site. But these days, it is one of the gems of the breathtaking Salford Quays development and a far finer and more fitting tribute to that eminent son than that bloody song from Brian and Michael.

Let's nail this canard immediately. L. S. Lowry never painted any flipping 'matchstalk men' or 'matchstalk cats and dogs'. He painted beautiful, detailed, childlike, haunting evocations of the streets, architecture and people around him. In fairness to Brian and Michael, whose tribute made number one in 1978, that wouldn't have made a snappy song title, and, yes, their song does mention Ancoats and the St Winifred's School Choir do sing 'The big ship sails on the alley alley-o' in a nod to the film of Delaney's *A Taste of Honey*. But surely this gormless ditty has contributed to a hackneyed stereotype of the north (I've lost count of the number of southrons who've asked me, chuckling, what 'sparking clogs' means and have I ever done it) and, worse, to an undervaluing of Lowry's unique talent.

Fortunately for Picasso, he never had some comedy Spaniards in sombreros singing a novelty hit entitled 'Ola, Signora, Your

Nose Ees On The Wrong Side Of Your Face'. Vincent Van Gogh did have a number one single about him called 'Vincent' but that was a lush slice of seventies cheesecloth balladry full of luminous imagery and sung tremulously by Don McLean. Brian and Michael, dressed as 1920s chimney sweeps and surrounded by urchins, were irredeemably rubbish and gave off that unwholesome whiff of 'Wasn't rickets and mass unemployment great?'

The Lowry Centre is a much better and hopefully more lasting monument to L S. It cost £94 million, just under a third of which came from the National Lottery. Next time you despair at the lines of shabby, defeated people in Asda blowing money they don't have on a one in fourteen million chance of freedom, remember the Lowry and think that it's not all wasted. For that sort of money you get an art gallery, two theatres, an interactive exhibition, a restaurant, corporate hospitality suites, a bookshop, a publishing house and a study centre. Arrived at by road and via a grim expanse of dirt car park, it's unprepossessing. But walk over the bridge, designed by Casado of Madrid and engineered by Parkman Ltd of Salford, and look back. At sunset or dawn, it's beautiful, 'like a futuristic ship crashed into the dockside', according to one proud guide I spoke to. But even on a raw March afternoon, it's impressive. The view from Pizza Express, I have to say, is limited, but the American Hot is terrific.

The Lyric Theatre within the Lowry has 1,750 seats and the largest provincial stage in the UK outside London. Big, big entertainment stars vie to play here. But for me the star of the building is Lowry himself. The dedicated galleries are on the north-facing side of the building to prevent damage from the sun, but light streams in from the promenade windows even from an opaque March sky. Salford began collecting Lowry's works in 1930 and has more than 350. What I love about the permanent exhibitions is that the full range of Lowry's work is on show. Not just the trademark (and wonderful) industrial townscapes but wistful, eerie portraits and sketches. My personal favourites are his seascapes, an obsession which he returned to again and again; vast empty canvases of remote horizons where sea and sky intermingle at the edge of the world. I find them as stately and spiritual as the most monumental Rothkos. An old art teacher of mine, Mrs Taylor, knew Lowry a little and once, accompanied by a friend's little girl, went to see him when he was an old man but still working in his studio and completing just such a seascape. Lowry asked the child if she liked it and she replied, 'It's too empty. It needs a seagull.'

'Put one in then,' said Lowry, amused, and handed her a brush. Horrified, Mrs Taylor went to stop the child but Lowry insisted and the little girl put a tiny stylised child's seagull – like a flattened McDonald's M – in the corner of the sky where, according to Mrs Taylor, it remains to this day.

I love that story. Some critics think that there's a wry irony in the fact that a withdrawn loner – he died a virgin, it's assumed – who 'inhabited a dark cave of the imagination', as one put it, should be celebrated in the shining futuristic creation of the Lowry Centre. I like to think of him as a genial old boy who would let a little girl paint a seagull on a canvas that he must have known was worth a fortune. That playfulness in him would approve of the fact that the Lowry rings daily now to the sound of kids doing workshops, going to and from pantomimes and concerts, pointing at his paintings and maybe thinking, 'I draw like that.'

On the other side of the Ship Canal from the Lowry, past the incongruous and dowdy Lowry Factory Outlet Mall, is another remarkable building: a huge, forbidding thistle of gunmetal splinters, gaunt against the Salford skyline. This is Daniel Libeskind's Imperial War Museum North, its dramatic design representative of a globe fragmented into three giant shards, reconfigured in pain and turmoil. It symbolises a world shattered by war and is both disturbing and strangely serene, like a battlefield long quiet.

Inside, it is a triumph of what you might call new museumry. There's enough interactivity to keep the most tartrazine-addled toddler happy. But there is real substance here; some powerful and moving exhibits that illustrate what a bloodthirsty century or two we've been living through. It's the small stuff that haunts: the documents of the disappeared, passport photos, ration books. That said, Renato Giuseppe Bertelli's 'Continous Profile', a futurist bust of Mussolini, is an amazing piece, that famous profile turned into an abstract 3D whirl of speed; for a second you can see the seductiveness of it all before you shake it off with a shudder.

Leaving the building I find that high winds have shut the towering 'observation shard'. A shame; I'd like to have seen Salford Quays from up there and maybe gazed across the Irwell to Manchester itself and tried to pick out on that crowded, blossoming skyline yet another new monument to Lowry's memory.

Whatever you feel about the Lowry Centre, the Lowry Hotel does seem to come wreathed in irony; a fabulous opulent watering hole and five-star hotel named after a man who painted, ahem, matchstalk kids sparking clogs or huddled factory workers shuffling and scampering to their shift. If you arrive, though, as I did, in the most biblical hailstorm even rainy Manchester can muster, it's an irony you can get to enjoy as the top-hatted, smoothly professional doorman opens your car door, shelters you with an umbrella and guides you into the airy, ultra-modern foyer before disappearing with your keys to valet park you somewhere snug.

Gratifyingly, there are original Lowry sketches on the walls of the bevelled corridors. My room is an understated but masculine symphony of red upholstery, black mahogany, brushed steel and burnt umber leather. The windows are huge; from them you can see how the hotel curves, hugging the bank of the moss-green Irwell. You can see the balconies and the mast that towers rakishly above the river. The bed is the size of a tennis court.

The River Room restaurant is run by Marco Pierre White, one of the first of that now ubiquitous, faintly tiresome modern tribe, the celebrity chef. Our waitress is slightly cool, bristling slightly at every query with the very Mancunian air of someone who thinks she shouldn't be doing this. At one point I hear her complain to a colleague that a diner is 'mithering' her, a uniquely Manc word meaning 'bothering'. She clearly thinks she should be running her own health spa or duetting with Kanye West but she does get the food right. (Minted pea soup with crab and pear, followed by watercress risotto and then coconut panna cotta with spicy roast pineapple, if you're interested.)

The *Lonely Planet* guide to this infuriating, invigorating power-house of a city says: 'Manchester is looking up. Gone are the Dickensian days of grinding poverty. Gone too the gloom'n'doom of the 1980s indie punk scene and its Joy Division pessimism: over the last 15 years the city has developed a champagne-for-breakfast insouciance and an almost giddy attitude towards fun.'

I quite liked that Joy Division pessimism actually, rather more than I think I like 'champagne-for-breakfast insouciance'. The tramps in Piccadilly Gardens were always pretty insouciant by lunchtime anyway, though not often on champers. But I love the fact that Manchester is showing off, something it's always been very good at.

In his classic 1950s folk song 'Dirty Old Town', Ewan MacColl envisioned a dream for his native Salford, a dream that seems to have been realised. 'We're going to make a good sharp axe, shining steel, tempered in the fire. We'll chop you down like an old dead tree. Dirty old town, dirty old town.' Manchester and Salford are still mucky kids at heart but having been mithered by Mam and had their faces wiped with spittle on some big civic hankie, they've scrubbed up dead smart.

* * *

It's a Sunday evening in May and it's raining in Manchester. We cross the bridges from Salford, pass the G-Mex and St Peter's Fields on the right and turn onto Deansgate as the lights are coming on, park the car by Quay Street and follow the crowds through the drizzly dusk to the foyer of the Opera House. There's a Cup Final buzz in the air, a palpable dizziness and thrill. We've come into town in our droves, pallid girls and boys in quiffs, mums and dads, lads and ladettes, to welcome back an old friend. Morrissey is in town and therefore, like moths to a flame, so are we.

As part of his evocative selection of introductory music, there's a punkish version of 'You'll Never Walk Alone', the anthem of Liverpool FC. Something in the air sours; a couple of rows behind me, five or six lads rise up angrily and join in with the derisive and combative Manchester version. 'Sign on, sign on…' they jeer. I was at Finsbury Park in 1992 when Morrissey took to the stage draped provocatively in a Union Jack and, for his pains, was pelted with coins and bottles. Within two years, the Union Jack had been denuded of all inflammatory power, commodified into a tacky Britpop/Spice Girls/Oasis/New Labour logo. But then it was still seen as the flag of the far right. Morrissey's was a defiant gesture of blithe disregard for acceptance. He's still winding people up, the stirrer.

Back on stage at the Manchester Opera House, he tells us how he came here in 1974 to watch Mott The Hoople supported by Queen ('they were quite good, actually') and, for a moment, he's just a kid again in love with a dream, like we all are. He introduces his band, Cockneys and Angelenos all, and says conspiratorially, 'They're not northern but I hope you won't hold it against them.' At one point, there is a sweetly maudlin snatch of 'Sally, Sally, Pride Of Our Alley' (Gracie Fields). Then he brings up the ticklish matter of 'You'll Never Walk Alone'. 'I know some of you weren't happy with one of the songs on the interval tape. Well, it does go back a lot further than football, you know.' This does nothing to placate the aggrieved, who keep up a low-level fusillade of abuse until other sections of the audience, who've been chanting 'Morrissey, Morrissey, Morrissey' to the strains of 'Here We Go' all night, turn on the dissenters and threaten them with violence.

Morrissey ends his set with a version of 'How Soon Is Now', which contains a signature closing flourish: 'There's a club if you'd like to go, you could meet somebody who really loves you/So you go and you stand on your own, and you leave on your own/And you go home and you cry and you want to die.' Tonight, this plaintive, private mantra of despair, which when we first heard it pierced every one of us here, I imagine, is bellowed lustily in unison, a clamorous roar that could challenge the Stretford End. There's an irony there all right. I hope Morrissey laughs about it, as we laugh about it later, on cold leather seats, as we head down ghostly arterial roads to the real Lancashire.

Mills and Bhuna

Bulgarians think the town of Gabrovo is funny. Pop into a bar in Sofia or Plovdiv and tell them you're on your way to Gabrovo and the clientele will slap their stocky thighs and spill their plum brandy in mirth. In Germany, they find the city of Emden a hoot; well, you know what they say about East Frisians. Parisians used to tell jokes about the hopelessly provincial Toulouse while in the United States, the very mention of Peoria, Oshkosh or Dubuque – hick towns, as they are known – is guaranteed to split the collective sides of the David Letterman audience.

I come from a hick town. There are 100,000 people there, a third of a million if you count the borough, and at the time of writing we are the only town in Britain to have a Premiership football team and a Super League rugby side. But we are eternally, perennially, irredeemably hick. I only have to tell people in Guildford or Maidstone or Purfleet where I'm from and they begin to chortle, rolling the name around their mouth like an Uncle Joe's Mint Ball. Wigan: the Gabrovo, the Emden, the Oshkosh of Britain.

I don't mean the above to sound defensive but I bet it does, particularly if you're reading this in Aylesbury. I feel about Wigan like I feel about Catholicism, like some do about Hartlepool United or folk music. Being steeped in it, I'm allowed to make fun of it; I can sit around with like-minded friends and laugh about the lack of a decent Thai restaurant in Whelley or the townie beer monsters on King Street, or for that matter the flaws in the notions of purgatory or transubstantiation. But woe betide any 'outsider' who rattles our cage. Like a south central gangsta bandying the 'N' word with his homies, we have the credentials. We've earned the right to self-deprecate the hard way. We're allowed to take the piss. But if anyone else should – God forbid, a southerner – then hackles rise, whatever hackles are. I'm not proud of this. It's just the way things are. Outsiders making fun of our home town is fighting talk where I come from. Mind you, everything is fighting talk where I come from. I come from Wigan.

Even one of my favourite writers couldn't resist having a pop. On his famous *English Journey*, J. B. Priestley noted, 'Between Manchester and Bolton, the ugliness is so complete that it is almost exhilarating. It challenges you to live there. That is probably the secret of the Lancashire working folk; they have accepted the challenge – they are on active service.' Of course, there speaks a Yorkshireman.

Eddie Waring didn't help the cause of Wigan's acceptance into polite, smart society. A famous rugby league commentator of the seventies and a small chap with a bizarre voice to boot, he was unequivocally daft, progressively more so once he became Stuart Hall's straight-ish man on *It's a Knockout*. His baroque style became a staple of bad seventies impressionists. 'Ah-Wig-anne … in the ah … hyooped sharts…' For years afterwards, if you didn't actually have a sense of humour, you only had to say 'Ah-Wig-anne' in the correct dopey intonation to get a cheap laugh, before you moved onto Pakis and mothers-in-law.

You can't argue with the fact that certain northern towns just sound funny. Because our place names reflect our Viking origins, the sounds are often guttural and wild to the gentle ear of the Home County dweller. Into this category, we can put Oswaldtwistle, Barnoldswick, Cleckheaton and Heckmondwike, places which actually sound like driving hail on a tin shed or the clacking of ill-fitting false teeth. Others appeal to the eternal schoolboy who sleeps within every one of us: Ramsbottom, Scunthorpe, Grimsby, Goole, Penistone. Wigan, though, isn't that side-splitting a name if you think about it. My town has been a comedy staple for many years purely by virtue of its associations – chiefly poverty, pies and piers.

Our associations with poverty stem from a visitor we had once in the 1930s. Eric Blair was a well-to-do southerner, an old Etonian who served in the Imperial Police in India. But his experiences there and among the poor of Paris and London changed him for ever. He cast off Eric Blair and became George Orwell, who in the mid 1930s travelled to Wigan at the instigation of the Left Book Club to write about the working class of the depressed north.

He lodged in various parts of the town and was appalled at what he saw. He couldn't believe the circumstances people lived in, or the vile and dangerous conditions in which they were expected to work. His descriptions of the hovels and slums of Wigan and the conditions of the pits and factories are written with a kind of cold rage that echoes down the years.

Orwell was the exact opposite of the modern left-winger, that delicate flower who marches against foreign wars and gets exercised over smoking bans but will not dirty his hands with anything as grubby or difficult as class and capital. He had little time for what we might call political correctness, multi-culturalism or moral relativism. His sympathies lay with those poor bastards at the bottom of the heap, below the bottom actually, lying on their stomachs chipping coal in water and blackness or, when they couldn't do that, wheezing in damp beds in the back streets of Wigan. As he wrote in *The Road to Wigan Pier*, Orwell knew that it was 'so much easier to feel yourself a Socialist when you are among working-class people. The working-class Socialist, like the working-class Catholic, is weak on doctrine ... but he has the heart of the matter in him... The profoundest philosophical difference is unimportant compared with saving the twenty million Englishmen whose bones are rotting from malnutrition – the time to argue about them is afterwards.'

The Left Book Club hated *The Road to Wigan Pier*. They even tried to prevent publication. Publisher Victor Gollancz inserted a foreword distancing himself from Orwell's attack on the intellectual left. Orwell was vilified in the pages of British communist and socialist literature. He didn't care. He was too busy getting shot in the throat in Spain fighting for freedom, an altogether more dangerous assignment.

Though he was posh to his bones, Orwell's sympathies always lay with the working class. He had no time for George Bernard Shaw and his ilk, 'the more-water-in-the-beer socialist' as he scornfully called them. He liked a pint and a fag. So he'd be delighted to know that we've named a pub after him.

The Orwell stands on the jetties of Wigan Pier between an old mill that's now a concert hall and the backstreets of Miry Lane, presumably a swamp once, maybe even when George lodged here. It's never been a local of mine, though I did go through a phase in my early twenties of dropping in to clean out the money in the quiz machine on Monday lunchtimes after daft drunks had been feeding it all weekend. It's an ordinary boozer really. However, it's always been the most controversial alehouse in town.

When it was proposed that Wigan should have a pub named after the man who made us famous – and that's with all due respect to Dave Whelan, Billy Boston, Ian McKellen, Paul Jewell, Richard Ashcroft and the rest – a great many of the town's more clueless council types almost burst their aldermanly waistcoats in a mass harrumph. Hadn't he run the town down at every turn? Emphasised the emphysema and stressed the squalor instead of perhaps pointing out the excellent surrounding countryside or state-of-the-art bandstand in Mesnes Park?

Having never read *The Road to Wigan Pier*, they had, naturally, missed its point; an occupational hazard of not reading, listening to or watching things you pontificate about. It's a sustained polemic, a tour de force of reportage intended to inflame and anger. It's not a flipping tourist guide. The Wigan that Orwell found in 1936 was a grim, beleaguered slum (so was a great deal of Europe actually – designer outlets and frappuccino bars were pretty scarce back then). Orwell didn't flinch from telling the leafy shires of southern England just what life in the north was like. But he never sneers, he never mocks. *The Road to Wigan Pier* is a call to arms, not a hatchet job.

Some people have just come here to sneer and mock, though. Charles Jennings's 1995 book, *Up North*, is essentially an extended sarcastic diatribe intended, one assumes, to amuse people from Streatham. I found it about as funny as leprosy but then I'm a northerner; presumably too doltish to appreciate its withering wit. Jennings' book, it seems to me, is exactly what the misinformed think Orwell's is: lazy, contemptuous hackery from a posh, soft southerner. He considers visiting some other towns with 'resolutely northern handles' like, of course, Ramsbottom and Oswaldtwistle, but eventually picks Wigan because Jennings has read half of *The Road to Wigan Pier*. 'Mostly Wigan is a lot of hilly streets with gales blowing down them and lots of beaten-up people,' he concludes. You get the picture. And he's wrong. I think he must be thinking of Pendle.

I think Jennings, like Wigan's dozier officials, misreads Orwell as a scornful attack on the town. He cites a famous passage about the food on offer at his lodgings. 'The meals at the Brookers' house were uniformly disgusting... However tactfully I tried, I could never induce Mr Brooker to let me cut my own bread-and-butter; he would hand it to me slice by slice, each slice gripped firmly under that broad black thumbs. For dinner there were generally those threepenny steak puddings which are sold ready-made in tins. For supper there was the pale flabby Lancashire cheese and biscuits.'

I have to say that I'm with Orwell on Lancashire cheese; anaemic, crumbly and tasting faintly of soap, the only way my grandmother could get me to eat it was by melting it on sausages. The reason she was so keen for me to consume the stuff was that she seemed to regard not liking it as an act of regional treachery tantamount to wearing a cravat or voting Conservative.

But, come on, British food in general must have been frightful in the 1930s. Lunch at The Ivy was probably cold brown Windsor soup followed by fillet of shoe leather with boiled turnip followed by lard and junket. It doesn't surprise me that Mr Brooker was sticking his dirty thumbs in the butter. It probably gave it a bit of flavour.

When southern gourmands discuss the shortcomings of the north, their plump lips pursed in displeasure, food is often chief among them. They may have a point. Even when I was a child in the sixties and seventies there was a deep-seated suspicion regarding people who got too excited about food, as if it spoke of an overtly sensual nature and moral laxity, like cigarette holders and bisexuality. Food was 'jackbit', 'scran' or 'nosebag'; fuel to be consumed in haste, taken to work or school wrapped in that unpleasantly greasy 'greaseproof' paper that bread used to come in.

Vegetables were boiled to within inches of their lives. If a trace of flavour remained, it was regarded as troubling evidence that the wretched tuber or crop hadn't been 'done' enough and would probably give you cholera. Every Sunday, a low green cloud of sulphurous cabbage would hang in the house all day, making even a reasonably cheery toddler's thoughts turn, by early evening, to the gentle consolations of suicide.

Home cooking never had the wholesome connotations to me it had to others. My aforementioned grandmother spent half the week baking and, bless her, the results were always terrible. Her blackcurrant tart was a glutinous mess of acidic fruit encased in flaccid pastry. No wonder I was so keen on convenience food. When I was about eight, I went to some kind of trade show in Wigan Park where Heinz, paternalistic local employers of thousands, had a food stall. A nice lady offered me a small plastic pot of a new line of theirs, Spaghetti Bolognese in a tin. I thought my head was going to explode. I felt like Ken Kesey and the Grateful Dead must have done when they first took acid. Whole new vistas of monosodium glutamate and preservatives opened up to me. About six months ago, in an effort to get a Proustian rush, I bought a tin of the said Spaghetti Bolognese. It tasted like cold, rancid fishing bait. But back then, to a small boy weaned on leathery cabbage and doughy tarts, it tasted like liberation. I had tasted the future and it worked, Mum.

Some people, particularly of the older generation, get very partisan about northern food. The more disgusting its provenance, the more robust they get in its defence. Take tripe, for instance. Ever had it? Don't. It's absolutely vile. But my grandmother was forever trying to get me to eat it. Corrugated, slimy, cow's stomach lining drenched in malt vinegar? Yummo! Hand it over with all speed, Gran!

Often the wholesome names of Lancashire foods disguise their essential horror. Trotters, which sound quite cuddly, are boiled pig's feet. Haslet is basically compressed pig's face and is quite simply one of the most repulsive things I have ever tasted. Don't even get me started on brawn and tongue.

Black puddings, mark you, are something entirely different.

A prince of foods and deserving of a fuller discussion in a little while. But one food more than any other has become proudly, humorously emblematic of the north in general, Lancashire particularly and my home town of Wigan specifically.

There are competing theories as to why Wiganers are known as Pie-Eaters. According to one, we acquired the name not because of our love of the pastry savoury, but from Wigan's abject collapse in the General Strike of 1926. Apparently, Wiganers took what managers offered, ate the humble pie that was being served up, and helped to break the strike thus gaining the contempt of workers in surrounding areas. The story goes that, in an act of defiance, Wigan folk reclaimed the 'pie-eating' insult and transformed it into a battle standard.

Personally, I'm very sceptical of this. I can't find any historical evidence for it and it sounds suspiciously like a terrible slur put about by Boltonians and jealous St Heleners. The truth, I fancy, is far more prosaic. Wiganers just really, really like pies. Hey, what's not to like? We can reel off the various bakeries and the top marques of this lovely lardy universe as if they were a mantra. First there are the major players of the pie world: Galloways, Greenhalgh's, Holland's, Sayers, Rathbones. Then there are the spirited independents like Twiss in Ince, Mr Muffin in Shevington and The Old Bakehouse in Orrell; real connoisseurs will take a bus trip to stock up on fare from these cult mavericks.

At the other end of the spectrum is that problematic, paternalistic pastry pariah Greggs. When John Gregg began making and selling pies in the 1930s, he had a single shop on Tyneside with a bijou bakery at the rear. When he died suddenly in 1964, his son Ian abandoned a legal career to take over the business. Smart cookie. Or pasty. Greggs now has more than 1,000 UK outlets and profits approaching £50 million per annum. But since they are not a Wigan pie maker, our respect is always grudging. They're too mainstream, too ubiquitous, too homogenous. They ruthlessly annexed the excellent Birkett's of Cumbria, whose Garlic Mushroom Slice was fabled among hungry northern vegetarians. And there's that difficult reputation as caterer in chief to Chav Britain, the staple diet of the hoodie hordes and the Trisha tribes.

Yet surely all northerners must secretly relish the fact that there is a Greggs in the West End of London and one tucked amongst the organic delis and import record shops of ultra-fashionable Portobello Road. This is the kind of relentless capitalistic expansionism we can live with, the northerning of the Home Counties, the light crusting of the soft south. There is a Greggs in Brighton, hardening the arteries of all those dance instructors and out-of-work actors. There are Greggs in Stratford-upon-Avon, at the nation's cultural heart, and in Cheltenham, where the beautiful, coltish daughters of the ruling class soak up their champagne with a Mexican Oval Bite. Greggs have even opened up a Belgian front with branches in Antwerp and Leuven. One day, there will be a branch of Greggs on the Champs-Elysées and the north will laugh. For the Reich of the Steak Bake will last a thousand years.

But here is a memento mori for the current Mr Gregg. Beware hubris and pie pride. Mark well the cautionary tale of Poole's Pies of Wigan. For years Poole's was Wigan's pie shop par excellence and non pareil. Every lunchtime the queue would snake down Station Road as hungry nurses, students, pensioners, policemen, accountants, teachers, brickies, drunks, laundresses, lighthouse keepers and loblolly men waited for their 'jackbit'. Then in 1998 came what has been described as The Wigan Pie Event Horizon. Bloated beyond all common sense by years of success, the Poole's empire somehow contrived to collapse in on itself in a huge calorific supernova, shrinking into a black hole like a dying star. No light can escape from the intense pull of a real black hole and so, appropriately enough, it was with Poole's Pies. All their shops disappeared overnight, their windows painted with whitewash so the townsfolk could not block the pavements nostalgically perusing the dark interiors. Wigan Warriors rugby club went into freefall almost immediately and have never recovered, though you can still get a Poole's pie at the van outside the JJB on Latics matchdays. Strong men queue there now for a Large Meat and Potato, heads bowed in silent remembrance of the days when Poole's were king. Pies cometh before a fall.

Our enthusiasm for pies has been immortalised in many a joke. What do you call four pies on a stick? A Wigan kebab. Why do meat pies have a hole in the top? So that Wiganers can carry them to parties like a six-pack. My favourite concerns a Bolton man who breathlessly tells his workmate from Wigan about a new lunchtime offer at the local pub. 'A pie, a pint and a woman. 80p.' The Wiganer seems unimpressed. '80p!' repeats his workmate excitedly. 'Hmm,' declares the Wiganer warily. 'Whose pies are they?'

When I go home for the football and stop off at my mum's for a cup of tea, she always sends me on my way with pies straight from the oven wrapped in tinfoil. Still warm by half-time, my mates, my dad and I fall upon them with gusto as we dissect the first half's events. Wiganers feel, in their hearts, that there is no social that cannot be significantly improved by a pie.

But however much we love them, we know that it's these kinds of associations that both define us and somehow restrict us. It's one of those emblems, like whippets, clogs and flat caps that keep us in our place. A cosy but marginal place well away from the centres of power and the heart of the culture. A place that is forever 1932.

Wallace and Gromit live in Wigan. Did you know that? 62 West Wallaby Street, Wigan, Lancs. Before you ask, no, it's not a real street, though there'll be councillors who think we should have named after a street after them rather than George Orwell. But I'm not so sure. It's all very sweet and everything but essentially on the same old faintly patronising riff. Wigan, and by extension Lancashire, is quaint, parochial and a little behind the times. Maybe I'm being too sensitive; I do love the fact that Wallace reads *Ay-Up* magazine to catch up on celebrity gossip. It doesn't help, I guess, that the other foodstuff that Wigan is indissolubly linked with is a powerful ovoid of mentholated treacle rejoicing in the name of Uncle Joe's Mint Balls. They come in a bright red tin with a picture of a bibulous, rakish fellow in a top hat (Uncle Joe, one assumes) on the front. Their legendary kick was celebrated in 'Uncle Joe's Mint Balls', a song by local folkie Mike Harding: 'Uncle Joe's Mint Balls keep you all aglow/Give them to your granny, and watch the bugger go.' At any given moment, thousands of tins of Uncle Joe's are criss-crossing the skies in the holds and luggage racks of jet planes en route to tearful exiled Wiganers in Pensacola, Bogotá and Vladivostok.

If you didn't know where the Santus Toffee Works was located, you could find it by smell. It's tucked away on Dorning Street between Wigan Wallgate station and the Pear Tree pub and the whole street is suffused with a heavy, sickly-sweet perfume. 'What's that smell?' asked my friends Anita and Tony on a recent visit to Wigan. 'It's gorgeous.' And I suppose it is if you're just passing through or you're six years old. But what must it be like to live next door to Uncle Joe? Every day must be a kind of Christmas morning, cheering at first and then somehow cloying and claustrophobic, like living off selection boxes for ever. It must get into your washing and drive your dog mad.

Anita and Tony are 'in telly'. They wanted to see Wigan because they were developing a project set in the town. The sun was shining as we met at Wigan North Western station – we have two, you see – and I took them for a stroll in what Bill Bryson was 'truly astounded to find … a handsome and well-maintained town centre'. No need to be shocked, Bill. Your predecessor Celia Fiennes, a travel writer of 1698, found it 'a pretty market town built of stone and brick'. You could never call Pemps pretty, a nightclub not far from Santus Toffee Works. It looks like an abattoir, or possibly a nuclear bunker for minor North Korean civil servants, a shuttered and windowless hellhole. Who would think then that this was once, maybe still is, one of the greatest nightclubs in the north, ruled as a personal fiefdom by the formidable Barbara, who stood guard in fur coat and riding crop and personally chose who, from the enormous queue, would be blessed with admittance. Here you could dance to Gwen Guthrie, Mantronix and Grandmaster Flash till dawn, at which point, if you were one of Barbara's chosen few, she would send out for bacon sandwiches for breakfast. Now that's a nightclub, Peter Stringfellow and Ministry Of Sound.

Cross the road from Pemps and you're in King Street. In an attempt to make this fabled, barbarous thoroughfare more Bourbon Street than Bigg Market, the council have inlaid a kind of plaque featuring a guitar and some musical notes in the pavement. A broken bottle of WKD and a half-eaten doner would have been more in keeping. Even at ten on a fine sunny morning, just the ambience of the street makes me feel slightly drunk and weirdly in the mood for a fight and a quick shag. This is where Wigan comes to let off steam in one of several dozen clubs and bars. If it's not a bar, it's a takeaway. One sports huge and hugely incongruous black and white pictures of Audrey Hepburn and Bob Marley. If it's not either of those, it's a solicitor's. Wonder if they stay open late at weekends?

Market Street is where celebrated Wigan Casino DJs Russ Winstanley and Richard Searling had their Northern Soul record shop (called, cryptically, Russ and Richard's). Every Saturday afternoon I spent my pocket money here on ultra-obscure seven-inch singles on long-defunct US labels. In the eighties, it became an indie record shop under the auspices of Alan, the town's leading skatepunk. He called it Alan's. We're crazy like that in Wigan. Here in the mid eighties, I spent my part-time lecturer's wages on Jesus And Mary Chain and Shop Assistants records. I always enjoyed that continuity. As we turn into Market Street, I'm saddened that the shop appears to be gone.

There's a record shop across the road, though, so I pop into Elite Vinyl (Dance Music Specialists) to ask about Alan. The girl in Elite Vinyl has, like most twenty-first-century Wigan girls, a sunbed tan so deep and chocolate brown she wouldn't look out of place in Rawalpindi. She tells us, in an accent soft and broad and wide enough to gently punt on, that Alan now has a bike shop on Market Street.

The tail has wagged the dog. Wagged the dog right off, in fact. Alan always had skates and bikes as a sideline; now they've become his bread and butter. There's not a twelve-inch copy of 'Sheila Take A Bow' to be seen. I haven't seen Alan for ten years but we start talking as if he'd just popped into the other room to put the kettle on. He makes some wry references to my 'media superstardom'. He talks about how his grandma spilt tea on his old Slade albums. He talks about buying Bowie's *David Live* for £9.99 and leaving the sticker on as evidence of the unbelievable cost of nearly £10 for a record. He tells me about Frank Sidebottom's recent triumphal return to live work at Darwen Library and how this week he's playing a Hotpot Supper in Leyland. Not for the first time on these trips, I get a real pang of homesickness. I want to come back here and eat hotpot in Leyland watching Frank Sidebottom. I never want to queue for the lifts at Goodge Street Tube station again.

We have lunch at Mr Chips of Hallgate. There is a 'sit up and beg' bike advertising the shop propped outside. The ladies have white hats and smile like the sun coming out and call me love. The actual sun does come out and Tony, Anita and I decide to sit outside at some pavement tables. They have chips, steak pie and gravy. I have another great northern delicacy, the steak pudding. I once asked for one of these in a chip shop in Bermondsey and the proprietor looked at me as if I was mad. 'A facking pudding? What, a Christmas facking pudding?'

A steak pudding, as any fule kno, is a sort of dome of suet filled with minced beef and gravy. It is sometimes known as a Babbies Yed (Baby's Head) for its resemblance to that soft, vulnerable appendage. Containing an adult male's recommended calories for a week, they are not high on any nutritionist's '5-A-Day' list. But when you really fancy one, nothing else will do. This lunchtime, I really fancy one. We eat with plastic forks in balmy spring sunshine; across the street, the Memorial Gardens are a riot of blossom, where for generations winos and truants have drunk industrial-strength ciders from bottles the size of U-boats. All is well with the world.

Sated and happy, we drive out to Skelmersdale, where I used to earn those part-time lecturer's wages back in the mid 1980s. Because of its Brutalist architecture, concrete walkways and houses on stilts, and the defiantly anti-Thatcher culture of the area, we used to call it the People's Republic of Skelmersdale.

Skem goes back a long way, though, to the ninth century when it was settled by a Viking called Skjalmar, hence Skjalmar's Dale. It was long established by the time it featured in the Domesday Book. 'Old Skem' is how locals now refer to the typical Lancashire pit village which in the sixties became absorbed within a huge new town built to accommodate the overspill from Liverpool slum clearances. Sociologically, it's fascinating; the red Ribble single-decker bus turns a corner just through Upholland

and suddenly you go from Lancashire into Liverpool, from wild woollyback badlands to Scouse street life.

Skem sits astride the ghostly M58, Britain's most underused motorway, and the whole town is a fork wound round the spaghetti strands of various bewildering traffic systems. It's the town of a thousand roundabouts, the largest of which is known as 'Half Mile Island'. There's not a traffic light to be seen. When I worked here, the locals had a mildly politically incorrect joke about the lack of Asian families in the town. Apparently it was because there were no corners for them to open shops on. Nothing thrived here in the seventies and eighties. When the subsidies ran out, all the major employers left town and abandoned the people to years of poverty, drug abuse and crime. Now those metaphorical green shoots of optimism can be glimpsed. The shopping concourse or 'connie' has been cleaned up; most of the shops are open and busy; the indigenous packs of scrawny wild dogs are gone.

I've not been back for nearly twenty years and as we begin to negotiate the ramps and slip roads near the town centre, I feel a strange sensation in my chest. I loved it here. Every economic and political cudgel had been used to bring these people to their knees and they simply would not submit. You threw them out of work and they responded in a variety of ways. Some of them signed on, went underground and smoked dope all day listening to Pink Floyd's *Meddle*. Some of them became, shall we say, entrepreneurs in the town's thriving black economy. Others, from sixteen to sixty, single mums, scallies out of school and car workers thrown on the scrapheap like last year's Lada, decided to go back to college, which is where I came in.

I can see it ahead of me, the college. Here I spent afternoons talking about Max Weber and Emile Durkheim – sociologists, not Bayern Munich wingbacks – and nights at wild parties in council flats and estate pubs. I was in my early twenties and most of my students were my age. It's still the most rock and roll job I've ever had. Like I say, I loved it.

There's a new receptionist now and feeling a tad self-conscious I try and justify being here by asking after some of my old colleagues. Notorious roué Keith Platt is gone, leaving a trail of betting slips behind him. Gareth the Marxist Mathematician is gone (two years ago, headship somewhere probably). Lovely Pat, the gentle Scouser with the waist-length hair, is gone. All gone. Would I like to leave a number? No thanks. Time to move on, I think.

On the edge of town, unsignposted and shy, is another symbol of the town's spirit. You wouldn't have Skem down as a religious citadel, a place of pilgrimage, a Lourdes or a Mecca. But it is the British headquarters of a major world religion, one that has contributed a great deal to the town's fortunes and for its pains has been left high and dry by its parent church.

Followers of Transcendental Meditation or TM (or, as it's a trademark, TM™) tend to get chortled at on a regular basis. This is due largely to their belief in something called Yogic Flying. From what I've seen of it, Yogic Flying should probably be called Really Energetic Yogic Cross-Legged Jumping. I'm loath to join in the chortling, though. For one thing, some of the chortlers believe pretty rum stuff of their own, such as virgins having babies who can rise from the dead or that cutting bits off your baby's genitals tells God that you love them or something. A spot of low-level flying seems fairly believable and humane by comparison. You pays your spiritual money and you takes your choice from the range of arcane magic on offer, as far as I'm concerned.

I have other reasons for feeling indulgent about TM. George Harrison was into it and if you were in The Beatles you can pretty much do what you like in my book. Also, TM has been rather good to Skem. When the Maharishi's people came in 1980, no one had a shred of faith in the town. Now looking around the gleaming new Stansted-airport-style shopping centre, a far cry from the grim old connie, there are no vacant outlets and hardly any spare business space in the town. The Maharishi European Sidhaland, as the Skem TM community is officially known, has even been awarded Best Practice in Urban Regeneration by BURA, the British Urban Regeneration Association.

I arrived in town five years after the TMs did and by then 'the trannies' had gone from being thought of as freaks to fondly regarded local curiosities. It was rumoured that the good vibes the TMs generated through meditation had brought down the crime rate. More practically, Skemmers welcomed the cash and jobs they brought to town: the gym, a business centre, new houses and, most significant of all, a new school.

The Maharishi School of the Age of Enlightenment has been the TM's big, unqualified success in the community. It's housed in a lovely stone barn in a quiet corner of Skem. As a school, it's completely non-selective, which makes its dazzling academic record even more amazing. Anna Selby, in *The Times* magazine of September 1998, 'watched in disbelief as a class of eight- and nine-year-olds went into their classroom after playtime, sat at their desks and started working before their teacher arrived'. Three years ago, every member of Years 10 and 11 won or was runner-up in a national poetry competition. Last year all the pupils got ten or more GCSEs at C grade or above, one of a handful of schools in the country to achieve a one hundred per cent top pass rate. It ranks consistently in the top 2.5 per cent nationwide in league tables, a ranking that puts Eton and Harrow to shame. Anecdotally, I can add that a friend of mine's daughter, a timid, introverted little girl who was struggling in the local secondaries, has blossomed since attending the TM school. Wags can chuckle at Yogic Flying but no one can belittle the achievements of this school, where the kids meditate as part of their daily routine. No one here is worried about knives or truancy. Maybe John Lennon was right and the Maharishi allegedly did try to put his hand up Mia Farrow's skirt in Rishikesh. So what? Lennon was an old fraud too. He got an airport. The Maharishi gets a really cool, successful school.

Half a mile away from the school is the Golden Dome, built the year after I left town and something the 'trannies' are touchingly proud of. It cost approximately £400,000, was inaugurated on 19 March 1988 and is a 10,000-acre space where between fifty and a hundred people start and end each day with a spot of meditation. Yes, there's some Yogic Flying here, apparently on designated flight paths so that you don't get nasty mid-air collisions. They say it is full of a 'lively silence'.

It seems the current Maharishi could do with lightening up a little. In a froth over Tony Blair's role in George Bush's Middle Eastern adventures, he has ordered the cessation of all TM teaching in Britain, describing us as a 'scorpion nation'. This seems harsh, since he's not done the same thing to America itself. I guess the yankee dollar is stronger than his Eastern principles. Many of Skem's 400-strong TM community, not unreasonably, wonder why their home country has been singled out and the US left alone. Whisper it, but many are simply carrying on as if nothing has happened. Good for them, I say, and good for Skem. I'll come back again in another twenty years and see how you're getting on. By then I hope to see you all sailing gently over the connie.

* * *

Skem scallies are West Lancastrians, eyes turned to Liverpool and the coast. They think of the whole hinterland of East Lancashire as an undulating moorland dotted with dark, sooty towns and villages populated by bucolic dolts. Accrington, Blackburn,

Bolton, Colne, Nelson, Oldham, Ramsbottom, Rochdale, Wigan; a rolling rhotic mantra of Peter Sallis vowels and gently dupable woollybacks.

I can't think of a more 'wool' way to travel than a tram. Except maybe a pit pony. Today, I'm sitting on a tram en route to just such a town, a real dyed-in-the-wool woollyback town where the people eat unspeakable parts of animals and watch the rain sheet in from the Pennine hills.

You can tell a real native of Shrewsbury by the fact that he says Shrew as in the little vole thing rather than as in Shrove Tuesday. East Midlanders say Durby not Darby for Derby. Only an out-of-towner says Theydon Bois as in the French for Wood rather than the English for Boys. These are shibboleths, markers of identities, and generally the more refined the pronunciations the more obvious it is that, well, you're not from round these parts, are you, boy? Or maybe Bwah.

My tram is taking me to Bury. Not Berry. Not the fruit. Not what you do with dead people. Burry. As in… Well, anyway, it's a very nice tram though its proper and rather soulless name is the Metrolink. It's one of the new fleet that operates out of Manchester heading north and south and west to Altrincham and Bury and Eccles. We clank gently out of Piccadilly station and swing round by the new Piccadilly Gardens stop. This is Manchester's very own Berlin Wall, a daunting-looking grey concrete erection that obscures the garden completely from one side. The Mancunians I've spoken to say that the new high-luminosity lighting and towering wall have discouraged the tramps and Special Brewheads, who used to treat the gardens as their very own Groucho Club. Seen from Deansgate or a passing tram, it looks like it would only need a few Alsatians and an armed guard or two to make it look like something from Sven Hassel.

The tram leaves the city centre and passes through Crumpsall and Heaton Park before heading for the relative greenery of Bowker Vale and Besses o'th' Barn. Here a huge unruly pack of schoolkids pile aboard; young lads reeking of Lynx with puberty raging in their faces and hormonal energy to burn. Then suddenly they fall silent and meek as little lambs. Into their midst has come a girl a year or two older than them, very pretty and standing three inches taller than most of them. On her blue blazer lapel is an enamel badge reading Transport Monitor. Whenever a fight or shouting match or *Lord of the Flies*-style beastliness threatens to break out, a disapproving glance and a flash of her eyes is enough to silence them instantly. Whoever thought of this strategy – putting in charge of the vile little oiks a tall, clever, cute girl that they all clearly worship and are desperate to impress – is a genius. Can't we make that man or woman head of the police force?

Bury is the end of the line, a busy town buttressed by low hills. The escalator on the platform is broken and harassed staff are having to placate mutinous old ladies with bulging shopping trolleys returning from the fleshpots of Manchester. Quite why they bothered though is beyond me. Five minutes' walk from Bury station is a shoppers' mecca, a retail nirvana rich with exotic bargains, a fabled bazaar, a veritable souk of the north. Come with me to Bury Market.

You emerge from the station through clusters of acned youths trying to pick up girls via time-honoured and elaborate mating rituals of kicking wastepaper bins and random headlocks. A flurry of signage offers directions to some of Bury's major attractions: the regimental museum of the Lancashire fusiliers, the East Lancashire Railway, the Met theatre. But you could follow your nose to the market, where black pudding, oven bottom muffins and even more arcane delicacies await.

Everyone in the north-west knows of Bury Market. They come from as far north as Barrow and Kendal and from the south lands of Stafford and Cheshire. They come for Cristiano Ronaldo posters and cheap 'bottom-uplift' knickers, they come for spirit levels and shampoo, for batteries and cut-price trainers. Whatever your heart desires, you can get a cheap version of it with an unconvincing logo at Bury Market.

'Off the market' has become a sniffy term of abuse these days: a synonym for shoddy, the sort of place where 'sad' kids get fake Adidas gear or rip-off Louis Vuitton. This seems unfair to me. True, I wouldn't buy my new suit for the Oscars from Bury Market, but where else can you get such a bewildering range of produce so flipping cheap? I saw an elderly man buying an old-fashioned shaving brush, an egg-timer and a quarter of humbugs from two adjoining stalls. Now that's what I call one-stop shopping, Mr Bluewater.

Where Bury Market excels, though, is food. In the new Fish Market (built on the site of the old NatWest bank) you can gaze, slightly unnerved, at the dead, sightless eyes of row upon row of sea bass and snapper, mackerel and trout lying in state on funeral dais of crushed ice and parsley. The stalls are staffed by either blonde girls in full make-up who you just know are dying to get out of that white coat and into their skimpy glad rags this weekend or cheery rubicund men holding up what look like conger eels and joshing in ribald style with housewives. All of them adhere to Maconie's first law of market trade: cheeriness is proportional to the gruesome nature of the wares being handled. The grislier the fare, the gayer the banter.

Feeling a little weak, I decide to have a nice sit down and a cup of tea at Big Jim's Café. It's directly opposite the market barbers where dour men reading the *Daily Mirror* and lads in snide tracksuits get their hair cut under pictures of male models.

From the stonewash and Jason Donovan barnets, these pictures have remained unchanged since 1987. Then, running a finger down their collars for stray hair, they go to Big Jim's for a mug of scalding, dark tea, a buttie and the sports pages. Bliss.

I feel a bit out of place in Big Jim's, though. My clothes are ever so slightly too smart and I'm carrying the manbag and a notebook and I'm the only person in the place not smoking. I wait self-consciously in the queue and read the signs behind the counter. One of them, apparently quite seriously, warns the staff against describing a pictured food item as 'a meat and potato pie'. It looks to me very much like a meat and potato pie but because of its composition, it seemingly can't be described as such for fear of contravening EU takeaway food regulations. It is, in fact, 'a potato and meat pie', and must be announced as such. Heads have rolled at the Ramsbottom branch over this, it seems.

I decide to order an oven bottom muffin, Bury's second greatest contribution to world cuisine. Quite why the oven bottom should be such a superb point of origin for muffins I don't know. Strictly speaking, I wouldn't even call them muffins. They're more like floury, fluffy baps. But whatever the provenance, the people of Bury are fiercely proud and enormously appreciative of them. At Big Jim's, they come with a range of fillings of varying degrees of calorific clout and grease factor, each looking appallingly tasty and artery-furring. I plump, and I feel that's the operative word here, for a Breakfast Special – an oven bottom muffin filled with bacon, sausage and egg. Furnished with this, I squeeze on to the corner of a table occupied by a clutch of goths. The place is full, crammed with representatives from every section of Bury's working classes: schoolkids, pensioners, young mums, burly middle-aged blokes, couples with buggies. I can't help thinking that this isn't how things should be in the middle of a Thursday afternoon but my glum reverie is suddenly, excruciatingly, interrupted when I take a bite and a geyser of searingly hot yolk erupts, scalding the roof of my mouth. All attempts at blending into the background are now scuppered as I swear unintelligibly through a cauterised mouth of oven bottom muffin and incinerated pig. A few people even look up from their *Daily Mirror*s. Silently weeping, I pretend to have an urgent appointment with a new socket set at the discount hardware stall.

Even oven bottom muffins play second fiddle in Bury's culinary orchestra to the food that made Bury great and that Bury makes great. It is a delicacy that sorts the men from the boys, the lads from the jessies, the north from the south. In Bury, they say that you can still see kids in buggies eating them in their hands like huge dark ice lollies. The French know it as *boudin noir*. It's *morcilla* in Spain, *biroldo* in Italy and *kashanka* in Poland. But we know it as black pudding. To paraphrase Dick Emery, ooh, you are offal ... but we like you.

It crops up in Book 18 of Homer's *Odyssey* and in his *Iliad* when the Greek general Agamemnon was said to have fed his army on blood and onions, a powerful combination of iron, protein, carbohydrates and sugars. The Romans' skill at engineering displayed itself in their terrific aptitude for sausage making. They took the blood and onions recipe, put it into skins and thus introduced the black pudding all over their empire with each country developing its own regional variant on the blood sausage. Ours is very akin to the German *Bludwurst* and our undisputed capital of the cult of the black pudding is Bury.

There are black pudding outlets all over Bury Market. I buy a bagful at an indoor stall that promises Chadwicks Original Black Pudding. The lads on the stall inform me, though, with a touching earnestness and clearly very keen not to take any false credit, that they do not make these famed black puddings. No, they are merely licensed to sell Chadwicks puddings in the indoor market. Chadwicks themselves, the Leonardo da Vincis of the blood sausage, can be found outside.

I don't need to ask directions. I just look for the queue. I had intended to do an interview of sorts with the proprietor but soon realise I have no chance. It would be like interviewing Pele mid-dribble or Mozart mid-sonata. Every shred of concentration front of house (presumably somewhere else unspeakable things are happening in huge vats) is taken up serving at breakneck speed the blood-crazed townsfolk of Bury. I slip in line and quickly learn the lingo. 'Lean' means without those white bits of fat studded through the pudding. Each to their own, of course, but for me if you're tucking into a membranous bag of congealed animal blood I reckon it's a bit late to start going all macrobiotic. A 'two' is two puddings linked together, a 'four' naturally is four, a six is presumably for parties. I buy two fours of fat and a two of lean for when I next have a waifish supermodel over for full English breakfast. By the time I leave the market, I feel slightly queasy, like a portable abattoir, weighed down with carrion, gore and carnage.

If you want to know just how seriously Bury folk take their puddings, here's a couple of titbits for you. The regular test for colorectal cancer – there's no easy way of saying this but it's to do with blood in stools – is basically unreliable in Bury as the natives eat so much black pudding that their tests are often falsely positive. Also, if you have an afternoon to spare, you can find online all twenty-six pages of fine print documentation referring to a dispute between Chadwicks Original Black Pudding Company and a company with the temerity, it seems, to call themselves The Bury Black Pudding Company. Chadwicks acolytes from around the globe were outraged. Fortunately the courts settled the matter before blood could be spilled. Well, more blood, anyway.

But I would leave Bury even more burdened with exotic fare. On the edge of the market is a delicatessen. Not any old delicatessen, though. Maybe the best deli I'd ever seen. My eye was caught by the queues and bustle and pavement tables and a sign promising two lunchtime specials: Lamb Kleftiko and Wiener Schnitzel. I had to take a look.

It felt like I'd strayed into a proper *kafenion* in the back streets of Nicosia, Warsaw or Istanbul. I half expected leathery old fishermen playing with worry beads and sipping tar-black coffee or mint tea or Ouzo. There was every kind of spicy sausage from kielbasa to chorizo to braunschweiger. There were glistening honeyed baklavas, rich, custardy Galaktoboureko and slices of plum cake that you could put on weight just looking at. There were cheeses from Cyprus, Bulgarian brandies and hams from Spain. There were even tubs of schmaltz, the rendered chicken fat that's indispensable to real Jewish cooking, all being snapped up by the cosmopolites of Bury. I had to find more space in my manbag, I can tell you.

Outside the shop, a tanned man in his sixties was diligently and paternally arranging the pavement tables in neat rows. I knew that this had to be the proprietor. George Katsouris came to Bury Market from Cyprus thirty-five years ago and is now a fixture, no, make that a treasure, in the town. 'We sell anything a little ethnic and we sell to anyone and everyone. Lancashire people, people from far away who are homesick, people who are curious.'

If this deli was in Camden or Brighton, we northerners would never hear the last of it. Smug Sunday broadsheet columnists would be forever telling us how popping down there was part of their Sunday morning routine, how they couldn't knock off their 500 words without some of George's Hungarian poppy seed cake and real Turkish coffee. As it is, it's in Bury so you'll never read a word about it in the *Observer.* Maybe that's for the best.

The lovely ladies at the tourist information centre didn't have to ask me where I'd got my baklava from. Everybody knows George, it seems. Those columnists from Brighton and Camden probably find the very fact that Bury has a tourist information centre rather hilarious, but apparently it needs one. 'We're perfectly situated for a weekend. If you like the outdoors, we're in the foothills of the Pennines, and if you like shopping and clubs, we're a tram ride from Manchester.' While I was browsing the souvenir pencils and postcards of Sir Robert Peel's birthplace, an American couple came in, researching their family tree. Bury native Henry Wood was a Quaker who, escaping religious persecution, left Lancashire by boat in 1683 at the age of eighty to set up a community in the New World with his family. Combining his surname with that of his home town, he called that new community Woodbury. It's now a city of 11,000 people, the county seat of Gloucester County, New Jersey, and Bury has become a prime destination for genealogists in baseball caps and big shorts.

I wend my way back to the tram, sorry, Metrolink stop, via the old railway station, now home to the East Lancashire Steam Railway and one of Bury's top tourist attractions. It looks good from the top of Bank Street steps if you're a trainspotter looking for a snap. I was rather distracted by the fact that an old boy in a Bury FC replica shirt fell spectacularly down these steps while I was admiring the view. By his vague yet voluble demeanour and florid complexion, I guessed 'Tommy' had spent the afternoon on licensed premises. It's very easy to do that in Bury – there's a pub every few yards, it seems. As with every city-centre pub in the north, most go through a name change every few months in a desperate attempt to appear new and hip and 'cutting edge'. Thus, proper pub names – those evocative pairings of Fox and Hound, Eagle and Child, Bird and Bee, those mythical Red Lions and Golden Hinds, those obscure dukes and earls – are disappearing.

They're being replaced by weird, unattractive appellations designed to appeal to Lynx-wearing Smirnoff Ice drinkers. The Royal – good solid name, steeped in history, places the pub as central to decent civic life as a hospital or school – is now called S77. Why? It sounds like some bloody form you'd fill in to get inoculated against diphtheria. I'm actually surprised there isn't a bar here called Diphtheria. There's one called Siberia, formerly Peelers & Waldo Peppers. Apparently, as it's in a basement, it has to close for several weeks every winter due to flood damage. But the advantage is that the decor is always brand new.

The north can make no claims on exclusivity where pubs are concerned, obviously. The Rovers Return might be Britain's most famous pub but it is surely run a close second by the Queen Vic. Southern pubs used to be different in my experience – dimple glasses, pictures of the queen, agricultural implements – but these days the British pub has become homogenised from Newquay's Steam Lagers to Newcastle Brown. It's one long pub crawl from Fleece and Firkin to Slug and Lettuce and they all look the same.

No, where the north does stand out is in the matter of the working men's club. The south has clubs, of course, but they are more likely to revolve around golf or tennis or some other sport, or perhaps the services, such as the British Legion or maybe the Conservative Party. The working men's club is essentially northern in character and image. Odd because they were started by a southerner.

Henry Solly (1813–1903) was born in London, the son of a successful railway mogul. His father wanted him to work in business too but Henry, bless him, was 'conscious of intolerable disorder all around me, and an overpowering desire to right all the wrongs in the universe'. One of these wrongs, as he saw it, was widespread 'wretched and degrading bondage to the public house' among the working classes and out of this grew the invention of the Working Men's Club and Institute Union in 1862. These were 'dry' venues which Solly believed would provide recreation and create an informal teaching situation, 'where more serious matters could gradually be introduced'.

Eventually, though, under pressure from the working men themselves, who were working up quite a thirst during all this gradual introduction of serious matters and informal teaching, Solly gave in on what became known as the 'The Great Beer Question'. After 1865, booze became available in working men's clubs, fortunately for Bernard Manning.

Southern in origin, it was the north that embraced these clubs enthusiastically. In fact they eventually became synonymous with the northern night out, chiefly because of a TV show called *The Wheeltappers and Shunters Social Club*.

On reflection, *The Wheeltappers and Shunters Social Club* was the kind of meta-textual, high-concept, reflexive irony that could have E4 or BBC3 schedulers of today drooling. It simultaneously mocked and celebrated the institution of the working men's club, managing to have its cake and yet eat it with gusto. Actually, it wasn't cake, it was pies. At some point in every show, Colin Crompton, as the morose, flat-capped concert chairman, would clang his bell and announce, 'T'pies have come,' a moment of fleeting pleasure in what you felt was a bleak night out.

But the genius of the show – and I think genius isn't too strong a word – is that while holding up the institution of the working men's club to general ridicule, it simply shoved out an hour's worth of club-style entertainment and got ten million viewers. Bernard Manning telling mother-in-law jokes. Bradfordian Afro-Caribbean comic Charlie Williams with routines that were essentially a modern version of 'spookin' it for de white folks', mute magicians in scarlet sequinned jackets who were always putting their fingers to their lips, girls in plunging necklines with pageboy cuts singing '(I Never Promised You) A Rose Garden'. Rubbish, really, but immensely popular and the sort of stuff Garry Bushell is always trying to get back on telly, inexplicably.

As a small and impressionable boy I quite liked *The Wheeltappers and Shunters Social Club* because I was a devotee of Crompton. Resembling a suicidal stand-up in a Samuel Beckett play, he made Archie Rice look like Norman Wisdom. Jowly and hang-dog, with a disastrous, wispy comb-over and permanently 'dripping' Number 6, he would deliver material that extracted bitter mirth from the futility of existence and the impossibility of happiness. One of my favourites was his long riff on the grimness of the dying Lancashire seaside resort Morecambe where 'they don't bury their dead, they stand them up in bus shelters' and the town turned out every Wednesday afternoon to watch the bacon slicer, 'lovely girl'. Chief among the town's attractions were boat trips around Heysham Head. 'They don't come back,' said Crompton in a tone of nihilistic resignation. 'They don't want to.'

The Wheeltappers, though, a world of yellowing Formica tables, bingo callers and pie and pea suppers, was a very particular and partial picture of clubland. If you had visited Batley Variety Club in the early seventies you might have thought you'd stepped through a wormhole in space from a small mining town in Yorkshire to Las Vegas. It was the Broadway of the north, a huge purpose-built club in a Yorkshire mill town (foundation stone laid by The Bachelors, Christmas 1966) that played host, in its heyday, to stars like Shirley Bassey and Louis Armstrong. They would have been driven down the A653 by proud owner and larger-than-life bingo baron Jimmy Corrigan. Rumour had it that he offered Elvis a hundred grand for a week at Batley in the late sixties. Colonel Tom Parker replied that £100,000 suited him but what about Elvis's fee? Gracie Fields was coaxed out of retirement twice – a dubious achievement, if you ask me – and

Roy Orbison played there several times, on one trip acquiring a wife in Leeds. Maurice Gibb married a waitress at the club. It was the Caesar's Palace of the West Riding. Corrigan wanted to give people what was for the time high-class entertainment at Yorkshire prices. He was forever encouraging staff to 'sell' the chicken in a basket as it was about the only source of profit.

The halcyon days of Batley and the rest are gone. Last Christmas, having a pint in a moribund lounge bar of a social club in Wigan, my dad reflected on the death of the institution. 'Twenty years ago, this place would have been packed,' he said, indicating a knot of middle-aged men sipping mild. 'It's not just television either. People wanted entertainment: singers, comics. Your generation just wants to dance or get drunk. And you like to eat out. We didn't eat out. It would have been a ridiculous idea. Something only posh people did. It was wasting time when you could have been playing bingo or listening to some bloke telling Irish jokes or a fellow in a bow tie singing "My Way".' Ironically, the last successful working men's club in Britain is probably the Phoenix Club in Peter Kay's *Phoenix Nights*, a comedy about a failing social club, enjoyed by people who wouldn't know a full house from a meat raffle.

Meat of varying provenances comprises my souvenirs of Bury. Apart from my delicious cosmopolitan haul from Katsouris, no one is terribly impressed. Or hungry, it seems. Now if I'd gone to a different corner of the market, or another part of town and shopped at a different shop, maybe, I'd have come home with another kind of Lancashire delicacy. Smoky dahls and fluffy naans, juicy bhajis and spicy chanas, curries rich with ghee and aromatic with cumin and coriander. Mmm. I can't help thinking that I'd have been a lot more popular if I had.

My mum gave me the first Indian food I ever tasted. She worked in a cotton mill alongside many Bangladeshi and

Pakistani weavers and, one winter night in the late seventies, she brought home a little gift of some home cooking that a young man had given her as a thank you for some favour. There was a Tupperware container full of a thick yellowish stew, some lumpy little brown dumpling things and several flatbreads wrapped and rolled in silver foil – dahl, pakora and chapatis essentially. My mum and dad examined each one with extreme caution, sniffed at the contents and recoiled a little at the warm, pungent spices, having been weaned on starch from which all flavour had been ruthlessly boiled away for fear of poisoning. I sat and ate it all in one go. I grilled the chapatis like toast, not knowing what else to do with them, slathered them with butter and then dipped them in the dahl. I thought I'd died and gone to heaven. Or, more accurately, wherever Muslim people went.

Delighted with how his cooking – or maybe his mum or sister's – had been received, he would send me my own bijou customised takeaways once a week or so. I'm ashamed to say now that, because my benefactor's nickname at work was Charlie, he became known in my house as Charlie Chapati. It wasn't meant as a slight; it was said affectionately if anything and I was only a kid. But I know how it sounds now – patronising and trivialising. I should have bothered to learn his real name but I was too busy gorging myself on his lovely food. It went on for years, by the way, long after I'd left home and gone away to college. I'd go home for the summer and within days, Charlie would have sent me another thick roll of puris or paratha, which I would eat standing at the grill at one in the morning, having drunk a gallon of Burtonwood's Top Hat Bitter.

Charlie must have been part of the second or maybe third wave of Asian immigrants who'd come to Britain to work in the mills of Lancashire and Yorkshire. Britain's relationship with the subcontinent is everywhere murky and complicated and the world of textiles has some of the darkest, bloodiest threads running through its warp and weft.

Cotton spinning was a technology borrowed from India and then mechanised in Lancashire during the industrial revolution. King Cotton and King Coal ruled our lives and kept us shod and housed for a hundred years. Every member of my immediate family, including me briefly, worked in one or the other industry. By the 1960s, new technology and the drive to maximise profits meant that Courtaulds and the like wanted to run their mills twenty-four hours a day. As a kid, I remember excited, apprehensive talk about the new 'continental shifts'. There were three a day, 6 a.m. till 2 p.m., 2 p.m. till 10 p.m. and 10 p.m. till 6 a.m. People didn't mind 'six-two'; Lancashire workers were early risers by nature and it meant you had most of the day to yourself. 'Two-ten' was less popular, as it seemed to fill the day, but you could make the last hour in the pub or get home to put your feet up for a while, and you did get a nice lie-in.

Everyone hated 'nights', though. You were going to work when people were settling down to an evening with the telly or going to the pub or club and your sleep was always interrupted by kids like me playing football in the street. The epic football games of my childhood were forever having to switch venues at short notice when an irate woman would come to the door telling us to 'play somewhere else, don't you know our Ronnie's on nights'.

Like Ronnie, the profit motive never sleeps. Desperate to keep the looms and carding machines throbbing and rattling day and night, the textile barons sent agents to remote Pakistani villages to recruit workers. There was a rich, cruel irony here. A century and a half earlier, Britain had cut off the thumbs of Bengali weavers to maintain Lancashire textiles' competitive edge in British-ruled India. Now we needed both their skills and their willingness to work the graveyard shifts. For their part, the young Pakistani men were largely happy to come. The mills were warm, the money was good. For a while, both communities existed in a state of tolerant scepticism.

Elsewhere in the world, though, in grim sweatshops across Asia, women and kids were working longer, harder and for much, much less. The British textile industry was doomed, particularly since the days of muscular protectionism of British industry were long gone. The new political paymasters in London spoke of a 'leaner and fitter' Britain while featherbedding themselves with dubious sell-offs and fat bonuses. The rest of us, whether we spoke 'Lanky' or Urdu, whether we were born in Karachi or Keighley, could go to hell. We did.

As the mills declined, entire towns ossified and decayed. White and black were united on the scrapheap, where there was little racial discrimination. Asian communities were forced into the local service economy, brothers pooling their savings and setting up shops or curry houses or turning to minicabbing. Across the Pennine hills, from Oldham, Burnley, Accrington and Blackburn to Bradford and Leeds, the Pakistani and Bangladeshi communities were among Britain's most impoverished. Trouble simmered quietly in the cobbled streets and run-down estates.

Arthur C. Clarke thought 2001 would be all about hands reaching out across the galaxy and civilisations coming together across unimaginable distance. In fact, the first year of the new millennium showed that human beings haven't really come very far since we were apes bashing away at bones in the desert. The year 2001 wasn't about ingenuity and destiny, it was all about stupidity and horror and man's capacity for slaughtering each other over competing varieties of mumbo-jumbo.

In the summer before 9/11, though, Britain had its own lesson in the clash of cultures. After years of decline, neglect and ghettoisation plus the provocation of the parasitic far right, the north burned. It burned as it had done twenty years before, but then it had been disenfranchised and riot-happy white and Afro-Caribbean youths, the traditional 'troublemakers'. This time it was the Asians, who for years had kept 'their heads down and their noses clean', as one young Bangladeshi lad I worked with put it. Not any more. Bradford burned, Oldham burned, Burnley burned. The pissed-off kids of my old friend Charlie Chapati were mad as hell and they weren't going to take it any more.

That's one way of looking at it, of course. Others were less inclined to be sociological. Areas of Oldham and Burnley had become 'no-go' areas for whites, they said, and the police turned a blind eye. The blue touchpaper was lit when an elderly white war veteran was beaten senseless for straying innocently into a park in a predominantly Asian enclave of Oldham on his way home from a rugby match. Quick as ever to capitalise on misery, fascists came to town. They dressed in good suits these days but were as ugly as ever and bent on trouble.

Riots blazed across the Pennine towns. Asian youths fought pitched battles with police. Pubs were firebombed, cars torched. Five years on, in May 2006, reports on the mill town riots were published. All the usual suspects were blamed: deprivation, lack of integration and shared values. Failures were systemic, problems institutionalised, lessons had to be learned. On the day the report was published, I took myself for the first time in many years to Oldham.

First impressions were inauspicious. In fact, it was the only really deflating arrival I had anywhere in the north. I disembarked from the Manchester train at Oldham Mumps station. Perhaps I'm overly delicate but for me, it doesn't bode well when the town's main station shares its name with a uniquely unpleasant childhood glandular disease that wreaks havoc with the testicles.

I make my way to the ticket counter to inquire about connections later in the day and find the kiosk 'unpersonned'. Then I notice that there is in fact an employee of Northern Trains in there, but he has pushed his little stool as far to the right of the window as it can possibly go and has his back pressed against the wall and his eyes tightly shut. I can't tell whether he's asleep or not but certainly he has taken every measure possible to avoid the sight-line of any potential customers. This is irritating but also kind of funny, a throwback to the days before customer service when Britain was truly a proud nation of skivers and jobsworths.

Out of the station, there is a distinct lack of any helpful signage, this in marked contrast to Warrington's glittering prom-ise of 'cultural quarters' or Wigan's mysterious 'The Way We Were', which turns out to be a museum. The station also seems to be built on an impenetrable one-way system-cum-flyover that's wreathed in exhaust fumes. There's a selection of subways, none signposted, all of them looking like a terrific place to get murdered. The town's women must detest them.

Taking my life in my hands, I cross the arterial road, travel-ling hopefully, as Robert Louis Stevenson would have it, rather than with any firm notion of arriving anywhere. Eventually I see a sign of sorts. It's a huge faded insignia painted on a railway bridge and it reads: 'Welcome to Oldham, home of the Tubigrip bandage.'

Towns hereabouts straddle and burrow into the Pennine foothills and so the streets are often built at calf-strengthening gradients. I pick a likely-looking one and aim up to the crest of what logic dictates must be the centre of town. It's a depressing slog past shabby shops and a grim-looking niterie called the Niagra (misspelling presumably intended to chime with Viagra) Fantasy Bar. On the awning is a silhouette of a reclining hottie but the building's general appearance would suggest that it caters for men whose fantasy is enjoying a spot of pole dancing in an abandoned butcher's shop. It looks about as sexy as mumps.

The locally famous Coliseum theatre is now surrounded by a garish clutch of fun pubs and variants of the Poundland 'cheap shop' concept. Poundworld. Poundville. Former Soviet Pound Republic. United Pound Emirates. Poundistan. Like many of the north's market and mill towns, Oldham seems to have become a shrine devoted to binge drinking and discount shopping. (My favourite remains Penrith's splendid Quids Inn.) On Yorkshire Street, every other building is some kind of drinking den. I am told by one publican, relishing the gallows humour, that this is 'the second most violent street in Europe'. 'What's the first?' I ask. He doesn't know. My guess is King Street in Wigan but even that, unlike Yorkshire Street, doesn't have a *M*A*S*H*-style 'battlefield hospital' triage centre for patching up combatants from the running battles. You have to say that does do wonders for a street's 'hard' credentials.

The Victorian town hall, though clearly once an impressive structure, looks like it hasn't seen a mayoral address or heated debate about bus routes in years. But there are muscular pillars and imposing steps and at the top a blue plaque that reads: 'Here Winston Churchill began his political career.' 'Winny' gave his inaugural acceptance speech on these steps when first elected as a Conservative MP for the town in 1900. If that seems odd for a Lancashire cotton town, well, Oldham has never been as dyed in the wool as you might think. The town's most famous musical son was William Walton, a northerner who spent his whole life disguising every trace of Lancashire in his make-up, dressing in floppy hats and cravats and writing imperial marches for coronations. He ended up every bit the establishment pillar as Winston. They do things their own way in this corner of Lancashire.

By the way, I say 'most famous musical son' with all due respect to the Inspiral Carpets. The last time I was here I spent the afternoon in a pub interviewing that agreeably clubbable band. The Inspiral Carpets were routinely lumped in with the Manchester bands at the height of Madchester, a designation they sensibly didn't argue with. But a few moments in their company, with their wary, wily humour and broad accents, convinced you that they were quintessentially Oldham.

Nowadays quintessentially Oldham could mean 'Alf's Rooftop Balti Palace', a name that would surely lure any red-blooded visitor after a few jars. Or X-Hibit Designer Shoes, the kind of ugly/quirky nomenclature that is supposed to be funny and is actually profoundly depressing. Eventually, I find a vaguely useful sign. It points to 'Gallery Oldham', so I take a right at yet another fun pub promising yet more big-screen Sky Sports action and 2 for 1 offers and go looking for culture.

Gallery Oldham turns out to be pretty marvellous. A classy bit of modernist steel and glass in the midst of tat and run-down Victoriana. It's the only library I've ever come across which seems to have a nightclub inside. It was taking delivery of crates of those flavoured vodka drinks (for people who don't like alcohol but want to get utterly trashed) and seemed to be called Rude or possibly 365. A large banner proclaimed 'IT'S ALL ABOUT HOUSE MUSIC', which reminds me of those strange lines from the 'Hokey Cokey'. About putting 'your right leg in' and 'your right leg out' and 'that's what it's all about.' Is that really what it's all about? Surely there's more to life than that.

Inside, pretty much all of the actual galleries are closed but I'm starting to get used to this kind of minor disappointment. The girl who politely explains that I can't use my wireless laptop link because I'm not a library member has an accent that's broad

'Lanky' with an exotic descant melody in Francophone, a pretty winning combination, I have to tell you. I began to ask increasingly redundant queries just to listen to her voice. Nearby, an elderly lady is asking after a local history book on an Oldham factory: 'I do hope you have it. Both my grandfathers worked there.' Sadly they don't but she reserves it for 80p. 'Can it go to Lees library? I live there, you see.' In the Local Studies section, a loud cheery man seeks help in his quest to investigate his Irish roots. 'My grand-father was born in 1818. But that's all I know. Would you do the research for me?' With unfailing courtesy the librarian points out that he has to do the actual research himself but that two nice ladies from 'the Society' come in every Wednesday from two till four. Also, she gently advises that the marriage certificate he's brought with him is in fact a death certificate. 'Green one's marriage, love, black is death.' As I travelled around the north, I saw hundreds of these small everyday acts of kindness and they never failed to cheer the spirit and make me quietly proud. Some of the clichés about us are true. We are friendlier and more help-ful. And if you don't agree, we might glass you, of course.

While trying to earwig this exchange, I pretend to look in a book of old photographs and find myself drawn in. There's a fantastic picture of a Failsworth milliner with a giant sign over-looking the canal that reads 'Finest Stetson Hats'. How popular were they in 1950s Oldham, I wonder? A steeplejack called Joe Ball built a castle with ramparts and towers and gargoyles in the middle of a terraced street. Someone demolished it in 1961. How could they?

Finally, there's a picture of the famous and now disappeared Help the Poor Struggler pub, whose landlord was one Albert Pierrepoint. Albert helped more than a few poor strugglers in his time; helped them struggling all the way to the gallows and trap-door. He was Britain's last hangman.

Walk through the Crime and Fantasy sections and at the back of Gallery Oldham you can sit on a nice blue Ikea settee and look through a huge display window across the town. You can see the vast old cotton mill that I worked in for a week when Courtaulds were unsuccessfully training me as a manager. You can see not far behind it the big whale-backed Pennine ridges reminding you that Oldham is very nearly hill country. Completing what is essentially modern Oldham in a single sweeping vista, you can also see the grand golden dome of a mosque.

That mosque will be frequented, I imagine, by many of the people of Glodwick, a predominantly Asian area. When I asked the taxi driver to take me there I half-expected him to blanch, as if I'd asked him for Harlem or Watts, so pervasive is this stuff about racial ghettos. As it was, he just looked a little pissed off and beckoned me in. He was maybe hoping for a fare to Aberdeen.

The W is silent in Glodwick, as it is in Smethwick, a neighbour-hood it has much in common with. According to the BNP and the *Daily Mail*, it's one of the notorious 'no-go areas' of Oldham, a sort of Islamabad of the Pennines where white men fear to tread. This May morning I am one of the few white faces on the street and, though I feel conspicuous, I don't feel unduly nervous. Up north, there's always been the feeling that Oldham (and Burnley) is much less racially tolerant and integrated than nearby Rochdale. So maybe there are other parts of Glodwick where I wouldn't feel safe. But I'm starting to suspect that my minicab driver has dropped me somewhere where he knew I – and of course he – would be comfortable. Or perhaps the intense cloying heat in his knackered cab plus the overpowering scent of Magic Tree air fresh-ener had driven him mad. I'm not bothered. I browse the trays of gulab jaman in a sweet shop, that obscenely sweet syrupy confec-tion that you can feel furring your arteries as you look at it. I opt for a marginally healthier pakora and watch Glodwick go by.

I notice a few camera crews and young women in smart suits talking earnestly into radio mikes. As the report on the Oldham riots of 2001 is out today, the media has come to town getting their 'today Glodwick is peaceful but five years ago, these streets were the scene of some of the worst rioting in British history as simmering racial tensions erupted in this quiet Lancashire mill town' pieces done for the six o'clock news.

For the record, and it'll have to be a pretty vague kind of record, I'm afraid, what did happen five years ago is still some-what murky. An old chap did get horribly, comprehensively battered by a gang of Asian youths but it's by no means proven that it was a racist attack. Some say that in the ensuing mayhem an Asian woman was attacked too. What's indisputable is that a mob of Asian youths attacked several pubs in the Glodwick area. 'There was just a big gang of them,' said Paul Barrow, landlord of one. 'They all charged in, kicking us, punching us and then proceeded to attack all my customers with whatever they had in their hand – stools, bottles, glasses.' A firebomb came through the window causing panic among the regulars, some of whom were elderly ladies. The landlord was quick to add, though, that his clientele included Asians. 'They were absolutely disgusted. They had to defend themselves like everybody else.' The pub, by the way, is called the Live and Let Live.

As I nibble my pakora, I watch a smartly dressed Asian man being interviewed by one of the equally presentable young women reporters. She calls him a community leader, which always makes me tremendously suspicious, whatever the community being led – white, black, gay, straight, Asian, Afro-Caribbean, traveller or whatever. Having never seen the job of 'community leader' advertised in a job centre, I assume now it's a euphemism for 'busybody', a type common to all communities. For some reason, they've moved on to the subject of the so-called 7/7

London bombings and he's trotting out the now obligatory line about 'the need to understand the root causes of this problem. What makes these young men so desperate that they must blow themselves up'. Oddly, I don't seem to recall any such hand-wringing about the motives of the IRA. Maybe I missed it but I don't remember seeing government spokesmen talking of the need to understand 'what makes these young working-class Catholics blow up soldiers'. In fact, I distinctly recall that 'stringing the bastards up' was 'the only language they would understand'. How kindly and thoughtful we have become.

I leave Glodwick in another minicab, this time with an Asian driver, hired from a run-down office next to a halal takeaway on the Glodwick Road. My driver's name is Ahmed and he tells me that Glodwick isn't as bad as people make out. 'There's good and bad everywhere, my friend. People are basically the same.' I notice his Magic Tree air freshener and the sweltering heat of his cab and reflect that he's right.

I pop back into the library and see if the riots and their aftermath are being addressed here in any significant sense. They aren't, which perhaps isn't surprising. It's a tough subject to turn into an attractive exhibition or snappy theme week. 'Oldham: Lancashire's premier racial trouble spot! Try our fun quiz and treasure hunt!' Dialect poetry is less problematic and altogether more cuddly and Lancastrian. Leafing through a book of it, I find this:

> *To some folks things are never reet*
> *but as have alwus towd um*
> *They'd seech a while afire they leet*
> *On owt as grand as Oldham*

Could you follow it? The gist is that you'll go a long way before you encounter anything as fine as Oldham. I can't say I'm completely convinced but I do like a bit of civic pride. I sit in the blue Ikea chair and look out across the town again. Beyond the houses and chimneys and mosques, the Pennine moors rise under what is now a glowering sky. Beyond those lonely hillsides lies Yorkshire. For a Lancashire lad, it's a slightly troubling prospect. There are ominous clouds over Saddleworth Moor. It's where I'm headed next. It's dark up there.

Cardboard Box? You Were Lucky

So Seth retires from the colliery in Barnsley after forty years working underground and his wife Mavis decides he deserves a really special treat. At great expense, she organises a trip to Caesar's Palace, Las Vegas, to see Bob Hope, acknowledged as the world's greatest stand-up comedian. After a sumptuous meal in their five-star hotel, they take their seats for what turns out to be the night of a lifetime. Hope is on fire, at the top of his game; wisecrack follows wisecrack, one-liners and ad libs pour from him. The audience is in tears and, after two hours, many of them are faint with laughter. Bob leaves the stage to wild applause, returns, does a half-hour encore of never-before-heard material and then announces that tonight will be his last performance. He leaves again to a twenty-minute standing ovation.

In the hotel bar later, over a fine old Scotch, Mavis says, 'Well, what can you say? Las Vegas. Bob Hope. That has to be the night out of a lifetime, eh, love?' Seth pulls a face and shrugs. 'Ah well, I suppose it were alreet for them as likes laffin'.'

I love this joke. So do all my friends. However, you may not even get it, particularly if you're from Yorkshire. Because it's a joke 'for them as likes laffin'. Good-humoured, twinkling, charming people with joie de vivre and an appetite for the finer things in life. Lancastrians, in other words.

The rivalry between Lancashire and Yorkshire is not like the rivalry between, say, Arsenal and Spurs or Cardiff and Swansea. It's not merely a petty neighbourly dispute about overhanging leylandii or a childish piece of civic grandstanding. The Lancashire/Yorkshire vendetta has its roots in a war. A proper war, with armies and battles and pikestaffs and axes. Forty years of bloodshed and mayhem. Cities ransacked and looted. A seventeen-year-old Yorkist earl beheaded and his noggin placed on a spike on the gates of York. At the Battle of Towton, near York, 20,000 men were killed, the greatest recorded single day's loss of life on English soil. The country was plunged into anarchy from the walls of London to the bridges of Berwick-upon-Tweed. It prompted our greatest writer, old Willy Waggledagger himself, as my English teacher used to rather racily call him, to write in *King Henry VI Part I*, 'And here I prophesy: this brawl today shall send, between the red rose and the white, a thousand souls to death and deadly night.'

You can read all about those crazy feuding Plantagenets and Tudors, Lambert Simnel and princes in towers in proper history books. It's a hell of a story; a bloody gory one too. All things considered, though, what's amazing is not that the rivalry persists half a millennium on but that it is now largely a matter of jocular banter and cricket matches rather than Molotovs and hand-to-hand combat in the streets of Halifax and Burnley.

In these quieter days, Lancashire and Yorkshire rub up against each other uneasily and awkwardly like big, jealous, brawling, north country brothers. They sulk and sneer at each other across the wildest, most romantic countryside in England and bridle when the boundaries shift and one of them loses a village or river to the other.

We each nurture deeply held prejudices against one another. They think that we are soft and a bit silly. Easily led and somehow lightweight. We think they are humourless and mean-spirited, arrogant and dull. Compared to us Lancastrian bons vivants, we say, waving our pints for emphasis, they are suspicious and cold. At which, they slam down their tankards and declare that they are simply shrewd, self-reliant and nobody's fools. They storm out in a huff and a harrumph and we realise that they never bought a bloody round. Typical.

Let's be honest, many of these traits and impressions 'tykes' seem only too keen to cultivate. These are a race, after all, who say of themselves with apparent pride, 'Yorkshire born, Yorkshire bred, thick in the arm and thick in the head.'

I like to think of myself as a man of the world, a cosmopolitan free-thinker unshackled by petty prejudice. I like to think of myself as this, much as I like to think of myself as a skilled and breathtaking lover, an unsung song-writing genius and the best attacking midfielder England never had. In fact, I know that I nurture some awful prejudices. Should the personal defects of anyone from a rogues' gallery of Britain's most appalling individ-uals be mentioned, from Sir Bernard Ingham to Jeremy Clarkson, Jimmy Savile to Peter Sutcliffe, Paul Daniels to Geoffrey Boycott to Peter Stringfellow, I simply shrug and say 'Yorkshireman' in the belief that this will explain everything. I will not accept that John Humphrys is Welsh or that Jeremy Paxman is, well, whatever he is, until I see birth certificates. Listen to them. Look at them. They just have to be Yorkshiremen.

But, honestly, Seth, I'm joking. Really I am. What are these churls set against Jarvis Cocker, Alan Bennett, Ted Hughes, Simon Armitage, Paul Heaton, Mick Ronson and the other sons of York who I love and admire? Maybe these are the few dozen exceptions that prove the rule.

For better or worse, and I have to say it's the latter, Yorkshire has become emblematic, axiomatic, symptomatic of the north in the hearts and minds of the south. It speaks of bullishness, lack of sophistication, dour self-sufficiency. The words that spring to mind are 'bluff' and 'no nonsense'. And that is a myth. Billy Liar?

Peter Tinniswood? Penny Lane? Morrissey? The Happy Mondays?
Alan Garner? Wordsworth? The north is a land of dreamers.

I'm not saying it's all Yorkshire's fault but Yorkshire has built
a cottage industry – it's a little cottage on t'edge o' t'Dales, nowt
fancy but it's grand, lad – on singing its own praises in a queer,
back-handed way. From Gervais Phinn and his wholesome homi-
lies of Dales schools to Bernard Ingham's canonical claptrap
about the Yorkshire spirit to Roy Hattersley's florid reminis-
cences, Yorkshire is happiest when talking about Yorkshire, using
'plain language' and 'speaking as they find'. What some might
call meanness, they call 'being careful'. They enshrine these
values in folklore about themselves, like the Yorkshire Prayer:

Hear all, see all, say nowt.
Eat all, drink all, pay nowt,
and if thy ever dus owt for nowt,
All-us do it for thee-sen.

And in this apocryphal note left for a Wakefield milkman:

When you leave the milk please put coal on t'fire, let t'dog
out and put t'newspaper inside t'door. P.S. Don't leave
any milk.

George Orwell, a softie from the south but one who fundamentally took the side of the north during its darkest days, could get
a bit tetchy with them:

A Yorkshireman in the south will always take care to let
you know that he regards you as an inferior. If you ask
him why, he will explain that it is only in the north that
life is 'real' life, that the industrial work done in the north
is the only 'real' work, that the north is inhabited by 'real'

people, the south merely by rentiers and their parasites. The northerner has 'grit', he is grim, 'dour', plucky, warm-hearted, and democratic; the southerner is snobbish, effeminate, and lazy – that at any rate is the theory.
'North and South', *England Your England*, 1937

Well, it seems as sensible as superstrings and black holes, to be honest, George. Yorkshire's capacity for contrived curmudgeonly bluff has even been caricatured by Yorkshiremen themselves. In the book *Billy Liar*, Keith Waterhouse pokes fun at the cult of Yorkshireness. Billy mocks the writings of a *Stradhoughton Echo* writer who styles himself 'Man O' The Dales' who praises 'honest native buildings' and 'gleaming cobbled streets'. Billy instead sees 'rugged Yorkshire towns with rugged neon signs and rugged plastic shop fronts... Have you ever realised that your blunt Yorkshire individuals are in fact interchangeable like spare wheels on a mass-produced car?' Similarly, in John Braine's *Room at the Top*, he writes of the hero's hometown thus: 'Bluntness was the fashion... Everyone behaved as if they were under contract to live up to the tradition of the outspoken Yorkshireman with the heart of gold underneath the rough exterior.' The worst of it was, he'd add, that underneath the rough exterior their hearts were as base and vicious as anyone's from the suave and treacherous south.

Perhaps the most famous piece of Yorkshire mockery ever was delivered in part, though not written, by one Michael Palin of Sheffield.

First Yorkshireman: Ahh. Very passable, this. Very passable bit of risotto.

Second Yorkshireman: Nothing like a good glass of Château de Chasselas, eh, Josiah?

Third Yorkshireman: Eh, you're right there, Obediah.

The Four Yorkshiremen sketch is often wrongly assumed to originate from *Monty Python* when in fact it was first heard on *At Last It's The 1948 Show* and was written by John Cleese, Graham Chapman, Tim Brooke-Taylor and Marty Feldman. It's come to sum up the county and its culture for a generation, to put the tin hat on it, as they say in Bradford. As they sit in luxurious surroundings enjoying fine wines, the four Yorkshiremen attempt to outdo each other in ludicrous one-upmanship about their childhood deprivations.

Boastful, needlessly competitive, prone to exaggeration and revelling in their own poverty, mental and physical, this is the caricature of Yorkshire that even Yorkshiremen have come to cherish.

They come across like Texans, or at least the caricature of Texans once beloved of British wits: smug, fulsome, well-fed individuals saying 'call that a waterfall/desert/tunnel' and telling you that back home they have faucets/golf bunkers/cat flaps that size. Tykes will indeed often tell you that Yorkshire is the Texas of Britain. The comparison extends beyond the character of the natives. Yorkshire is huge, easily Britain's biggest county. Six thousand square miles of it, from vast undulating moors to sprawling conurbations. Lancashire is only a quarter as big, something which Yorkshire folk love to tell us Lancastrians in a kind of 'pitying smirk at the urinal' kind of way. It's seven times bigger than Nottinghamshire and thirty-six times bigger than Rutland. That reflects its origins as a territory of the Vikings, who were so expansionist in outlook they made Tesco look positively bashful. It's got three chunks to it too: the famous Ridings.

It was even bigger before 1974, when a notorious shake-up of regional government saw it significantly and savagely pruned. In the north-east, around Barnard Castle and Bowes, it lost a chunk to County Durham and Cleveland and gave up Dent and

Sedbergh to Cumbria, resulting in the bizarre anomaly that the Howgill Fells are in the county of Cumbria but part of the Yorkshire Dales National Park. In the south-east, the upstart region of Humberside pinched the bits around Hull. But most galling of all to true tykes is the loss of most of its territory west of the Pennines to us Lancastrians. Yorkshiremen will talk of the day that they ceded Saddleworth to the old enemy with the same shame and sadness that a Serbian talks of Kosovo.

Saddleworth and the moors lie nor'-nor'-east from Oldham. You'll do it in half an hour, even on our ravaged public transport system (thanks again, Margaret) and quicker still if, like me today, you're travelling by car. It's becoming more and more popular with walkers and tourists, as evidenced by a new Brownhill Countryside Centre located on the long climb out of Oldham. Initially, it appears that the opening times on the door suggest otherwise. I try the door but it won't budge. Just as I'm going back to the car, an elderly lady appears shouting, 'Ey, we're open. I were just on t'toilet, love,' in a voice that sounds like old sandpaper marinated in caustic soda. 'I thought I'd better lock it, you know, in case…' In case of what? I want to ask. In case one of those infamous masked gangs of armed fudge and cycle-trail leaflet robbers come down from Huddersfield and ransack the place? But she seems a nice old soul so instead I admire the displays of children's art, wander upstairs and look at some embroidery and leave with an armful of maps and brochures and fudge.

But though Saddleworth isn't far from Oldham in the grand scheme of things and gets its gas and electricity and mail from the resolutely Mancunian Denton and Stalybridge, it is a world away from the mills and bhuna of the new Lancashire. For a while they spun wool here, traditionally the preserve of Yorkshire folk, but when that failed, they diversified, leaving the old industry to fade and the bleak moors to reclaim the landscape to the joy of locals and ramblers. Don't be put off by the approach along the main A road where the moors look pitted and grimy and you are suddenly confronted with the gutted and derelict remains of the Horse and Jockey pub. Dotted across this landscape are a succession of lovely, sooty-faced villages clinging to the hills, with buildings the colour of toffee and full of nooks and crannies. Delph, Dobcross, Diggle; gorgeous places, each sounding more like one of Trumpton's firemen than the last.

Isolated by their height and relative remoteness, Saddleworth folk have always had a reputation for making their own fun. There are a plethora of youth clubs and amateur dramatic societies, cricket clubs and male voice choirs. There are a clutch of decent pubs. Locals will tell you that this self-sufficiency in entertainment stems directly from rotten weather and isolation. Though the coming of the 4X4 and the dreaded Chelsea tractor has liberated Pennine folk to a degree, a few days of snow can make it feel like Siberia. So there's no point looking to the fleshpots of Rochdale and Oldham for your kicks.

Chief in the area's social calendar is Whit Friday, 'band day' as my friend John Leonard, who lives in Dobcross, calls it. For him, it's one of the highlights of the social calendar, involving a barbecue, guests galore and concerted consumption of beer. On Whit Friday morning, contingents from all the Saddleworth villages parade into Uppermill for a church service, after which comes the serious business of brass band playing and beer drinking. The contests proper start around six in the evening by which time the less dedicated bands might find their technique stymied by the potent produce of Messrs Marston, Theakston and Boddington.

John is keen to point out, though, that 'it's not quite like that scene in *Brassed Off* where they have the babies in haversacks and everyone's too pissed to play. That's funny but it's not strictly accurate. These are serious musicians for one thing and there's a lot of money at stake in the various competitions through the day. Someone like the Black Dyke Mills band can earn more on that one day than selling out the Royal Albert Hall.' In 2006, there was almost thirty grand in prize money at stake.

When the south looks north, when its documentary makers and film directors frame their shot of the mill chimneys and the slate roofs and the mint ball factory, they can already hear the soundtrack and always it is the sound of a brass band. That warm roseate glow of sound is the north in a handful of notes. As a kid I hated brass bands. They belonged to the same order of things as 'parlours' and 'antimacassars' and 'larders', a chilly, pre-central heating world that was in effect an endless Sunday. They conjured up sickly children in tin baths by the fire and women in shawls waiting at the pithead for the inevitable bad news about the roof fall.

Now I love them. Clearly it's me who's changed, not them, because brass bands don't change. By long-standing tradition, they comprise twenty-seven players playing three basic types of instrument – valved metal stuff like cornets and euphoniums, trombones and percussion. The movement has its roots in the Industrial Revolution at the turn of the nineteenth century and the comings of organised industry and, with it, organised leisure. While the big cities had picture palaces and theatres, the smaller towns and villages, like Saddleworth, had to make their own fun and 'banding' was part of that fun.

Soon, the factory and mill owners realised that brass bands were a great way of keeping the workforce out of the pub for a couple of hours. The employers began to sponsor and support the bands; supplying instruments, music, conductors, trainers and funds. The employers did well out of the arrangement – a leisured, sober workforce and something to boast about to old Sourbutts, whose band didn't know their Holst from their elbow

– and the workers had something they could take pride in. Instrumental prowess became a matter of family honour; some babies had a cornet in their mouths before they had a dummy. Top cornetist Harry Mortimer once said, 'I don't think I was even asked if I wanted to learn – it was as much a matter of course as cleaning my teeth or polishing my boots.' Brass bands are still a vibrant part of working-class culture in the north but their origins lie in a more paternalistic world; one of jobs for life, stable communities, living in one village all your life and towns built by wealthy, portly men with mutton-chop whiskers.

On the Saturday after Band Day, the Saddleworth Beer Walk is held. This is a huge fundraising event where participants walk around Saddleworth in fancy dress, stopping off at many of its pubs along the way for half a pint of beer or lager while spectators chuck money at them. Saddleworth also hosts what has become the largest Festival of Morris Dancing in the whole of the United Kingdom, at which point we should pause for giggling.

Now I like morris dancing a lot. I suppose I'd classify it as a guilty pleasure. I've never tried it, adhering to Thomas Beecham's principle that one should try everything once except incest and morris dancing. I like it in the way I like folk music and proper beer and all that kind of stuff, however geography teacher-ish it makes me sound, because it has its roots in real communities and the English landscape and the people involved in it are generally adorable. But mainly I like it in the perverse way that I like seventies progressive rock and Pot Noodles; precisely because they are all Aunt Sallies for those snickering southern studenty comedians. In their vernacular, it's 'sad'. It's for 'losers'. (This usually from someone whose wardrobe runs to three T-shirts, can't cook and hasn't had a proper girlfriend since 1997.) My idea of heaven would be watching a group of beefy tanked-up morris dancers lay waste to the Soho House club, sending TV commissioning editors fleeing, possibly on micro-scooters.

But back up here on the hills between Oldham and Huddersfield, where are we? Yorkshire? Lancashire? A Pennine no-man's-land? Writing in 1968, local journalist and TV presenter Graham Turner found locals who claimed the Wars of the Roses weren't dead and one man in particular who pointed to the moors and said, 'That hill, it's like the Berlin Wall.' And you know what they say: the only good thing that ever came out of Yorkshire is Standedge, the local name for the road out of Yorkshire. Saddleworth politics has been equally contentious down the years, with a strong Tory and Liberal tradition in sharp contrast to most of Lancashire. But when I ask my friend John if we are now in Yorkshire he says yes, unequivocally and without hesitation. 'They have a Real Yorkshire Society in Saddleworth. They tour the pubs and walk the old boundary and a lot of those pubs still have a white rose emblem behind the bar. Quite a few people put West Riding of Yorkshire as their address. They won't admit to coming under Oldham. They don't talk like Yorkshire people though. They still say "abowt" and "rowndabowt". When you get over the hill into Marsden it's all different.'

So I go over the hill into Marsden through a drifting sheet of fog and rain. Occasionally, a sodden sheep or embattled pub looms out of the murk. Everyone's headlights are on at three on an April afternoon. Living here must have been wild and precarious once. John Wesley came here in 1757 and said, 'A wilder people I never saw in all England.' So maybe that wasn't a sheep I just saw huddled on the hillside by the trough. You can understand why there's little allegiance with the valley dwellers of Oldham, safe and snug way down there.

Marsden is a big beefy village or a small town depending on your perspective and it's a paradise on earth for transport history spods. If your future husband gets sweaty-palmed at the idea of tunnels and turnpikes, you might find yourself honeymooning here rather than Rome or Paris. Blind Jack Metcalfe of Knaresborough (I'm not making this up) built three turnpike roads up here in the late 1700s. I would have thought blindness was a pretty formidable obstacle for a career in surveying and road-building but what do I know, since the third of Jack's turnpikes is still in service as the modern A62. We'll be lucky if the Virgin Pendolinos are still running next year.

Best of all, though, is the Huddersfield Narrow Canal, opened in 1811, which runs from Marsden to Huddersfield. The Standedge Tunnel, the longest, highest and deepest canal tunnel in Britain, is seven feet wide and three miles long and it used to take 'leggers' four hours to push a narrowboat through, lying on their backs and using their legs only. John Noakes used to recreate this every other week, it seemed, on *Blue Peter*. As you drive across the moor, you can see enigmatic, striking monuments dotted across the landscape, the ventilation shafts for the tunnel. At the prosaically named Tunnel End, there's a visitors centre – more fudge and leaflets – and a chance to board the Marsden shuttle, a narrowboat that you can take on the short trip through the tunnel. You can even hire it for parties if you like.

It was launched, literally and metaphorically, in 1991. A brief, largely forgotten TV incarnation as a riverboat captain aside; why on earth David Essex? It's not as if his name even sounds like Fred Dibnah so it can't have been a bad line to the agent. His name in fact is Essex, not a good start for your Yorkshire boat-launching celebrity candidate. Never mind. I hope he sang 'Rock On' as he manned the tiller. That's my favourite.

You won't go hungry or thirsty in Marsden. The Luddites used to drink here, planning their next act of mass sabotage, and it's still a fine place to booze away an afternoon when you should be working, even if you don't actually smash up a lathe or anything. There's a great little micro-brewery at the Riverside Tap (seven beers, go nuts, sample them all, then you'll be singing 'Rock On' on the Marsden shuttle). Then if you can get in, you can have a good feed at the justly famous Olive Branch, a 'restaurant with rooms'. I like the idea of a restaurant with rooms. It makes me think of stunned diners, unable to walk after the bread and butter pudding, being carried up to bed like babies.

Marsden is the hometown of one of our best contemporary poets Simon Armitage, whom I first met when we used to work together on Mark Radcliffe's late-night Radio 1 show. The show ended at midnight and Simon, like Ian McMillan, another terrific Yorkshire poet and regular guest, would head back home by BBC minicab over the Pennines from the Manchester studios. Neither of them minded the winter snows and getting home in the small hours. But after one occasion when Simon realised his driver had fallen asleep at the traffic lights in Saddleworth, they drove themselves. Or better still, we'd all stay in the Britannia Hotel and get drunk.

Simon has written evocatively about these parts, their isolation, their debatable status, that sense of being a fragment of the rough urban north cast carelessly skywards into the province of sheep at the top of the world. His website bears the cheery injunction: 'Welcome, from the long lifeless mud of the Colne valley.' His poem 'Snow Joke' tells the story of a motorist, 'wife at home, lover in Hyde, mistress in Newton-le-Willows and two pretty girls in the top grade at Werneth Prep', who becomes benighted and snowbound while in a reverie on the moors and is eventually found by local drinkers who 'heard the horn moaning like an alarm clock under the duvet'. In his poem 'It Ain't What You Do, But What It Does To You', a touching lyric about finding the magical in the everyday, he writes of 'skimming flat stones across Black Moss', a local reservoir, 'on a day so still I could hear each ripple as they crossed'. His book *All Points North* is definitely the second book about the north that everyone should read.

But one quietly eerie poem about this landscape addresses that shadow, that distant echo of horror that will always hang around these uplands now. It's in *Zoom*, his debut collection, and is called 'On Miles Platting Station'. Armitage describes the view from an early-evening train traversing these moors:

> *high enough to see how Ancoats meshes with Beswick*
> *how Gorton gives onto Hattersley and Hyde to where*
> *Saddleworth declines the angle of the moor...*
> *the police are there again boxhauling the traffic*
> *adjusting the arc lights. They have new evidence tonight*
> *and they lift it from behind the wind break, cradle it along*
> *their human chain and lower it carefully down*
> *into Manchester*

The poem describes with a delicate horror the reopened investigations into Britain's most notorious murders. Saddleworth Moor is where Ian Brady and Myra Hindley disposed of four of their young victims during their sadistic killing spree of the mid sixties, dumped them in ravines or nameless places, buried them in shallow graves. In the late eighties, acting on information from Hindley herself, police began to look for two more suspected victims, Pauline Reade and Keith Bennett. They found the little girl. Keith Bennett's remains are still unrecovered.

I did some work with a camera crew from near the area recently and when Saddleworth was mentioned the cameraman said, 'Saddleworth? Lovely place but the kids get under your feet.' There wasn't a groan, no embarrassed clearing of the throat. Just a sudden appalled and utter silence. Media people are generally fairly unshockable; it's almost a badge of honour in these days of 'dark' comedy. But no one makes jokes about the Moors Murders. Alongside the Yorkshire Ripper but more reviled, they are the north's darkest, nastiest secrets, the source of an enduring miasma of evil that swirls around Saddleworth and Chapeltown. The passage of a hundred years and the fact that they are illuminated by hissing gaslight to the clop of a hansom cab has meant that Jack the Ripper's crimes have become safely packaged into just another exhibit on London's tourist itinerary, even though the murders were savage and chilling. There will never be Moors Murder tourism. They have a special, inviolate place in the national psyche. That place lies in the north. Nineteen sixty-six was not just the year of Moore, Charlton, Hurst and triumph in north London. It was also the year of Brady and Hindley and wickedness beyond belief in Manchester.

Everyone in the north of my generation grew up in the shadow of the Moors Murders. When we were told not to speak to strangers, to run home from school on dark winter nights, to avoid nice-looking ladies wanting our help looking for lost dogs or gloves, we knew it was not just idle parental blather or daft talk from Nan. We knew that horror and evil had come out of the dark, sounding and looking just as northern as our own kind, looking for kids like us and finding us, in Ancoats, Gorton, Ashton, the places where we lived and played and went to school. For kids like me from towns like mine, the bogeyman was not a nameless fear or a vague shape under the bed. The bogeyman had a name, two names, normal names, and the bogeyman's two faces stared at you out of the newspapers, hair full of peroxide and brilliantine, eyes full of pure and pitiless evil.

Poor, lost Keith Bennett aside, the story is maybe beginning to recede into memory. Hindley is dead, unmourned, Brady a caged, sacred monster who'd rather be dead. If you want to know the whole grisly story, find a copy of Emlyn Williams' brilliant and sober study *Beyond Belief*. In it, he describes how in the end it was Myra Hindley's sister and impressionable teenage partner David, whom Brady tried to lure into his world of fascistic fantasy, who alerted the police when they realised just what kind of a world it was. That couple were The Smiths. Williams describes them as this several times and I've always thought that maybe that's how the greatest of Manchester's bands came by their name. Certainly their song 'Suffer Little Children', tender and ghostly at once with its famous 'Oh Manchester, so much to answer for' refrain stands alongside Williams' book as a sombre and seemly remembrance of hideous events.

Slaithwaite is a lot more heart-warming. It's a town which, if you're a devotee of heart-warming Sunday night drama, you may already know. A glut of these shows have given many Yorkshire towns and villages a little added USP on the marketing front. The daddy of them all is Holmfirth, the village where old men behave like little lads and baths are forever being turned into rudimentary flying machines with hilarious consequences as the home of *Last of the Summer Wine*. LOTSW – as I'm sure someone must call it – has been running for twelve hundred years and predates the coming of the enclosure system. I haven't checked this; I'm just going off a gut feeling. I'm not going to tell you what it's about as it is utterly unthinkable that you have not seen it. I will just say that it has become fashionable to mock *Last of the Summer Wine* for its recycled plots and sickly 'aren't we all daft oop north' humour and this is one occasion where I am happy to go along with metropolitan fashion. It's rubbish. My mum and dad love it, though. If you do too, make a pilgrimage to Holmfirth and you can have chips at Nora Batty's old café. I actually did this once with Billy Bragg, the ratlike pop group Bros and Radio 1 DJ Mike Read, for reasons far too complex to go into now. Similarly, Goathland in North Yorkshire has a cute little narrow gauge steam railway system, a big village green, a couple of pubs, and is known to millions as Aidensfield in *Heartbeat*. *Heartbeat*, like its successor in the schedules *Where the Heart Is*, is twee and toasty and melted buttery and must save the NHS a fortune in Mogadon. Don't go there on a Bank Holiday Monday unless you want to be trampled underfoot by the massed nice ladies of the Nick Berry Fan Club looking for things 'he' might have touched.

And Slaithwaite, a tykeish, likeable little country town which straddles a tributary of the Colne Valley, is transformed by the magic of television into Skelthwaite in the aforementioned *Where the Heart Is*. Locals watch it with the sound off just to spot each other's allotments and houses. Half the buildings cling to the steep sides of the valley like lichen, half – like the huge old Titanic Mill, now chic apartments, of course – sit brooding in the hollow like a troll. I'd provide more evocative detail but by now lacerating sheets of hail (just like those old plastic strip curtains your auntie used to have) have completely obscured the town. It stung your face like ice-cold buckshot and filled your pockets with freezing water. This then is the Colne Valley. In May.

A few sodden pieces of paper have been left blowing about in the bus shelter. These turn out to be several copies of a leaflet entitled 'Walking Round Slaithwaite', presumably abandoned by a drenched rambling party who are even now warming up with a Jameson's in the snug of the Silent Woman or the Shoulder of Mutton. But this leaflet does tell me that Slaithwaite is the only town in Britain to have a canal running along the main street. Lean out the cabin door and you can probably grab a Greggs pasty.

Before we leave the subject I should say that a night or two later I was recounting my trips in these parts to some friends from Wakefield and at the mention of Slaithwaite they began to roll around on the floor slapping themselves in near parodic mirth. Apparently it isn't Slaythwayt but Slawit. So they said, anyway, but I've since learned that at least four separate pronunciations are in regular use. It's different from pub to pub, it seems. Typical bloody Yorkshire orneriness, if you ask me. These kinds of lexical traps are waiting to ensnare unsuspecting southerners (and Lancastrians), so you should also know if you're heading north and east that Linthwaite is Linfit and Appletreewick is Aptrick and that they'll laugh at you in Chichester on South Tyneside if you pronounce it with an itch rather than an eye. Not as much, though, as I laughed at my New Zealand friend Brendan's first attempt at Clitheroe. You had to be there. But you can guess.

As Slaithwaite or Slawit or Slewitt, or whatever you call it, recedes in the rainy rear-view mirror, we begin to enter what the French might call Le Yorshire Profonde: Deepest Yorkshire.

The comparison here, at first ridiculous, between the rough-hewn, hail-hardened tykes of Yorkshire and the indolent gastronomes of the sun-kissed Dordogne, actually makes sense. Yorkshireman and Frenchman alike share a stubbornly unreasoning pride in simply being a Yorkie or Frenchie. They believe they have the best food, the best rugby teams, the most beautiful women. They share an almost mystical attachment to their native land. Just as the wine-growers and peasants of the Languedoc believe no one is their equal in the cultivation of the grape, so Yorkshiremen think that their beer has no equal but is similarly, mystically, bound to the soil, like the friend of my editor who loves Tetley's bitter of Doncaster but says that 'it dunt travel'. In other words, it only really tastes right in Yorkshire. The French call it 'terroir', the sacred, inexplicable union of weather, ambience, landscape and history that imbue a region and its drink. Yorkshire calls it things being 'proper'. (I would like it greatly if Yorkshire adopted the French term though. Then I could have a pet theory about a Yorkshire Terroir. Thank you. Goodnight.)

Deepest Yorkshire fans out before you now; north, east and south are Bradford and Leeds, Barnsley and Rotherham, the Dales and the Moors, where the caps are always cloth and the chips are always Harry Ramsden's and livestock cowers on the hillsides waiting for Ted Hughes to stride among them with his notebook or Christopher Timothy to come and put his hand gently up their bottom. J. B. Priestley said, 'From such heights, you look across at hills that are constellated and twinkling with street lamps,' adding, 'If the towns of the West Riding were as brilliantly illuminated as Los Angeles, they would run excursions so people could see these patterned hills at night.' That was in 1933. Now, of course, these great cities fizz like LA with electricity and from the right Pennine heights in the right dusk you can see them strung out across the east of England like clusters of fairy lights. Nothing remotely fairy about them, though, obviously, owd lad.

In the south sits Sheffield, and Sheffield is a curio. Graham Turner described it as 'a great city with an international reputation which is capital of nowhere'. The south of the city is pretty much in Derbyshire and the wild and woolly north-easterners of Redcar and Middlesbrough regard it as essentially the Midlands, all soft hills and Daiquiris on the terrace. Because of its origins as an agglomerate of hamlets and villages in a bowl of seven hills, it's always been thought of as fiercely individual and slightly 'other', even by its near neighbours. In Barnsley, Doncaster, Rotherham and Chesterfield, they call Sheffielders 'Dee-dars' because of their unique and slightly daft pronunciation of thee and thou. Some Sheffield folk will smile tolerantly at this, others will smack you in the mouth. When Rotherham looks down on you, some would say you're in trouble. I would never be so rude. But I will say this of Rotherham, Sheffield's smaller, sourer, more ingrown neighbour. An American visitor I knew watched a head-scarved Rotherham woman who could have been anything between thirty and seventy walking home with her shopping, leaning into a gale, carrying cheap plastic bags over a concrete bridge between two of Rotherham's uglier estates. She said that it was like a bleak vignette from one of those forgotten chemical towns in the former Soviet Union.

Sheffield may not be as northerly as Irkutsk or Murmansk but whatever the Geordies think, it's surely the north. If Sheffield isn't the north, what is? Think how the town grew rich, not on accounting or tailoring or anything smooth and white collared but on two hard, hard materials. Coal and steel. What could be more northern?

Sheffield still makes steel. In fact, it makes more than at any other time in its history. You just wouldn't notice the fact any more as you wander its streets and pop into its latte bars. The skies are no longer black and streaked with fire, the foundries no longer clang. Martyn Ware and Ian Craig Marsh of The Human League claimed that it was a Sheffield childhood soundtracked by booming turbines, forges and hammers that led them to make their own percussive electronic music. Sheffield's pretty quiet now but if you want to rekindle the foundries for an afternoon, you can visit the Sheffield Millennium Galleries and a room devoted to steel craftsmanship. Alternatively, you can pop over into the former Soviet Union, or Rotherham if you prefer, and visit Magna, an award-winning and frankly breathtaking science adventure centre set in the former Templeborough steel works.

Mention of The Human League should remind us that Sheffield has been mighty industrious and hugely successful in the production of that other great British export, pop music. It's produced two very different Cockers – Joe raw but Jarvis wry – who have both captured the different voices of the city's working class. At the time of writing, youthful sons of the city the Arctic Monkeys are enormously fashionable and successful thanks to a witty, punkish take on modern Britain and particularly modern Sheffield viewed from the bottom of a bottle of Smirnoff Ice. They're very Sheffield. I love their line, 'Ask if we can have six in, if not we'll have to have two,' ('Whatever People Say I Am, That's What I'm Not') which must be utterly opaque to folks in certain places but is instantly recognisable to anyone who's ever had drunken discussions about how to divvy up cabs.

Mainly, though, Sheffield means electronic music, maybe because of those relentless inhuman foundries which, like Stanlow, might even be glamorous if you don't have to work there. It's an impressive list: The Human League, Heaven 17, the Thompson Twins, Cabaret Voltaire, Dave Ball of Soft Cell, and more latterly the wonderful Warp Records, original home of the Yorkshire bleeps and bass scene now sadly relocated to London just as Motown moved to sunny LA from their own northern industrial town of Detroit.

I'd like to think that it was this illustrious, slightly off-kilter lineage that led to someone deciding that the National Centre for Popular Music should be built in Sheffield rather than in Liverpool or London. Both these cities wanted it apparently and what with The Beatles and, er, Spandau Ballet, both could lay claim to it.

What no one had stopped to think though was that a National Centre for Popular Music was a very, very bad idea, one engendered by a brief rush of national cockiness called 'Cool Britannia'. In that horny golden dawn, a newly priapic Blighty felt all youthful and sexy again after the deathly Ice Age geron-tocracy of the late Tory years. We had a new young guy in Number 10, champagne receptions with Noel Gallagher and the

Spice Girls and a general mood of coked-up overconfidence buoyed by a bulging macho package of Lottery money.

The National Centre for Popular Music gave the lie to that old adage, 'If you build it, they will come.' They did build it in 1999 – four huge horrible tin drums with spouts on top – but no bugger came, to use the local parlance. It had to close down within a few years, saddled with enormous debts. Before it did I visited it and a depressing afternoon it was too. It didn't help that my Sheffield minicab driver curled his lip with contempt when I told him where I was headed and offered the opinion that it would be far better if his old mates who'd got jobs there were smelting or soldering rather than 'poncing abaht with Phil Collins posters'.

He was right. It was rubbish. It somehow contrived to have all of pop music's cheesiness without its sass and vigour, all of pop's populism without its charm and fun, all of pop's earnestness without its passion and power to move. The highly individual Scottish musician Nick Currie aka Momus called it 'a glorified shopping centre, a feebly educational day out for the kids... A scenario in which all creativity, all rebellion, all originality have been co-opted by a horrible consortium of music industry people. It's hypercapitalism in league with the government and academia. It stinks. Here, no matter what buttons you press, you basically get the same conformist shit.'

It's difficult to improve on that beyond making the obvious point that Britain doesn't need a centre for popular music; our houses and schools and clubs and bedrooms and streets are already that. Like Sheffield makes steel, Britain makes pop. It's what we do. It's in our blood, handed down from generation to generation like a monkey wrench or a pair of greasy overalls. Anyone remotely interested in doing this and doing it properly is already doing it in a bedroom with a computer or in a garage with a pawnshop guitar, not 'poncing abaht' in front of a video screen pretending to be Will Young. I'm sorry for the people who lost their jobs (sixty-nine to be accurate) but no one mourned its passing. Like the Millennium Dome, it stands as a monument to the arrogance of the people who think they know what 'the people' want.

Bradford got it right, probably to Sheffield's chagrin, when they opened the National Museum of Photography, Film & Television in 1983. That quickly became the most visited national museum outside London, attracting an average of 700,000 visitors each year. This was a quietly significant moment in what I think of as the northern renaissance. The museum is an offshoot of London's Science Museum and was something of a test case. Some in Islington and Hampstead would have loved it to fail but it flourished, proving that there is an appetite north of Watford for more than rugby league and shin-kicking contests, great fun though they both are, of course. Far from faltering through the nineties, it embarked on a £16 million expansion programme. When it reopened in 1999, it attracted over a million visitors the following year and Bradford folk are now as proud of their elegant curved glass landmark as Sheffield are queasy about their tin white elephant.

Unlike the NCPM, the NMPFT was based on a sound practical selling point: you can't watch rare archive film or look at pioneering photographs or gawp at a massive IMAX cinema in your front room whereas you can listen to Jo Whiley or play your Sex Pistols records. There's still the usual knee-jerk worshipping at the altar of interactivity but at least it's fun. You get to play with cameras and read the news. Plus there is stuff you might conceivably want to see like John Logie Baird's original telly – I had one quite like it as a student – or what is regarded as the world's first example of moving pictures, Louis Le Prince's 1888 film of Leeds Bridge.

It was the reason I first came to Bradford with a gang of media studies students in the late 1980s. After we'd spent the afternoon pretending to be newsreaders and cricking our necks at an IMAX film of the Grand Canyon (IMAX cinemas are great but there's only a slim canon of subjects that really work: moon launches, Mount Rushmore, etc. You wouldn't want to see Ingmar Bergman's *Scenes from a Marriage* like this) we sampled the delights of Bradford. Delights aplenty there were too, particularly if you liked Indian food. I still remember the looks on the faces of our party upon entering one of the city's many fantastic cheap and cheerful curry cafés. We were seated at a table with the cutlery chained to it and scanned a typewritten flyer offering us sheek kebabs at 10p a pop and chicken bhuna for a quid. John Burke ate so much that the waiters came out and marvelled at him in quiet amusement. Then he asked for a doggy bag.

Bradford has long luxuriated in the smells and tastes and voices and colours of half a world away. It was built on wool and buying wool means travelling the globe. It's been said that you may meet a florid man sipping a whisky and soda in a Bradford saloon bar who looks as if he has never been further than Morecambe. But in his pocket he may have the timetable for the Istanbul sleeper. Bradford has always been a city of travellers. The textile men bought from Australia and Argentina, they sold to Belgium and Beijing, and the result was a city that was a funny mix of the bluff and the cosmopolitan. Barbara Castle and J. B. Priestley are one kind of Bradfordian: humane, liberal, doughty. Composer Frederick Delius was another: patrician, urbane and of German stock like many Bradfordians. Bradford's famous bohemians include the Californian exile David Hockney and Billie Whitelaw, Samuel Beckett's favourite actress.

Bradford gets very angry when casual observers overlook its proud, individual character and assume it to be a continuation or even worse, a suburb, of a certain other city ten miles west. It doesn't help that the local airport sports both their names. But it rankles with Bradford; especially these last few years. While Bradford gets docudramas about inner-city riots and criminology, Leeds – flipping Leeds! – gets Harvey Nichols, café culture and *Guardian* features about its bloody fusion restaurants.

Here's an illuminating little episode. A decade or so ago, I went to Leeds to interview a band (I've forgotten who, sadly) and took a minicab back to the station on a hot summer's day. I sat in the back with the window down as we waited at traffic lights and a couple of likely lads walked by, giving me a grudging, contemptuous look. Then one walked over and, leaning almost into the car, snarled 'RICH BASTARD!' at me.

Back in London, even my editor James Brown, a Leodensian himself, laughed in a rueful sort of way. Here was the north, no, maybe here was Yorkshire in a nutshell; bitter, envious, aggressive, impoverished, the kind of place where if you take a four-quid taxi ride, you're a pampered aristocrat.

I thought about this on my most recent trip to Leeds as I reclined on fat, plumped pillows on a handmade maple bed in the penthouse suite of 42 The Calls. The bedroom was enormous, hewn from stone and, as the whole building was a converted corn mill, buttressed and criss-crossed by the original dark wood riveted beams. The in-room hi-fi was tuned to some serene Ravel piano music on Radio 3, which mingled with the sounds of the River Aire below me and the swoosh of the hot water from the deluxe shower room. I realised, with mild annoyance, that I'd left the recessed plasma widescreen in the living room switched on and that I could still hear Ray Stubbs on *Grandstand*. Never mind, I'd go through in a minute just as soon as I'd finished my Bombay Sapphire and leafed through the menu one more time. White Crab Meat in a Saffron Aioli looked nice, as did the

Sautéed Calves Liver with Crisp Pancetta and Roast Shallots. But, you know, I really ought to eat out. I was, after all, in Leeds, Britain's most improved city, the gentrified jewel of the new north, the Barcelona of the West Riding.

I have always had a special place in my heart for Leeds. During the 1970s, when most people detested it, I loved it for pretty much the same set of reasons: namely Revie, Bremner, Giles, Lorimer, Clarke, Yorath and Madeley. Week in, week out I went to watch Wigan Athletic vainly try to lift themselves from the gloom of the Northern Premier League into the rarefied glamour of League Division 4. But a twelve-year-old boy needs something slightly more thrilling in his football life than Tuesday night trips to Goole and Altrincham and so my other team were Leeds United.

I can now see what I couldn't at the time, namely that my beloved Leeds United were essentially the Nazis in Umbro, the Daleks dressed by Gola; a crack squad of inhuman automata with one purpose in mind, the ruthless subjugation of other life forms. Perhaps that's a bit strong. Let's say that they were a team of eleven J. R. Ewings; duplicitous, untrustworthy, conniving and, as in when they taunted a beaten Southampton with those thirty-two passes on *Match of the Day*, heartlessly smug. The press hated them and never had a good word for them, their dispassionate zeal and their Moonie-like teetotalism.

I loved them.

I'm not sure why, though. I think it may have been to do with Billy Bremner, who was little and feisty and a good role model for a shortarse and whose busy, combative style I could emulate in the playground whereas the technical virtuosity of George Best would always elude me. Or perhaps it was because they were northern but not obvious. But probably it was because no one liked them. Everyone in my class supported either Manchester United or Liverpool, both of whom I felt carried themselves with the irritating hauteur of the self-styled playboy. No one in my part of Lancashire supported Leeds even though they were a top side. So I did. Given that I also had a partisan thing about Björn Borg, who was similarly austere, loathed and all-powerful, a psychologist would have had a field day.

I didn't get to Elland Road much but my dad would sometimes take me to Blackpool or Burnley or Preston whenever Leeds came to town. Whenever they did, the away end would fill up with Leeds hooligans in white butcher coats daubed with the names of their heroes in marker pen. They were the most frightening thing I had ever seen. They may still be just that. And I've drunk in Redcar on a Friday night.

When Leeds won the FA Cup in 1972, I watched it lying on the rug at my Auntie Maureen's house watching her big new Rediffusion colour telly and my Uncle Brian said I was the most biased football supporter in Britain. I dimly remember them romping to the '74 Championship. But what I mainly remember are a series of crushing disappointments and a taste like ashes in the mouth. Ray Kennedy's goal at Spurs pipping us to the Championship when I was ten, probably my first introduction to the random existential cruelties of adult life. We lost again to Derby the year after, made worse by the crowing of Brian Clough. Then we lost the Cup Winners' Cup to AC Milan. Horribly, in 1973, 'plucky' Sunderland of the Second Division snatched the FA Cup from under our noses. Everyone in Britain thought Bob Stokoe and Jim Montgomery, the gallant minnows manager and goalkeeper respectively, were adorable except me. I brooded under the incessant 'chauving' of my school mates.

The European Cup Final of 1975 was the comically perfect denouement of Leeds' seventies saga of begrudged victories and bitter, mocked failures. Bayern Munich won by two goals to nil after some of the worst refereeing decisions ever; a cast-iron penalty turned down, a perfectly good goal by Peter Lorimer disallowed. Drunk with pain like a wounded animal – but mainly just drunk – the Leeds travelling contingent rioted in the streets of Paris. The club was banned from European competition and the team slid into a long, slow decline. I was lured away by girls, music, girls, college and girls, in that order.

So how nice to come back in happier times. The football team are rebuilding themselves – financial profligacy having nearly destroyed them again – and the city is abuzz. Of all the great northern civic rebirths of the last twenty years, Leeds has been the most talked about because it's been the most unexpected. From the vantage point of the deep, soft south, where it's always been synonymous with ferrets and watch-fobs and batter puddings and cloth caps, the idea of Leeds as a vibrant European city was first laughable then baffling. But get used to it, Giles and Sebastian. Deal with it, Henrietta and Imogen. Leeds is happening.

It started happening in the mid nineties. The hotel I'm staying in (42 The Calls) was an early part of it. Leeds' first boutique hotel, it began a city-wide trend for urban sophistication as well as the stolidly Victorian civic pride and wealth that had always made it a handsome city. Now it's handsome and sexy; a heady mix.

The hotel takes its name from the Calls district, a former stopping-off point for the barges on the Aire and the canal. Twenty years ago, when this was derelict and deserted, a single woman would have been insane to have lingered alone in this part of town. Tonight I can see from my window a young woman giggling and chatting on her mobile phone as she sits on the steps of Cuban Heels salsa bar. Some local naysayers have already begun to describe the Calls area as 'yuppified', which is intended as an insult but I personally prefer it to 'run-down shithole'. There are apartments here if you can afford them and, for the price of a

Cuba Libre or a plate of dim sum, you get the feeling of being in a cosmopolitan city. Look at the names: Hakuna Matata, Casa Mia, Sela, Dr Wu's. You could be in Milan, Tokyo or Seville, except the tans are from Tanfastic and there are a lot more tattoos.

If you fancy a tattoo or some vulnerable part of your body pierced or maybe some outlandish item of surfer apparel, then you should stop off at the Cornmarket, a fine old circular building with great curved galleries, on your way from The Calls into the city centre. I would have thought opportunities for 'hanging ten' or 'riding the big curl' were fairly limited in Leeds, which may explain why the surfing shop was pretty quiet of a Thursday morning.

The real market on Kirkgate was a lot busier. Leeds Market is one of those places that Alan Bennett really ought to eulogise more. It's a different kind of grandeur than the fabulous Victorian town hall or the art gallery – both favourites of the great man – but it has a magnificence all of its own, an Edwardian cathedral to commerce in green timber and high vaulted glass. Here for a century Leeds folk have come for bargains and for those items that you couldn't find anywhere else: parakeet cages, greaseproof paper, shaving-brush holders. A bit of sawdust on the floor à la Bury Market would have made it even more evocative. But like a lot of Leeds architecture, there's an endearing touch of the Hyacinth Bucket about the Market Hall, a certain raising of the nose towards the common herd. It was here in 1884 that Michael Marks first set up his stall with the slogan 'Don't Ask. Everything's A Penny', an early equivalent of Poundland, I suppose. Later, of course, in conjunction with Tom Spencer, they found that the way to Britain's heart was through underwear, microwaveable curries and those really great beef and onion crisps.

As I cross the bustle of Kirkgate and Briggate, curving spines running through the eastern squares of the town, I notice that the lampposts are festooned with exhortations of municipal pride and cheering messages to the citizenry. In Pyongyang or Rangoon, these would say 'Shoulders To The Wheel Of Progress, Sons Of The Proletariat!' or 'Workers Of Our Glorious City, We Salute You For The Sacrifice Of Your Monthly Rice Allowance'. But this being modern Britain and the placards designed by a marketing consultant in an Armley loft space, they say 'Leeds Is Thinking Positive. Are You?' and 'It's Your City, Use It With Pride'. I shouldn't sneer. Pride was an awkward character that the Thatcher Experiment was supposed to eradicate from the north, along with hope, joy and security. Nice to see that it failed.

Long before Thatcher was a malevolent twinkle in a Lincolnshire grocer's eye, Leeds was renowned for its superb arcades. Modern Leeds has continued this tradition in fine style, throwing a high stained-glass ceiling over Queen Victoria Street, or at least Brian Clarke Architects did. When the council announce that they're going to glass over some of the city's nicest, oldest shopping streets to make an instant arcade, you can understand the worry that the result could be some nasty hybrid of a tomato growers' polytunnel and a Center Parcs. I don't know what Alan Bennett thinks but Pevsner likes it and Maconie thought it singular and stylish, more like Brussels than *Bladerunner*. The shops were pretty classy affairs too. I almost bought a pair of leather brogues in one but on glancing at the price, I awoke to find a gaggle of concerned shoppers loosening my collar and offering me water. So I thought I'd leave it till next time. If you're determined to shop till you drop, The Light may sound spiritual and be next door to the Catholic cathedral but it's a temple to Mammon with a nightclub and a gym tucked inside.

It was round about here that I decided to fasten on to the end of a crocodile of visiting academics who were slinking through the shallows of town. Their plastic name tags read like

Peter Gabriel's 'Games Without Frontiers'; Sun Li and Sven, Pyotr and Giselle. A man with a clipboard and rimless specs addressed them in what seemed to be Dutch. They all laughed and then scuttled up a side street. I followed them right into the foyer of the City Varieties.

The City Varieties Leeds is the oldest extant music hall in Britain. It's tucked discreetly away on Swan Street between two major shopping thoroughfares and next door to one of the many, many places in Leeds these days where you can get polenta, gnocchi or red snapper for lunch. I imagine when Houdini and Charlie Chaplin played here they popped into the Grapes for a pie and a pint. Many another legend of variety has played here and the most famous gaze down from murals on Swan Street. In the confined space of the extremely compact foyer, two of the Dutch contingent of academics start to have quite a tetchy dispute that I can't follow. Perhaps it was about who was the best out of Roy Hudd and Ken Dodd.

The City Varieties looms large in my childhood and I guess that of many Brits between the ages of thirty and fifty for two reasons. Firstly it was the venue for the BBC's long-running show *The Good Old Days*, which ran from just after Agincourt to 1999. My nana loved this recreation of an evening at an Edwardian music hall with the same passion with which I hated it. As a toddler she would force me to watch it with her when she babysat me. Leonard Sachs, dad of Andrew, *Fawlty Towers'* Manuel, was the master of ceremonies and produced the most astonishingly prolix and grandiloquent introductions, full of terms like pulchritudinous and terpsichorean and coruscating and then, disappointingly, someone like Vince Hill would come on in a straw boater and sing an embarrassing song about dogs in the window. My nan loathed these verbose introductions, probably because they sounded to her puritanical Lancastrian ears suspiciously like showing off, a cardinal sin. They were the only bit of the programme I liked. Generally, I have always agreed with Alexei Sayle when he said that there were many competing theories as to why music hall died out – socio-economic, technological, etc. – but he thought it was because it was crap.

The show has long since disappeared from our tellies but lives on in a live version still going at t'City Varieties. On the bill are Stan Stennett, Jimmy Cricket, Johnny Casson 'the furtive funster', Ward Allen and Roger the Dog, 'Two voices in one accord'. Marvellous stuff, I'll wager, but not for me. 'Why not come along in costume?' asks the flyer. Why not drink a pint of caustic soda while you're at it, I think darkly.

If you're a child of the seventies, the other reason to remember and fear the name City Varieties Leeds was *Junior Showtime*, which also came from the hallowed venue. *Junior Showtime* was a variety show for kids and ran for five years till 1974 – extraordinary really, given that kids hate variety. It was hosted by Bobby Bennett, a man with a shock of Jimmy Savile-esque blond hair, possibly compulsory in seventies Leeds, and boundless reserves of gusto. Pauline Quirke and Bonnie Langford were on it most weeks, I remember, shrieking and cracking awful jokes or appearing in mirthless 'skits'. I could take the Daleks but this I did have to watch from behind the sofa.

The lunchtime tide of Leeds folk carries me down to City Square, a newly pedestrianised area being restored to how the Victorians would have known it before the car-mania of the sixties and seventies turned it into a polluted chicane. To the south is Leeds station, subject of an old indie ditty by the Parachute Men. To the west is Majestyk nightclub. To the north, far more glamorously, towers Number One, City Square. Here, in lofty air-conditioned splendour, tier upon tier of accountants and graphic designers, PR firms and new media companies climb up to the sky. It's more Manhattan than West Riding. Men in DKNY shades and women in fuck-me heels click through reception texting furiously, thumbs a blur as they go to get their three-bean and sweet potato wraps. It's all very sexy.

Feeling positively troll-like by comparison, I remember I have reason to post an old-fashioned 'snail-mail' letter and so am pleased to see on one side of the square a broad and august building that looks very like a superior Victorian post office. And so it is: the Old Leeds Post Office. Things are moving so fast in Leeds though that it is a mistake to assume anything postal might occur there now. No, the post office is about to reopen as Residence 6, an £8 million redevelopment. While the building's classical facade has been maintained, inside it's become twenty-three luxury one- and two-bedroom apartments, each featuring kitchen, lounge and en suite bathrooms as well as state-of-the-art entertainment systems. Valet parking and gym naturally. It's hoped that 'as well as executives … Leeds United's new signings will stay at Residence 6 as they househunt while opposing players will be encouraged to use the apartments before a game.' It's all a far cry from Jack Charlton walking his greyhounds down to the pub, something I'm sure must have happened.

Chris Dalzell, one of the project's grand fromages, has said, 'What we're putting in here is what most major cities don't have at the moment. We're a little bit ahead of the game. We wouldn't have done this if we didn't have the confidence in the city. It's raised the bar and what you'll find is that as we ratchet up what is provided, customer expectations will rise.' If the barman knows how to mix a martini as well as Chris can mix a metaphor, it'll be a great place to hang out.

There'll be 'al fresco dining' in the square itself, something that will supposedly bring to the city 'a European feel', presumably Madrid rather than Chechnya. And you'll be able to enjoy your spinach and ricotta parcels under some handsome if incongruous statues including the Black Prince and discoverer of oxygen Joseph Priestley. As I stand there admiring them and reflecting on the wind of change that's sweeping the north, a man with a whippet on a lead walks past me. A fabulous moment.

In the Henry Moore Centre, there are no pictures of whippets but there is an exhibition of Brazilian video installations. From here, you can stroll through a Perspex walkway to Leeds City Art Gallery, haunt of the teenage Alan Bennett and home to the finest collection of twentieth-century British art outside London. Their online literature encourages visitors to 'read … mingle … chat … laugh'. Personally I'd have put 'look at some pictures' in there as well but I understand that museums are now so terrified of being thought elitist, so desperate to be 'inclusive', that they have to avoid the unspeakable truth, namely that modern art isn't for everyone. Neither is John Coltrane or Bartók or the ghost stories of Robert Aickman or peaty Laphroaig whisky or English mustard. That's why they're so special and fabulous. Let's not patronise the public by wet-nursing them like this. A lot of great art is tough and elitist. But we're grown-ups. We can take it. So go to this fabulous gallery and look at the Stanley Spencers and Antony Gormleys and Frank Auerbachs and then emerge onto the grand parade of The Headrow, Leeds most impressive street, with your mind refreshed and thinking great thoughts.

Great thoughts of lunch in my case. The previous evening I'd dined at Bibi's, at the recommendation of the girls at 42 The Calls. They said it was the best Italian restaurant in Leeds and nothing that occurred or was placed in front of me made me doubt this in any way. It's a big, twilit, sumptuous, art deco room; the sort of place that Edward G. Robinson might have arranged a contract killing over a big plate of linguine. On a

Sunday night it was absolutely packed with families, courting couples and bohemians. There's live entertainment here regularly on a proper stage but last night's entertainment was provided by a live DVD of soul/jazz smoothie George Benson on a huge screen. It was weird but kind of fun.

Lunch was fishcakes and red onion and dolcelatte tart at Brasserie Forty 4 in The Calls. Like Bibi's it was completely full, this on a Monday lunchtime, and at the next table, a dissolute-looking couple chainsmoked and read the *Guardian* arts pages while ordering round after round of drinks: champagne, Baileys, cognac. It was a final nail in the coffin for any lingering stereotypes of Leeds and its people.

Looking back, I seem to have written an awful lot about Bobby Bennett and red onion and dolcelatte tarts and hotels and shopping and not much about Leeds' great cultural heritage and its continuation. I've neglected completely to tell you about Leeds Town Hall, one of the great, and I'm using a technical architectural term here, 'fuck-off' statements of northern Victorian might. I love these kinds of landmark. On its massive stone steps, generations of Leeds citizens have met lovers and snogged or smoked or read their lunchtime novels while eating a banana sandwich. Looking up at these mighty colonnades and sheer braggadocio in stone you can only shake your head at the thought that George Bernard Shaw said Leeds ought to be burned down and John Betjeman said it was an ants' nest. Some nest. Some ants.

In truth, when it comes to old Leeds, Alan Bennett's done it all before and far better than me in *Telling Tales*. I'd rather tell you about new Leeds, the Leeds of Corinne Bailey Rae, Forward Russia and the Kaiser Chiefs, the group whose brilliant 'I Predict A Riot', the north's new unofficial national anthem, paints an affectionately lurid picture of their home city and actually introduces the word Leodensian into a pop lyric. This is a town that seems almost drunk on its own newfound prosperity and vibrancy, and who, apart from jealous Londoners sweltering on the armpit line, could begrudge them?

Let me paraphrase Freddie Trueman, archetypal Yorkshireman, and his sign-off on the riot of polyester and best bitter that was the pub sports show *Indoor League*: 'Ah'll sithee, Leeds.' Very soon I hope.

Fur Coat and No Knickers

Late one winter's afternoon in 2005, after finishing a day of location work for TV in west London, I flagged down a black cab in an avenue off the Portobello Road. I was on the opposite side of the road from the taxi and so nipped across the street only to find the driver's side rear door locked against me and the cabbie making a weary gesture that I should come round to the pavement side. As I was carrying a heavy bag and snow was falling, I was loath to walk any further than necessary but I complied.

'How come I can't get in the other door?' I asked innocently.

'Because, mate,' he said with a roll of his eyes, 'I don't let people in that way. A passing car could catch my door.'

I pointed out that the street was deserted, that it was snowing and that I, the paying customer, was heavily burdened. But it didn't seem to matter.

'Look, no offence, but this cab probably cost more than your house back home, wherever that is, so I ain't taking the chance, all right.'

Snow or no snow, bag or no bag, I stepped briskly from the cab and went around to the cabbie's window. I said that on reflection I'd decided to seek alternative travel arrangements as I was reluctant to contribute in any way to the income of a man whose attitude I found frankly objectionable. I added that I wouldn't be using his service again even under the unlikely scenario that he was Britain's sole surviving cabbie and that he was fortunate indeed that my displeasure with him had not taken some more direct, physical manifestation. That was the gist of my message anyway. Having watched the blood drain gratifyingly from his face, off I went into the sleet.

I was absolutely flipping furious. Temple throbbing, fists clenching, cold sweat forming in the armpits; as angry as I've been in years. I hope the reason is obvious. Generally, I like London cabbies but here was one of that unpleasant few whose bigotry and ignorance extend to anything outside the M25. This bastard had heard my accent, deduced that I was northern and assumed that I was a peasant who lived in a backstreet hovel somewhere unspeakably far north of Rugby. What made this little scene all the more ironic was that I had spent the afternoon inter- viewing Stephen Poliakoff, the esteemed dramatist, and Ken Loach, the leftist film director. The cabbie would never see this interview as he would doubtless be watching *You've Been Framed* on ITV3, perhaps in a string vest, and probably thought Stephen Poliakoff was a midfielder Chelsea were after from Dortmund. Ken Loach might have put the whole thing in one of his films.

When the more ignorant Home Counties man thinks of the north, they see wheezing men in clogs and donkey jackets search- ing their trouser turn-ups for a dog-end. They see women in shawls waiting for the bailiff to take their tin bath. They see filthy children scouring the municipal tip like seagulls. They see strik- ing miners and ragged urchins. They see poverty.

The idea of the north as poor and primitive is rooted deep in the national psyche. It's a notion reflected in music, from 'Dirty Old Town' to 'Liverpool Lullaby' to 'Jarrow Song', in literature from *Hard Times* to Walter Greenwood's *Love on the Dole*, and in films from *The Full Monty* to *Billy Elliot*. All of these contribute to the belief that the natural condition of the northerner is desperate near-destitution or at the very least a life spent watch- ing the pennies.

Mind you, there's a certain factual basis for all of this. The Jarrow Marches weren't invented by Alan Price for his jaunty seventies hit; they really happened. Similarly, during the seventies and eighties, northern cities crumbled sometimes through wilful neglect. As whole industries were strangled, so were the towns that depended on them. In the case of steel, it was Consett and Irlam. Hundreds of pits closed and took their towns and villages down with them.

Not all southerners were as hard-hearted as Mrs T, sinister henchman Tebbit and monkish, demented cohort Keith Joseph, who once called for the compulsory sterilisation of the working class. I had family members at Golborne Colliery and during the strike, food parcels would arrive from sympathetic communities and individuals in the south. Being irredeemably Lancastrian in his outlook to food, my Uncle Brian, though grateful, was hostile. He was mildly terrified of the contents within; weird, inedible things like pasta, curries, herbs and spices. Even the tins of French onion soup and spaghetti bolognese (my old fave, remember) sent in solidarity from the Heinz workers at Kitt Green were regarded with suspicion. Rumour had it they'd become contaminated with flavour and tastiness and contained no pastry whatsoever.

So rather than waste them he passed the parcels on to me, then an impoverished student. Thus I played my part in the last great class conflict of the age. It was a sideline role in the drama, admittedly, eating Pot Noodles and tinned chicken madras in solidarity. Hardly as pivotal a role as Scargill or Mick McGahey or even Ian McGregor. But I was there. With a sachet of mango chutney.

Poverty and its close associates, rickets, diphtheria, alcoholism and whooping cough, form a goodly part of the comedy caricature of the north. We've even taken it on board ourselves. We like to think of ourselves as 'simple folk, poor but happy' and all that malarkey. Even before the coming of Roman Abramovich, Chelsea were generally disliked in the north for their 'Flash Harry' Kings Road playboy image. We don't like ostentatious displays of wealth. We can be quite parochial in this respect. In the mid 1990s, looking out at our wilderness of a garden, my wife suggested that we pay someone to come and tidy it up as neither of us had the time or inclination. Apparently, I reacted with shock and outrage. 'Hire a gardener? A gardener? OK, why don't we buy some top hats and monocles while we're at it?' Old habits die hard.

It's all bollocks. The north is rich. In the newly revitalised cities you can practically smell money. The restaurants are full and the girls are dressed in Vivienne Westwood. Of course there are sink estates and cars on bricks and urine-damp stairwells, but the south has its fair share of these too. London has the highest poverty rate in Britain and the two poorest boroughs in the UK are Hackney and Tower Hamlets. The capital has the highest rate of families living in low-income households at twenty-seven per cent. The south is no place to be poor. In fact, with its grotesquely inflated house prices and overcrowding, it's no place to be a nurse or a teacher. You get a London weighting, of course. But until it comes in gold bullion I'd still rather teach in Kendal or Keighley.

The days when visiting Chelsea and Arsenal fans would sing 'What's it like to have no job?' at Scousers or wave wads of money at Geordies are pretty much gone. Mancunians still sing 'In your Liverpool slums' towards the Kop but that's tribal hatred not socio-economic analysis. If you want some proper facts then how about these unearthed by Judith Holder in her book of the TV series *It's Grim Up North*. There are more private swimming pools in the north than in the south. They raise more money for charity in Cheshire than anywhere else in Britain. Geordies buy twice as much champagne per head than Londoners.

Regeneration has been a buzz word in the north for years now. There are bars called Regeneration which used to be called things like the Clog and Two Whippets or The Boilerscrapers Arms. It's hard to date exactly when the northern renaissance began. Some might say it was that moment, iconic and ironic, when Thatcher's government conjured up a 'Minister for Liverpool', the gorgeous, bouffanted Michael Heseltine, and sent him up north to bring us solace. Having just spent £10,000 on booze and nibbles at a birthday party for his daughter – a Lancashire semi's worth at the time – he popped up to Toxteth and launched a massive and frankly long-overdue tree-planting campaign. Naturally, he was carried back to his ministerial Jag shoulder-high through the streets of Liverpool 8 by tearful scallies in ceremonial Lacoste with an honour guard of grateful Bullmastiffs who now had somewhere to cock a leg.

All sarcasm apart, a fair bit of money, much of it European, did begin to flow to the regions in the late eighties. As the song has it, the north did pick itself up, dust itself down and start all over again. By the time New Labour came to power in 1997, Militant and Derek Hatton were a nasty memory and the new north was more about branding and ciabattas than class struggle.

And so it came to pass that, not far from the Orgreave coking plant where the forces of the state clubbed British workers for having the temerity to defend their jobs, not far from the roads where riot police stopped the free movement of British citizens, they did open the first branch of Harvey Nichols outside London. In the grand scheme of things, opening a branch of a posh department store may not seem to be as culturally pivotal as the great Miners' Strike of 1984. But blimey, the fuss!

When Harvey Nicks came to the Victoria Quarter of Leeds in 1996, broadsheet journalists in Fulham reeled. Reams of comment and columns were dashed off, much of it gently and perhaps unintentionally patronising. The *Lonely Planet Guide* began to refer to Leeds as 'the Knightsbridge of the north' (though we will only truly know, comrades, that the battle for sophistication has been won when they start calling Knightsbridge 'the Batley of the south'). All things considered, people couldn't have got more in a flap if they'd opened a branch of Waitrose on Neptune. Roy Hattersley said of the opening: 'I can't say it fills me with joy but it's a good sign.' Mind you, what would fill Roy Hattersley with joy?

We've never looked back, cocker. As we sip our frappuccino at a pavement café in Wakefield's Latin Quarter, taking time out from our job at the blue-sky-thinking consultancy, we reflect on how far we've come. Regeneration has become a gleeful mania in the north and my favourite current regeneration story reunites us with our old friend Anthony H. Wilson.

Tony and his partner Yvette Livesey were recently hired by an agency called Elevate East Lancashire to come up with some 'blue-sky thinking'. They may even have called it 'imagineering' with a fairly straight face. The intention was to regenerate Burnley and what is rather fancifully called the Todmorden Curve, the string of mill towns left to rot by economic mischance. These are the ones of which Brian Sewell once said, 'Are they worth regenerating? The best they can hope for is another plague, or a bout of Russian flu which depletes the population by twenty million. Then we could demolish them.'

Tony and Yvette have somewhat bigger and better ideas. In their twenty-page report which rejoices in the brilliantly anti-corporate title 'A Wish List. A Series Of Consummations Devoutly To Be Wished', they call for a fashion tower, a series of Philippe Starck-designed 'chic sheds', a canalside curry mile and a new name.

With a typical flourish, Tony suggests that the whole area be rebranded as 'Pennine Lancashire' which will, he hopes, become abbreviated LA style, to 'PL'. This then avoids calling the place East Lancashire: 'Anywhere with a compass direction in the name is a bureaucratic concept, not a place.' People in the West Riding and South Shields might disagree but you have to like the cut of his jib. The chic sheds will encourage hip young professionals to grow organic vegetables, the fashion tower will chime with the area's rich history of textile work and the curry mile will celebrate the influence of the large Asian community. They unashamedly evoke the name of Richard Florida, US regeneration guru, the man who identified the boom in the Pacific Northwest of America. In fact, Wilson is already talking, nineteen to the dozen, about Burnley being 'the new Seattle'. I love him for stuff like this and I hope he's right.

Being a creature of the media, Anthony H. knows that any attempt to change the image of the north fights against nearly a century of enshrined and ingrained imagery from films and tele-vision, a kaleidoscope – a grimy kind of kaleidoscope, admittedly – of representations that have shown the region not as one stereotype but rather a pick'n'mix of stereotypes like the old Woolworth's sweet counter: a bit of anger here, a scoop of whimsy there, humour, grit, sentimentality, all bagged up together like white mice, cola bottles and red liquorice shoelaces.

Back in the 1930s, the north could be seen on screen in different lights, depending on how it was being illuminated, by miner's lamp or toothy smile, by cold fury or warm glow. The cloth caps and mufflers looked the same but there are two differ-ent norths glimpsed in, for instance, *Love on the Dole* and the films of George Formby and Gracie Fields.

Walter Greenwood's novel *Love on the Dole* was written in 1933 in the middle of the worst depression the industrial north had ever suffered. It was set in Hankinson Park, Salford, where

Greenwood had been born and bred, and where he was 'burning up inside with fury at the poverty'.

It's not a cheery tale. There are no funny male strippers or anything of that sort. Just one family, the Hardcastles, being gradually destroyed by the scourge of unemployment. Son Harry can't find work and is disowned when he marries. Daughter Sally falls in love with a principled but ineffectual Marxist activist and is pursued by a local gangster. It was an instant commercial and critical success. Poet Edith Sitwell – later to collaborate success-fully with an Oldham lad called William Walton on something rather more refined called *Façade* – wrote, 'I do not know when I have been so deeply, terribly moved.' It was soon adapted for the stage and a riveting production opened at Manchester Rep within a year, a *Look Back in Anger* twenty years before its time, with realistic themes and language never heard before on a British stage. One reviewer said it had been 'conceived and writ-ten in blood'. It toured Britain with two companies playing up to three performances a day. A million people had seen it by the end of 1935 in, among other places, London, New York and Paris.

For all its impact, Ronald Gow's stage adaptation is much gentler than Greenwood's bleakly angry book. Gow said he 'aimed to touch the heart' and this he does while shying away from actually blaming anyone for the plight of the northern poor. It's just one of those things, basically, pitiable but unavoidable, like a little matchgirl's bronchitis. Even so, the British Board of Film Censors would not allow a film to be made for nearly ten years, fearing that this 'very sordid story in very sordid surround-ings' would inflame the workers into insurrection. It was eventu-ally filmed in 1941 with Deborah Kerr as Sally, by which time war had come and British society was convulsing anyway. And by which time we had Our Gracie and Daft George to take our minds off our wretched lot.

As you'll know if you've ever listened to Roy Hudd or Bob Monkhouse for more than twenty seconds, a great deal of northern humour and light entertainment of the inter-war era didn't travel. South of about Daventry, it became untranslatable, unfathomable, unintelligible. While southerners liked their humour spivvy and saucy, as exemplified by Max Miller (who we in turn found charmless and grating), our favourites, like the superb Frank Randall, 'never appeared to extend his bailiwick beyond his homeland of terraces and mills, chimneys and ginnels, whippets and ale houses, Golden Miles and Alhambras' as cultural historian C. P. Lee put it. Some did manage it, though, exporting a brand of regional daftness so successfully that it may well have been injurious to the north's health, contributing to a view of northerners as good-hearted simpletons with alarming dentistry and a penchant for the banjolele.

Like me, George Formby is a Wiganer. There may be other similarities, too; you'd have to ask my southern mates, I guess. Northerners generally have a problematic relationship with George. To some hard-liners among us, he's a Lancashire version of Stepin Fetchit in the 'coon' movies, an insulting caricature of a proud people; to others he was a gifted, skilful comedian, a shrewd businessman in conjunction with svengali wife Beryl and even a formidable weapon in the fight against Fascism. When he died, 100,000 people followed his cortege to his final resting place in Warrington where he was buried, little stick of Blackpool rock and all. Perhaps his greatest achievement was to make window cleaning seem an attractive career option. Oh, and winning the Isle of Man TT races and Grand National in most of his films, from what I remember.

Personally, I've always found toothy George a great deal more palatable than Gracie Fields, who, though long dead, cast a dark shadow over my childhood via various Sunday afternoon films. It wasn't just the bandsaw voice, the mawkish material and the asinine plots. No, even as a toddler, I had strong philosophical objections to Our Gracie, who always seemed to be leading a phalanx of dolts down the street while bellowing some ditty about 'getting back to work at t'mill and not grumbling'. Some of these prejudices were handed down from my gran. Like many of her generation, she was inexplicably keen on Fields's down-to-earth persona, a teeth-rattling combination of the shrill and blunt – but disapproved of her decision to relocate to Capri with her second husband, an Italian, for the duration of the war. For many northerners this was considered desertion and treachery. One assumes, though, that Fields was taken by the climate and cuisine rather than any deep political allegiance to Il Duce. Whatever, her career never really recovered, possibly because Elvis and The Beatles came along to invent real pop music and Fields's mawkish old guff fell out of fashion. Trivia fans, here's one for the pub. Grace Fields's real name was Stansfield but she was no relation to that other titanic Rochdalian songthrush, Lisa.

As a small boy I watched a lot of telly with my gran. Much of what my gran enjoyed, such as *The Good Old Days* and the grotesque Hughie Green, left me cold. Nothing left me quite as frosty and distressed as Gracie and George though. I like to think that even while I was still in a romper suit, I could tell that the pair of them couldn't sing in any meaningful sense of the word and that their outlandish, life-affirming adventures were unlikely to be replicated in any factory, mill or scout hut near me.

Sometimes, though, if I was lucky, BBC 2 would put on another kind of film of a Sunday afternoon and a different kind of north would be revealed to me, watching blue-faced before the 625 lines in the November dusk. These are still my favourite films. I never tire of them. They have provided me and Morrissey alike with some of our favourite catch-phrases and the British film industry with its crowning glories. That's the truth, as Albert Finney as Arthur Seaton would say. All the rest is propaganda.

Finney is a god in my house. As is Tushingham, Courtenay and Bates. Just as Kenneth Tynan said that he could never really love anyone who didn't love *Look Back in Anger*, I'd have trouble even working up the enthusiasm for a store-cupboard snog with anyone who didn't love *A Taste of Honey*, *A Kind of Loving*, *Room at the Top*, *The Loneliness of the Long Distance Runner*, *Billy Liar* or *Saturday Night and Sunday Morning*. This glorious swathe of films about the experience of love, sex, work and struggle among the working classes of the industrial north – I know Sillitoe's book of *Saturday Night and Sunday Morning* is set in Nottingham but Finney and his film are indisputably northern – came to be known as the British New Wave or, disparagingly, as 'kitchen sink dramas' by Terence Rattigan fans in cravats. After decades of Kenneth More and Noël Coward, of Anna Neagle and Pet Clark, of stiff upper lips and cheery Cockneys and London Pride being handed down to us, these films were electrifying, revelatory, astonishing. Here was life as it was lived in our towns and cities, filmed in a way that made our lives lyrical, sexy, vital, tough, tender and raw.

You can't watch the opening credits without being sucked in for the umpteenth time, best watched on a rainy afternoon with the drops pattering the windows and a mug of real tea. Whatever you're doing, you'll be transported back to that just pre-Beatle era, of sexual frustration and knitted ties, white Bri-nylon shirts, winklepickers, scooters and transport cafés and smoking on the top decks of buses and football papers on Saturday and squaddies and dodgems and always the hum of the lathes and the insistent throb of sexual desire in a cold, conservative climate. Sex is everywhere, in Bates's coal-dark charisma as he stalks the streets of Bolton, Preston and Southport in *A Kind of Loving*, in Finney's glossy, priapic quiff and bantam cock strut, in Tushingham's gamine, thrilled terror on the edge of adulthood, even in Courtenay's doleful, melancholic yearning for what Morrissey would call 'the brighter sides to life'.

I've met Tom Courtenay and Rita Tushingham, though I doubt if they'd remember. To them it was just another interview, I suppose. To me it was as if two of the gods had stepped down from Olympus for a chinwag and a cuppa. Tushingham is still as quirkily, owlishly beautiful as she was in *A Taste of Honey* and *The Knack*, and as gracious in real life as she was gawky on screen. Courtenay was frail and tired after a theatre performance but the perfect gentleman and still suffused with that enigmatic sadness. I told him that his book of letters home to his mum in Hull from RADA, *Dear Tom*, was a wonderful book and he seemed genuinely touched. I meant it; it's a lovely, heart-breaking hymn to maternal love and the spirit of the northern working class. Read it. But not in public, for the tears will flow like Boddingtons, believe me.

Finney has blossomed into a florid mandarin of the British stage but in 1960 he was as potent and sexy as Elvis; Elvis on the Irwell, if you like, a juggernaut of youth and beauty and virility. In *Saturday Night and Sunday Morning*, you cannot take your eyes off him for a second, even if you wanted to. You can see why Shirley Anne Field falls for him, even over stale cheese and pickles in that dismal backstreet pub. He was the son of an illegal street bookie from Salford, a situation ironically illustrated in the film itself. It was made in 1960 just before licensed betting shops reopened after a century of censure and in it Arthur Seaton, played by Finney, risks arrest by placing bets with bookies just like his dad. In my family, the story was often told of how my grandad got nicked in a backstreet game of pitch and toss, one of the few gambling activities the proletariat could indulge in, though strictly illegal. Meanwhile, at Crockfords and Whites, the well-to-do gambled fortunes on backgammon and roulette. We plebs had no common sense, though, so it was best for our social superiors to tell us what to do with our money.

I should mention Laurence Harvey, smooth, suave and rumoured to be gay star of the fabulous *Room at the Top*, if only for the wonderful episode that occurred on the set of *The Alamo* where he starred alongside John Wayne. Wayne disliked Harvey and made slighting references to his limey effeminacy whenever possible. Finally one day, noticing Harvey mince by, Wayne snarled, 'Can't you even walk like a man?' To which Harvey replied, 'Are you talking to me, Marion?' Wayne's real name, I should add, was Marion Morrison. Now that is true grit.

The north continues to be seen as both gritty and grotty though the golden age of its cinema probably ended round about 1963 and Lindsay Anderson's superb version of David Storey's *This Sporting Life*. By 1964, a new mood was abroad, of liberated escapist fun, captured in Tony Richardson's *Tom Jones*, Richard Lester's *A Hard Day's Night* and the early James Bond movies. The sixties were beginning to swing and writers like John Braine and Stan Barstow and characters like Arthur Seaton with their brilliantine and beer belonged to another, slightly shabbier world.

There's been nothing quite as good since, of course, nothing quite so poetic and powerful, but films about us still come around with regularity. These days, northern representations will be splattered with vomit, blood and other unmentionables and ring with expletives. But still we need the sweetener of either humour and music (in the case of *The Full Monty* or *Brassed Off* or *Billy Elliot*) or sex (*The Full Monty* or *Rita, Sue and Bob Too*).

The real auteurs of the north have, for several decades now, been working on the small screen. Bleasdale's *Boys From the Blackstuff* was as pungent and harsh a view of mass unemployment as Carla Lane's was glib and saccharine in *Bread*. Lane cops some deserved flak for her lazy stereotypes and barmy opinions but to be perfectly honest, northern comedies have always been a mixed bag. For every Jack Rosenthal or Clement and La Frenais, writers who knew and loved the north but could make fun of its foibles, who could get a laugh from just an expertly placed reference to Fenwick or Crumpsall, there's a *Last of the Summer Wine*, a drearily whimsical half hour in the company of some depressingly immortal Yorkshire geriatrics. But sporadically the region's true spirit still breaks through the vapid everytown that permeates TV culture. *Phoenix Nights* was as northern as a club singer with a lilac frilly shirt and his arm in plaster – something I once saw at St Cuthbert's Catholic Club – and *The Royle Family* was staggeringly good until it became engulfed and obscured by its own fart jokes. Paul Abbott, with shows like *Shameless*, has become the laureate of northern white trash.

By being sharp, savvy and Armani-suited, Anthony H. Wilson has appeared on TV regularly to confound our image of a northerner. Back in PL, Wilson's visionary schemes are still some way off. But the north has always had its posh bits, the bits that contradict our image of phlegm hawking, tripe eating and shin kicking. As Graham Turner once wrote, 'There are, and have always been, other norths, where these archetypes seem as alien as they would be in Virginia Water or Epsom.' These places like to think of themselves as 'a cut above', even if other northern cities and towns may view them as 'fur coat and no knickers'. Nowhere is more furry and these days quite possibly knickerless than Cheshire.

There's a lot of new money in Cheshire. But Cheshire's desirable status as the north's Hamptons or Beverly Hills is in no way nouveau. It's always been that little bit different, rolling greenery and gentle agriculture rather than smoking chimneys and booming foundries. Money made in Manchester has always bought fancy houses in Cheshire. Why? Because to the west was Salford, pits and chemicals, to the north, the darkened Pennine towns; only south was there a chink in the plate armour of the industrial north, the leafiness these industrial captains craved for their homesteads.

Cheshire has always had its gentry, its Cholmondeleys and Tollemaches. These were augmented at the end of the nineteenth century by the new class of successful businessmen and merchants. Little Budworth has the only polo club north of Bristol. There were two big Cheshire foxhunts before that particular little bit of fun was stopped. Even in the sixties, Cheshire's house prices rivalled the West End of London. Cheshire votes Tory to a large extent and defiantly so, even when the candidate offered is Neil Hamilton.

The real money is concentrated in the Golden Triangle; nothing to do with heroin or triads but an area bounded by Wilmslow, Alderley Edge and Hale and including Mottram St Andrew, where Rio Ferdinand holed up in splendid isolation after his £30-million transfer to Man Utd, and Prestbury, long regarded as one of England's richest and loveliest villages.

You can understand why someone would fall in love with Prestbury. It's exquisite. The gardens of the church slope gently down to the River Bollin, which murmurs through the village. A pretty main street overhung with yews boasts a chic selection of bistros, pubs, delicatessens and restaurants. The newsagent will tell you that, even with competition from required trophy-wife reading matter like *Grazia*, *Hello!* and *Heat*, Prestbury's most popular magazine is still *Cheshire Life*, a publication which oozes contentment with life's lot.

'Cheshire is a county of wealth, culture and elegance,' its website murmurs seductively, talking of the 'crescent of prosperity that runs from Wilmslow through to Alderley Edge, Altrincham, Hale, Prestbury, Bowdon, Knutsford and on to the stockbroker belt of the Wirral'. In the way that a skilled hotel doorman knows the good tippers and the captains of industry from their Vuitton and Longchamps luggage, *Cheshire Life* recognises that 'our affluent readers are keen to know about the best of fashion, interiors, motoring, antiques, education, hotels and restaurants.'

Prestbury isn't everyone's cup of green tea, though. My friend Rhys Hughes, a Radio 1 executive, moved there in 1997. He hated it.

'It was awful. I loathed every minute of the year I was there. It's the snobby north, and the snobby north is far, far worse than the snobby south. There are some "nouveaus" but basically Prestbury is old money and they're suspicious and insular. At the time, I had a shaved head and had just bought my first BMW so me and the missus would go down the pub and it would fall silent as we walked in. It was pretty obvious that the Golf and G&T set thought I was a Manchester drug dealer made good who'd moved out. A couple of footballers lived there too for a while, Cantona and Roy Keane. I think they hated it too. It didn't help that my next-door neighbour was a special constable. They're worse than the actual police, aren't they? Cos they're doing it in their spare time. Unbelievable.'

The odd footballer, Radio 1 producer and possibly drug dealer notwithstanding, Prestbury is old Cheshire money; sober, discreet, frosty. The nearby village of Great Budworth was the model for Stackton Tressel in the Hinge and Bracket TV series and you can see why. It's the sort of place where you feel Sicilian-strength vendettas smoulder at the bring and buy sale and expensive curtains twitch at twilight. But there's another Cheshire too, where the new money sloshes through the wine bars and tanning salons and jewellers and where bling is more important than breeding. This is the Cheshire of footballers' wives and its capital is Wilmslow.

Porsche, Porsche, Daimler, Aston Martin, Lamborghini, BMW, Aston Martin, Jag, Daimler, Alfa Romeo, Porsche. A rainy spring Saturday afternoon in Wilmslow and to amuse myself as I stroll along, I'm playing a little game of Top Trumps (Flash Car version) on the high street. In Chelsea you'd find the odd Ford Focus. In Surrey, they wear their clapped-out Merc or Range Rover like a badge of pride. But Wilmslow believes if you've got it, you should flaunt it, baby.

Strolling through Wilmslow on a Saturday afternoon, though, you won't instantly and automatically notice the sheer, heady wealth that surrounds you. The streets aren't paved with gold, there are no sedan chairs in Sainsbury's and the townsfolk don't sport hats made of rubies or anything like that. There's a Boots and a WHSmiths and even a Greggs if you look hard enough. But slowly, as it did in the town of Stepford, the impression grows on you that all is not quite normal. You begin to notice the quietly astonishing array of top-of-the-range cars. You spot that one street has nine estate agents. On the main high street, you realise that while most towns don't have one designer sunglasses boutique, Wilmslow has about six. One of them, stupidly massive, is clearly some kind of converted cinema. Just how afraid of the sun, or publicity, or hungover, can one town be?

Popping into the Oxfam shop, you now know that normal shopping rules no longer apply. Most Oxfam shops are not good hunting grounds for the brand conscious, unless the brands you crave are Mills & Boon, K-tel and St Michael. Not so the charity shops of Wilmslow. On every rack, there's DKNY, Versace and Armani. I saw the most expensive item I've ever spotted in a charity shop, a pair of rather nice Hugo Boss loafers priced £150. They didn't have them in my size, though, and anyway I was feeling a little nervous. This was the first charity shop where I've felt frightened of breaking something.

Back outside, I counted two more designer sunglasses boutiques, a shedload of solicitors – I guess divorce doesn't come cheap in these parts – and a jewellers where the very first item I looked at, a quite boring ring, cost £125,000. On the other hand, I didn't see a butcher's or a fish shop or a hardware store. I suppose if you eat Malaysian red snapper bisque at the brasserie every night or move house when the battery in the doorbell goes, you don't need such dull stuff as a butcher's. Not when the new Diors and Police have arrived at Designer Sunglasses Universe. I don't know how acutely Wilmslow feels this gap in its retail soul but one local opined to me that 'it's easier to buy a supercar than a sausage in the centre of Wilmslow'.

A little weakened, I lunched at Pizza Express. Having railed against the increasing homogeneity of modern northern street life, I'm now going to renege on all my principles by admitting that I don't mind if it means there's a twelve-inch American Hot in every town with my name on it. Besides, Wilmslow's Pizza Express is nothing like any other I've visited just by virtue of its clientele. At every table except mine there seemed to be several members of just-going-out-of-fashion boy bands, some slightly hard-faced beauticians and sundry variations on a theme by Victoria Beckham. Everyone wore shades, suddenly explaining the need for the superabundance of such stores. No one looked like they were planning to do any grouting later in the day, which perhaps also accounts for the dearth of hardware stores.

This was the real essence of chav, I realised. People with vaults of money and absolutely no taste. People with style can wear a bit of old coal-sack and make it look fabulous. The people in Wilmslow's Pizza Express were designer shod from head to foot but they looked like they'd got it off the market. Everyone was the colour of builder's tea, wore baseball caps and low-slung jeans, had white belts and tattoos and gold things dangling about their person. There was so much fibre-hold hair putty and spray tan and Chanel No 5 in the atmosphere that I kept glancing nervously at the flames licking at the door of the open oven. They were all probably really nice people. But the feeling that I'd walked into the gossip pages of *Chat* magazine was inescapable. Nearly put me off my doughballs. As I settled the bill, I looked out the window and saw a man in a high-visibility tabard. Bet it was Armani, though.

Leave Wilmslow southbound on the A34 and you are soon in the realms of mystery, with part of that mystery being how one small village can have so many gourmet delis and Ferraris. This is Alderley Edge, a place of fabled wealth and legendary warriors.

Recently those warriors have tended to wear the red of Manchester United, fifteen miles north of here, which is next to nothing in a Ferrari. David and Victoria Beckham lived here and at the time of writing, it is home to the flashy and mildly irritating Portuguese wunderkind Cristiano Ronaldo. This village, it's said, boasts more millionaires and drinks more champagne than any equivalent area in Britain. Once the money came from cotton, now it comes from celebrity endorsements, shirt sponsorship, shaving foam adverts and the odd spot of football.

Even before the coming of these mythic creatures, legends have clung to the Edge. I grew up with them as part of northern folklore as far afield as Wigan, a good half an hour's drive away. Long ago, a farmer from Mobberley on his way to Macclesfield Market was confronted by an old man in flowing robes who wanted to buy his horse. The farmer refused but the old man told him that he would make no sale at Macclesfield and he would meet him again on the way back. The farmer didn't sell the horse in Macclesfield and was met again by the old man on the Edge. This time, he took the terrified farmer to a great iron gate in the hill and there in a cave slept an army of men with their milk-white steeds. The old man explained that one day when England was in great danger, these knights would wake and ride out onto the Cheshire plain to save the country. But one of the sleeping army did not have a horse and that was why the old man wanted the farmer's. The old man is said to be Merlin and the sleeping army King Arthur and his Knights of the Round Table. When the local paper first printed this bit of folklore in 1806, two nearby pubs instantly changed their names from the Coach and Horses and the Miners Arms to the Iron Gates and the Wizard respectively. Shrewd business folk round here evidently.

These and other ghostly local legends have been used as the basis for classic fantasy tales by the author Alan Garner, a resident of Alderley Edge where his family have lived for 300 years. All Garner's books have been written in the same room. The legend of the 'King Under the Hill' begins his book *The Weirdstone of Brisingamen*, *Elidor* is set on Alderley Edge and *The Owl Service* takes place in nearby North Wales. As a kid I remember being terrified by the BBC Sunday afternoon adaptation. I still find Freddie Jones alarming to this day.

The very name Alderley has a mystical significance here; the Alder tree has long been worshipped as sacred in northern England. For a long time witches' covens from Manchester met on the Edge and marched about with flaming brands until adverse publicity drove them away. Every Halloween hundreds of masked and caped celebrants, filled with the spirit of WKD rather than Wicca, climb the Edge and perform their very own pagan rites, with the local police in close attendance.

In the right light on the right day, the Edge is an eerie place, a lowering, wooded hulk set against the grey Cheshire sky and the flat countryside around. On this day in spring, though, you get a fabulous view from Storm Point of the distant Pennines, and from the escarpment's northern rim the Cheshire plain comes to a sudden halt as Manchester rises in steel and glass, the Beetham Tower glittering in the crystal haze. Jodrell Bank tilts a lidless eye to the sky and way out west beyond Knutsford and Northwich and the curves of the M6 and M56 lies another honeypot, Chester.

In 1759, Samuel Johnson wrote to Boswell, 'Chester pleases me more than any town I ever saw.' Up until this year, I'd have had to disagree. Chester had bad memories for me. It took a delightful day in this beautiful old town to exorcise them.

Firstly, there was the afternoon my dad took us on a rowing boat on the River Dee. My mum, never a seasoned mariner, had some kind of panic attack and stood up in the boat screaming. She thought we were going to capsize and, even at six years old, I knew that standing up in the boat screaming was a great way to make this happen. We made for the bank as fast as my dad's oarsmanship would allow before we were all consigned to a watery grave.

More traumatic yet was the St Jude's Altar Boys outing of 1970. The trip, long planned and savoured, was a visit to Chester Zoo, and for weeks before I had imagined the delights of eating massive ice creams in the rank tang of the lion house. Family members had given me advance pocket money and I reckon I had a couple of quid at least on arrival at the zoo. It was a lot of money in those days – you could buy an ocelot and a 99 and still have change from sixpence. Within seconds, though, I'd contrived to lose the lot and spent the rest of the day manfully fighting back tears and licking other people's ice creams. Given that it was an altar boys' day out, it was a particularly cruel blow. My faith in a merciful and benevolent God took its first battering there by the penguin pool.

So I went back to Chester for the first time in decades in a cloud of apprehension. It almost instantly dispersed. Chester is beautiful. True, she's like one of those girls who know just how lovely they are; there's the faint aura of self-satisfaction about her. But hanging around her for a day or two really does lift the spirit. She seems to have become the first-choice destination for the young and pulchritudinous in general. Maybe since the advent of *Hollyoaks*, the sexy soap set among the town's gorgeous twenty-somethings, all the ugly people have been forced out to live somewhere else. Wrexham perhaps.

Chester and Wrexham hate each other, you see. Primarily it's because of football but there's class and nationhood simmering nastily in there as well. Stereotypically, Chester is English and bourgeois, Wrexham/Wrecsam is Welsh and working class. The towns are just ten miles apart.

A Wrexham fan called Paul Baker once told *FourFourTwo* magazine: 'I'd rather Chester didn't exist at all. I despise the club and a city which is full of people who are full of themselves.' In what might be the most tragic and misplaced show of pride ever, he continued, 'Cestrians are stuck up their own arses. We wear sensible clothes, they wear pink shirts and have gel in their hair. We go out on the steam. They just want to have a drink or two and chat up the ladies. That's why a lot of Wrexham girls go out in Chester – they like to be treated well and they know we're just pisscans.' Wrexham girls are pretty smart then, I reckon. I know where I'd rather spend my Friday night.

The two office girls eating their sandwiches in the chilly sun on a bench by the newly excavated amphitheatre used to live in Wrexham. They tell me this with a slight shudder. Our conversation had been prompted by the sight of my notebook. 'Are you an archaeologist?' they asked genially. Knowing full well I was never going to pull off any kind of ersatz Harrison Ford routine, I came clean. They were very helpful on the subject of the amphitheatre. 'It's half excavated and it could hold seven thousand people. It was the biggest arena in Britain, sort of like the Wembley or the Millennium Stadium of its time. We had a talk on it at college.'

There's a lot more on the amphitheatre at the adjoining tourist information centre. An American in a cattle feed baseball cap asks about the excavation and is pointed in the direction of the film show upstairs. 'It was the Dodgers stadium of Roman Britain!' I interject cheerily. This prompts Jenny, who I think was working there – she had a name tag but may have just been a freelance interjector like myself – to share some more facts about Chester. I write them down in my pretend archaeologist's notebook.

Chester's town hall clock has three faces but none on the Welsh side because it's said that Chester won't give Wrexham the time of day. According to an archaic law, a Chester resident can still shoot a Welshman found within Chester's city walls after dark. Chester is the only city in Britain to still be ringed by a complete wall. The circuit is two miles and according to everyone is the best way to see Chester. Henry James did it in 1872 and later remarked, 'Starting at any point on the walls, an hour's easy stroll will bring you back to your station. I have quite lost my heart to this charming creation.'

Convinced by Henry James and having bought a little leaflet on Jenny's advice, I decide to start my circuit at the Eastgate, busy pedestrianised heart of a busy town. There's a tiny green sandwich kiosk – what was once surely the smallest barber's in Britain – and by scooting up the steps you suddenly emerge high above the bustle of the street.

Below you are buskers, baskers, girls straight from *Hollyoaks* auditions, smart old ladies with tartan trolleys, businessmen with Marbella tans and black leather briefcases. At the side of you is a really fancy clock. Chester is very proud of this eccentric creation, described by Pevsner as 'a rusticated elliptical arch, on it jolly ironwork carrying a diamond Jubilee Clock, by Douglas, and surprisingly playful'. Surprisingly playful is a nice description. It's surprisingly popular too. Cestrians like to say that it's the second most photographed clock in Britain (after Big Ben, of course) and I can vouch for this. No matter where I positioned myself I ended up encroaching unwelcome into people's photographs. As I write this, there are people in Oslo, Seoul and Des Moines showing off their vacation snaps and saying, 'I have no idea who this bloke with the notebook is.'

Walking northwards along the wall you pass on the left a monolithic modern bell tower; pretty cool in a severe sort of way. On the right, less attractively, are the delivery bays of what I think was Argos. At strategic points along the wall, cute little plaques give relevant information about the sights. Understandably, they didn't bother with this. So it may have been Netto. (But I doubt it in Chester.)

Whatever, let's look left instead at the glorious cathedral grounds of the Deanery Field. In late March, there's snow on the ground under a cloudless blue sky and you suddenly feel a pang of envy for all these busy Cestrians on their lunch hour. A woman goes by with an incredibly tiny dog, roughly the size of a burly hamster. As I stare in disbelief, a Scouse bloke joins me in wonderment. 'How small is that dog? It's doing my head in!' With that he is gone.

Strolling on into a quieter corner, I embarrass a middle-aged American man who's climbing a tree to impress his lady friend. She insists I take his picture. His face is red with discomfort, exertion and pleasure and I didn't blame him one bit. It was just the sort of day for climbing trees in snowy churchyards to impress girls.

I paused for reflection at the King Charles Tower, so named because here Charles I watched as his cavalry were routed at the nearby battle of Rowton Moor. In modern Britain, we're forever fretting about how violent and feral and barbaric our cities have become. So it's always educational to remember just how savage and bloodthirsty the good old days really were. Today Chester gets invaded by nothing worse than a few drunken Wrexham supporters and a phalanx of Japanese tourists armed with high-velocity Minoltas. But a few hundred years back, Chester and its people suffered appallingly as two sections of the British establishment tore it and themselves to bloody pieces. Chester was besieged for two years by Parliamentarians during the English civil war at dreadful cost to the townsfolk. Here's a letter written by one on 23 September 1642:

> Good Sir
>
> The latter end of your letter is somewhat comfortable in that you write there are some Dragoons coming into Chester for our relief, but surely they are not come, and now will come too late for we are all plundered and undone; I only desire you to pray for us and let us hear from you; the Lord fit us for these ill times, and worse which I much fear... To hear the pitiful shrieking, weeping and howling of women and children, did more trouble me than any thing else; God grace? I never heard the like.

And here's one from 10 December 1645:

> Eleven huge granadoes [grenades] like so many tumbling demi-phaetons threaten to set the city, if not the world, on fire. This was a terrible night indeed, our houses like so many split vessels crash their supporters and burst them-selves in sunder through the very violence of these descending firebrands... In a word the whole fabric is in a perfect chaos lively set forth in this metamorphosis. The

grandmother, mother and three children are struck stark dead and buried in the ruins of this humble edifice, a sepulchre well worth the enemy's remembrance. But for all this they are not satisfied, women and children have not blood enough to quench their fury, and therefore about midnight they shoot seven more in hope of greater execution, one of these last light in an old man's bedchamber, almost dead with age, and send him some few days sooner to his grave then perhaps was given him.

Not Srebrenica or Fallujah. Not Beirut or Darfur. Chester, home of *Hollyoaks*. A history of firebombs and firing squads and old men shot in their beds in cold blood. Next time the *Daily Mail* tells you the country's going to hell in a handcart, think. We may actually be moving slowly towards civility.

Built right into the city wall, high above the Shropshire Union Canal, is what must be the best located bookshop in Britain. Stepping inside adds to an already slightly magical air. A bell tinkles, a young bearded owner looks up welcomingly and a browsing girl turns with a smile from shelves groaning with out-of-print ghost stories and Arthuriana, which is what Gildas Books and proprietor Scott Lloyd specialise in. I instantly spot a copy of LTC Rolt's *Sleep No More*, a fabulous long-out-of-print selection of eerie stories set around canals, railways and deserted industrial locales. I lost my original on a late-night train trying to defend a single woman from a drunken businessman from Coventry – his company were called the General Asphalt Group, in case you fancy boycotting them – and I've been looking for a copy ever since. And here it is, placed there by fate, at the frankly very reasonable price of twenty quid. 'Make sure you have a proper look,' says Scott anxiously, 'there's a bit of water damage and the title page is missing. Otherwise it'd be more like a hundred and fifty quid.' I pass a pleasant half hour in this quaint corner of Chester and leave with several other of Scott's recommendations under my arm.

I stop and read one of old LTC's spooky stories in a spot called Pemberton's Parlour or the Goblin Tower, a sort of big arched bus shelter built into the wall. This would seem an ideal spot for young Cestrians to learn the arts of love or to experiment with controlled substances but for the fact that the council have put a massive gate on it. Piqued, someone has thrown a Greggs wrapper and a can of Red Stripe over the gate. Serves them right. I'm sure old Mayor Pemberton would rather his parlour were being used for a bit of youthful hi-jinks than left mouldering behind chains. Maybe not, though. Back in 1730, John Pemberton built this tower so he could keep an eye on his work-men below, so he sounds a bit of a sourpuss.

In the distance are the Welsh hills as you turn left along the wall and head down past the Roodee, prettiest racecourse in England, to the Watergate. I've only been to the races once, Ladies Day, Aintree 2003, at the invitation of Granada TV, and I lost all my money while Jimmy McGovern and John Parrott made a bloody fortune. Typical bloody Scousers. But if I do ever go back to the races, it'll be at Chester, where I can at least go broke in gorgeous surroundings.

The Watergate, by the way, is a legacy of when Chester was a port. Not just any old port; the busiest in northern Britain, no less, taking regular deliveries of olive oil and fish sauce for the homesick Roman garrisons pining for a change from cabbage and spuds. Then with spectacular bad luck it silted up and the trade moved away to ports with actual water in them. Chester's history tends to loom at you from unexpected corners; the old Spudulike on Bridge Street had a Roman hypocaust just behind the salad bar.

I walk past the Dee, scene of my mum's maritime disaster, and watch a man dressed as a Roman legionnaire waving an unconvincing spear at a party of kids in maroon blazers before my eye is caught by a public house. I'd heard a lot about this place as I'd chatted with Chester folk. The Albion Inn, below the city wall on the corner of Albion and Park Street, looks like a typical backstreet boozer albeit festooned with flags and black-boards. Get down to street level, though, and you become aware of the pub's unique character. The blackboard reads 'The English Pub At Its Unspoilt Best. Opening Times: If we are open, we are open, if we are closed, we are closed. No Chips. No Fry-ups. No U.H.T. No silly foil portions. No children. No plastic playground or music machines or big screens. Plenty Good Food. Real Ale. Good Wine. Family Hostile!'

This seemed slightly cranky and unfriendly at first. For one thing, 'No Chips' is just snobbery. If they're good enough for Nigel Slater and the bistros of Paris, they're good enough for a pub in Chester. But after half an hour inside I was willing to forgive them anything. You could say that the pub is themed, though I'd say it when the landlord isn't listening. 'Themed' usually means decked out as a Bondi Beach surf shack or festooned with agricultural implements in a poor approximation of a Connemara saloon bar. But not here. The Albion Inn just hasn't changed much since 1915. There are adverts for Fry's chocolate, cast iron fireplaces, William Morris wallpaper and tasteful reminders everywhere of the Cheshire regiment and the young lads who may have drunk a pint here after enlisting at the nearby drill hall, oblivious of the horrors to come.

All was peaceful that afternoon, though. I soaked up the gentle hum of conversation around me. A couple in muted linen, clearly having an affair, were talking about Debussy; some young office workers were raving about the Thai green curry; a cheery clutch of middle-aged men were bemoaning the fortunes of Chester City. I sat in the dappled sun, drinking my pint of real ale, leafing through a guidebook and tucking into my Tunstall Tortilla: black pudding, cheese and onion in a Staffordshire oatcake. I thought I'd died and gone to heaven.

It was hard to leave the Albion Inn but I did. I had to. I got a phone call from a radio producer friend telling me that a nice man from a bookshop in Chester had rung the BBC to say that I'd left my credit card there. And so I walked the whole circuit of the walls again, back to Gildas Books, slightly slower this time thanks to the added cargo of tortilla and beer.

Later and slower still, I made my way back to the station along City Road which, as a legacy of the railways I imagine, is lined with the kind of independent hotel that used to be quite swanky but have now been rather left behind by the modern chains. The Westminster, the Queens, the Belgrave; all going slightly to seed though still boasting 'colour TV in all rooms' and 'tea- and coffee-making facilities'. On the train, two appalling and very posh students from the Home Counties were discussing the rules to some game. 'It's f***ing wicked, yah, if you don't have a joker in your pocket, you have to drink a pint of beer out of your shoe.' They talk about the girls they're going to 'do' during Freshers' Week and then both take out copies of *Nuts* magazine. I take out my newly acquired, slightly foxed LTC Rolt and think again about building that wall from Bristol to Skegness.

* * *

When I was a child, I thought Wigan was a spa town. I thought this because we had a branch of Spar. I got my *Beezer* comic and Opal Fruits there. Later I learned that a spa town was something altogether grander and that Wigan certainly wasn't one but that Cheltenham, Bath, Epsom, Tunbridge Wells and Harrogate are.

But for the discovery of a chalybeate well in the late sixteenth century, Harrogate would have no greater an opinion of itself than Hunslet, Hull or many another Yorkshire town. But as the fame of its healing waters spread and so the fashion for 'taking the waters', so Harrogate prospered into the genteel, elegant, enormously pleased-with-itself place that it is today.

Its streets are wide and tree-lined, its houses Georgian and breathtakingly expensive for these parts and its hotels seem the sort of places where the linen is always starched, the waiters gouty and breakfast finishes at eight.

Perhaps this is a gross slur. Perhaps every room has a PlayStation and a plasma screen TV and they'll mix you a Screaming Orgasm at four in the morning. Perhaps blame Alan Bennett, whose famous *Dinner at Noon* documentary found him staying at the Crown Hotel Harrogate reflecting on the etiquette of tipping and poached eggs and *Country Life* magazine. I thought about climbing up the hill to see if he'd checked out yet but it looked a long way from the centre of town and my view of the route was obscured by the strikingly ghastly new conference centre whose design merged Tutankhamen's tomb with a Latvian recycling plant. I hope it's nicer on the inside otherwise I pity those poor sods spending three days in there talking about new directions in bacon packaging.

Maybe I didn't give it a chance but I didn't warm to Harrogate. Part tourist trap, part dormitory town, unwarrantedly snobby, it was 'neither mickling nor muckling' as Billy Liar might say in his cod-Yorkshire patois. This really was fur coat and no knickers territory. Walking up the steep drag behind the famous Royal Baths, you'll find those twee little shops that sell golliwogs and scented soap jostling for position next to dodgy nightclubs and a long-defunct pizzeria with smeared windows and a filthy facade. Harrogate, I mused, is a bit like a Georgette Heyer heroine with a bottle of alcopops shoved down her petticoat. She fancies herself but she's not as classy as she thinks she is. I decided that she was the Brighton of the north. On the subject of the famous Royal Baths and Pump

Room, I did think about taking the waters but when I popped in, there were a lot of red-faced men in towels and an overpowering smell of sulphur as if someone were boiling every egg in Yorkshire. Either the Crown Hotel had some very hungry breakfasters or Harrogate's celebrated liquid ponged as bad as I'd been warned.

If you do drink from the famous Old Sulphur Well at the Pump Room (known as the Stinking Well and reputedly the most sulphurous well in the world), the trick is to hold your nose. You might be able to get it down if you don't actually smell it. Better still, the trick is to avoid it completely. Until the coming of the Pump Room, the waters used to be dispensed by one Betty Lupton, octogenarian 'Queen Of The Wells'. Betty has gone but she gives her name to a famous Harrogate landmark, Betty's Tea Rooms, which has the august address 1 Parliament Street. Betty's is as much about old-world ambience as the menu – you can have a live Mozart piano trio with your rarebit although the nosh is very good and is described enticingly as Swiss-Yorkshire. An under-publicised fusion cuisine this, but I can recommend it. Try the spring onion and mushroom rosti with raclette or the Käseschnitte – 'A traditional hearty alpine dish, made with Gruyère cheese, white wine and fresh chives, served on toasted crusty bread.' Cheese on toast essentially but if even that sounds a bit fancy for you, you can wash it down with a pint of Black Sheep.

I once knew a girl who worked at Betty's for a summer and she said that there was something about the starchy, lacy white uniform that drove men wild. She was forever fending off amorous middle-aged punters in cardies and her boyfriends were always asking her to wear it at home. Maybe that's why the book you can buy about the history of Betty's is called *Hearts, Tarts and Little Rascals*. Probably not, though.

Though it will never be anything as vulgar as a franchise, there are six Betty's branches now – although the family firm has steadfastly refused to open any outside God's own county. Very Yorkshire, that. There's one down the road in Ilkley, a lovely little town which is in its own way just as classy as Harrogate but more subtly so and definitely shyer about saying as much. Ilkley folk seem to want to keep the place to themselves. I don't blame them.

However, having the world's most famous moor somewhat stymies them in this regard. It brings, in their Bank Holiday droves, the day-trippers, the tourers and the ramblers in their coaches and cars. It brought me too, ambling up the gentle slopes and through the bracken. If you're used to Pen-y-ghent in the Dales or the high fells of Cumbria, Ilkley Moor is a hands-in-pockets stroll along well-marked paths. But there's a lot up there to commend it. It's quite wild and woolly, littered with rocks – thrown around by a local giant after a tiff with the missus, so legend has it – and it has one genuinely weird and compelling place. This is known as the Swastika Stone. There in its own little enclosure high on the moor is an ancient carving that looks like the Nazi emblem done by some really stoned hippies; the unmistakable configuration but in soft, round, blurry curves like a Grateful Dead cover. It's been here since a millennium and a half years before Christ, and from it you can see the Pennines range away into the misty distance. But what's it for? No one's really sure, to be honest. Some think it's sun worship, some a fertility symbol. Terry Deary, author of the *Horrible Histories* kids' books, thinks it's a prototype four-armed boomerang. 'It's the earliest representation of a boomerang. There's nothing else it could be.' Next time I see him, I'll ask Julian Cope. He knows about these things and generally his feeling is that they're a lot less mystical and esoteric than we think. It's probably a bit of graffiti by a Pict who'd drunk too much fermented birch sap.

Dartmoor, Bodmin Moor and Exmoor might dispute my claim about Ilkley being the world's most famous moor but, think about it, do they have their own theme song? 'On Ilklah Moor Baht 'at' is sung lustily by Yorkshiremen everywhere and by the Yorkshire diaspora around the globe. It's sung by non-Yorkshiremen everywhere too, usually without understanding a word of it. Essentially it's a meditation on mortality and the cyclical nature of existence prompted by a bloke going for a walk with his girlfriend on the moor. Said bloke does this without a hat (baht 'at), which prompts the unnamed narrator to speculate that such behaviour will result in his catching a cold and subsequent death – from pneumonia, I imagine. But the cheery morbidity doesn't stop there. Then, says the sinister narrator, we'll have to bury you and the worms will eat you. In turn, they will be eaten by ducks. (Ducks? On a moor? Let it pass.) But in an ending that will please Buddhists, the ducks will be eaten by humans and the great wheel of life will continue to turn. Invigorated by the strong wind and feeling reckless and hatless, I sang a verse or two as I strolled along. A doughty rambler who I hadn't seen emerged from behind a tree and gave me a look as if to say, 'They all do that, you know.'

If the Swastika Stone didn't convince you that underneath the doilies and dainties Ilkley, like much of the north, has stuff that is old, dark and weird, then pop into the church. There's a saint with the head of a bull, a variety of phallic symbols, two Roman altars with runnels to carry away the blood after live sacrifices and what is thought to be a carving of the water goddess Verbeia clutching two very primordial-looking serpents. It's a long way from *The Vicar of Dibley*.

So, in Harrogate, Ilkley and their, ahem, ilk, the north has its Cheltenhams, Marlboroughs and Leamingtons, slightly faded, prone to tears after a few G&Ts but with a lot of class and still a hell of a looker. And in the golden triangle of Cheshire, it has its Cannes and Nice; suntans, beautiful people, yacht showrooms. But does it have its Islingtons, its Hampsteads and Hoxtons, its bohemian enclaves, what the Americans would call its 'crunchy granola' belt? The answer is yes, and not far from Ilkley, actually. If Yorkshire is Texas, then Hebden Bridge is its Austin; hidden in the hills, a groovy outpost of liberal hippy cool in the middle of redneck cowboy country.

It began in the late 1960s when the unassuming mill village of Hebden Bridge went into the same seemingly terminal decline as its neighbouring Pennine textile towns. The former workers fled to find jobs elsewhere and Hebden Bridge slumped; at one point in the seventies there was talk of terraced houses changing hands for the price of a night out. Whole streets were demolished. But as the mill workers deserted Hebden, impoverished hippies heard that here and ripe for settling was a lovely town set in beautiful landscape with artistic connections (Brontëland is over the hill in Howarth, Ted Hughes was born two miles away in Mytholmroyd and Sylvia Plath is buried on a hill overlooking Hebden). Word got around that you could squat in real stone cottages and sturdy artisans' terraces, grow your hair and grow your own without too much hassle. The hippies told their friends. They came, they saw, they set up juggling shops and wholefood delis and over three decades Hebden Bridge has blossomed into what's been called 'the Hampstead of the north'. The tolerant atmosphere has made it 'the lesbian capital of Britain' – ladies of Sapphic tastes outnumbering their hetero sisters by six to one, it's said – which has led the arguably local, definitely unhinged Bernard Ingham to call it 'tantamount to Sodom and Gomorrah'.

In a recent survey in *Highlife*, British Airways' in-flight magazine, Hebden Bridge was rated the fourth 'funkiest' town in the world behind Daylesford, Australia, the Brazilian town of Tiradentes and Burlington, Vermont. I've never been to any of those three – though I'm open to offers, naturally – but I have been to Hebden Bridge. I can vouch for its funkiness, man. My mate Terry's dad had a business delivering pop and crisps to pubs and clubs around East Lancashire and when we helped out, we'd often detour to Hebden Bridge just to soak up the boho atmosphere, sip half a bitter on the canal and sigh over hippy girls in faded denim. On reflection, maybe they were all lesbians. It didn't matter. This was the nearest to San Francisco I was going to get at seventeen, especially within ten minutes of the A646.

If you arrive by train and you're a romantic, you'll do a bit of billing and cooing over the cute little station. You'll feel sure you've just seen Trevor Howard helping Celia Johnson get something out of her eye. Actually, the real *Brief Encounter* station is Carnforth in Lancashire but that's been allowed to fall into disrepair, unlike Hebden's.

And then you're into Hebden itself, a relaxed, vibrant, pretty little town that's a riot of antiquarian bookshops and organic delis, if you can have a riot of such things. A vigil, perhaps. While never quite losing its Yorkshire bluffness, Hebden has become comically right-on. There's an alternative technology centre and a Montessori school, there are percussion workshops and Human Rights Awareness seminars. A gentle tide of lentils and natural fibres runs along the main street. If you listen hard enough, they say you can even hear a distinctly Hebden Bridge accent among the teenage kids of those original hippy incomers; a coolly offhand fusion of their parents' Estuary and the local Pennine accents.

One local resident, a writer called John Morrison, began to gently parody the town's achingly liberal credentials in a series of on-line columns that grew into three books: *View From the Bridge*, *Back to the Bridge* and *A Bridge Too Far*. He writes about recognisable local archetypes such as Willow Woman, a befuddled tree-hugger, and Wounded Man, 'not gay, exactly, but happy to pitch in if they were ever short-handed'. Wounded Man is a founder member of the Holistic Plumbers Collective who 'try to put plumbing problems into a more global context. Instead of just mending leaks or plumbing in washing machines they like to sit around at the customer's house, drinking coffee and consulting the *I Ching*. Only when they have fully explored their feelings do they make any effort to get down to work. By which point, in an unconscious homage to more conventional plumbing procedures, they usually find they've forgotten to bring any tools with them.'

If this hasn't made you warm to Morrison already, here he is on Hebden Bridge's sworn enemy Bernard Ingham, who's often railed against the town in print and on telly. 'The last time he was in town, chaperoned by a film crew, he announced it was exactly fifty years since he'd last set foot inside the Hebden Bridge Cinema... Bernard lambasted the lesbians and complained, bizarrely, that there were too many trees, before buggering off back to Purley where he belongs. Somebody please tell me why this buffoon isn't drummed out of town every time he shows his fat ugly face?'

In a bitter reversal of the sixties trend that made Hebden what it is, house prices are now spiralling and some fear the town is becoming a dormitory for the yuppies of Leeds and Manchester. Local activists are resisting this, though. One of them, Susan Quick, says: 'We refuse to contemplate the possibility of becoming a rich commuter belt and losing the very thing that makes Hebden what it is – all those weird and funny people who can afford to live here and do their own thing, the eccentrics, the off-beats and the drop-outs.'

Pippin and Sorrell and the other children of that first hippy generation can't afford to live where they were born. Two years ago, they took over Hebden's vacant tourist information centre – a site earmarked for redevelopment – and set up the People's Information Centre. Though their plight is not uncommon, you can't help wishing them well. Hebden Bridge is that rarity, a small town without small-mindedness. It would be sad if it lost its unique and heady aroma but it may be already happening. John Morrison says that, nowadays, 'If you see somebody mumbling a mantra, it's probably the FT-100 share index.'

Morrison has left town now, sold up and gone to the flesh-pots of the Lake District. We're leaving Hebden Bridge too. Having spent a chapter telling you that the north can be every bit as chichi, funky and 'bleeding edge' as your moneyed south, we now step into a different picture. Put your head through this hole, madam, and find yourself in a saucy postcard, where a diminutive balding man with a red face and an undernourished leek is having an amusing misunderstanding about sexual organs with a huge lady in a floral print dress. In the background you can just make out a teenage girl in a Stetson vomiting on the log flume. Just smell that bladderwrack, wee and stale Tetley's. I do like to be beside the seaside.

Beside the Seaside

I don't remember anything before Blackpool. A lot of people have probably said that, as they lie in intensive care waiting for the stomach pump. But what I mean is that Blackpool is one of my earliest memories. Right at the furthest, most distant outpost of recollection where the receding railway tracks of your memories meet as a pinprick on the horizon, there lies Blackpool. It's right there with my white plastic guitar with George Harrison's face on it and my next-door neighbour's Andy Capp cartoon books and the music to *Sunday Night at the London Palladium*.

Working-class Lancastrians go or at least went to Blackpool so often and so regularly – for day trips, holidays, stag dos – that it's impossible to date accurately when my first trip was. The mid-sixties, I imagine. Probably in a romper suit and on reins, always being likely to stray under a passing tram to Cleveleys.

I remember my first proper holiday there, in an abstract way, anyway. We were with my Auntie Molly and Uncle Cliff and cousin Steven. The boarding house was full of Scottish people. They were the first Scots I'd ever met and seemed tremendously exotic creatures to me, with their milky skins, freckles, outlandish accents, incendiary ginger hair and a massive capacity for a sticky orange fizzy pop that tasted like metal. One of them was a fat boy of about twelve who got so sunburned that he spent the rest of the week in bandages and cotton wool. Sotto voce, people were sympathetic but they did say it was his own fault. What with his skin and everything.

I thought I'd get some more accurate detail by ringing my mum. This, I now acknowledge, was foolhardy in the extreme. If you've read the interview with my mum about The Beatles in a previous book of mine, *Cider with Roadies*, you'll know just what to expect.

'Oh, that would be, oh, let's think, we'd just found out that we'd got that council house in Worsley Mesnes and so we were moving from your nana's – 1968, would it be, yes. Us and Molly and Cliff and Steven. On the front, right down by the baths… No, no, I'm wrong. It was nowhere near there, it was up Gynn Square, miles from the front. (Shouts off) What was the name of that hotel in Blackpool where we stayed with Molly and Cliff? Wait, I'll put your dad on.'

Then there comes the unnecessarily loud phone voice adopted by all dads of a certain vintage who still don't really believe that this newfangled contraption can possibly work.

'HALLO? HALLO? Hallo, cock! Now this hotel. It was called the Seagull and it was next to the Seagull coach garage. I don't know if it was the same firm…'

Instantly and clearly audible in the background my mother disputes this. 'No. No way, Peter. You're wrong. The Seagull garage was owned by a distant relative of Kathleen Ellison. We never went there with Molly. We were there with Maureen and Brian. Don't you remember? Walking down the prom we saw Theresa Mears with their Arnold. We were staying in a hotel in Gynn Square next door to a boarding house that was next door to Pat Marsh's brother-in-law Tommy. He'd just been signed off by the doctor…'

In case you think these kinds of conversation are an invention of Peter Kay's fertile mind, think again. This is how people in the north actually talk. If you're recounting a story, however trivial – be it a holiday in Blackpool or a recent visit to B&Q for rawlplugs

– everybody in the story must be identified by their family line-age or by some significant event in their life history. In this, we are true northerners, inheritors of the Eddas and the Icelandic sagas of our forefathers. In the Eddas, you might encounter Grolnir, he who slew the troll by the waterfall. In my mother's sagas, you may encounter Gerald, he who fell off a ladder at the Bleach Works. In this way, telling the tale of your recent trip to the chiropodist can take two hours. My mum and dad were still arguing when I gently replaced the receiver. By the way, there really was a Bleach Works in Wigan, which even after it was demolished gave its name to that particular part of town, as in, 'He's going out with a girl from up by the Bleach Works.' Evocative, eh?

But returning to Blackpool, I guess that I must have been there four or five times a year for the first dozen years of my life. In that I was by no means unusual. Different towns – in Lancashire and in Scotland – would have different holiday peri-ods or Wakes Weeks in which the factories would close for a fort-night and the town would pretty much decamp to Blackpool. Preston would have certain weeks, Blackburn others. Wigan's weeks were the same as Glasgow's, which made for a lively old time, I can tell you. Factor in countless day trips and all Lancastrians and most Scots of a certain socio-economic group got to know Blackpool as well as their own home town.

In the last couple of decades, I've hardly been back at all. Stone Roses and James concerts at the Winter Gardens in the nineties, the odd football match. I've not really had much cause to venture there, to be honest. That's the thing about the coast-line. You're never just passing through. You have to really want to go there. It puts off the faint-hearted. That's why Philip Larkin liked living in Hull so much. Journalists would set out to interview him and then seeing how bloody difficult it was to get to, would stay on the train and head for Newcastle to doorstep Basil Bunting instead.

So for the first time in years, I find myself on this chilly, drizzly spring morning aboard a packed Northern Trains sprinter service from Preston to Blackpool North. In the early years of tourism, travelling to Blackpool was a bona fide expedition, not for lightweights; two days from Yorkshire and a day even from Manchester. The situation was transformed in 1840 when the Preston and Wyre Railway was built and brought the cheap excursion trains from industrial Lancashire. Since then, almost any day of the year will find the spiritual and actual descendants of those early day-trippers and holidaymakers heading for Blackpool in search of some very northern r'n'r.

In its own way, the train and its passengers were as queer and colourful as a trip to the hill station at Darjeeling or overnighting on the Trans-Siberian Express. It was a kind of carnival on wheels. Less charitably, some might have called it a travelling freak show. Though maybe I was the freak. When I took out a book and began to read, the whole carriage looked at me as if I'd taken out a cuckoo clock or a lacrosse stick.

There were entire families who appeared to be in fancy dress. Surely that's not what they wore normally: Stetsons, gold lamé tracksuits, helmets with horns, replica football kits. It was a kind of uniform. They were dressed for fun. They had planned for fun with military precision and every shred of their being was focused on its acquisition. I found that quite sweet, but this early on a nippy morning on a grubby train, it was also kind of tough on the nerves. Everyone, young and old, was shouting. Some were arguing, some were demanding attention, some were shouting merely from the sheer unalloyed joy of being on a train to Blackpool. One man had a toy rifle. Two Asian girls were dancing to cheesy dance music from a radio on the table.

There was a shy-looking girl holding a giant furry prawn over a shoulder.

After all this, Blackpool North was a deadening experience. It looked less like a railway station than a decontamination plant. If this were your first time in Blackpool on the first day of a long-awaited holiday, you must surely wish you'd booked for somewhere else. A disused naval base in the Bering Straits, perhaps.

Blackpool, I've been told, has a large transient population and a big drugs problem. Everywhere there were signs telling me what would happen if I were caught taking crystal meth by the booking office or whatever. The gents toilet was like a vision of hell, lit with a sickly and unreal deep vermillion. This is anti-drug lighting, so called because you can't find a vein to hit in this light. Or maybe because everything looks so weird and disorienting that you decide you don't need any more drugs anyway.

But get out of the station and head down Talbot Road and things get better. After a few hundred Poundlands, a couple of branches of Greggs and several discount book shops, I spotted the North Pier. It could have been the big kid in me, or the race memory of the northerner, but suddenly my heart lifted and my step quickened. I was nine again. The sun came out. The amusement arcade beckoned. I had a pocketful of change and when it ran out, I didn't have to ask my dad for more. Bliss. Freedom.

I'm glad to report that amusement arcades haven't changed that much in thirty years. Yes, there are huge terrifying-looking machines that you have to be strapped into like a Navy Seal into a stealth fighter and where you attempt to eliminate the Vorgon race at unbelievable volumes. Yes, there are virtual reality games where cadaverous life-size zombies try to sever your head with a rusty scythe. But if you look hard enough you will find the treasures of your childhood and fall on them with fetishistic pleasure. There are still the Penny Falls, which are now ten pence obviously but still as blatantly fixed as ever; teetering piles of coins never quite cascading over the lip, perhaps due to the gobbets of superglue keeping them in place.

There is still a perspex box where you can signally fail to get a grabbing hand to ensnare some kind of gift. Once upon a time I seem to recall this was twenty B&H or some kind of rubbish 'Swiss' watch but now it's a disfigured gonk. It doesn't matter. It's not the prize, it's the tantalising Sisyphean swing of the grabber that lures us, a lesson in the ultimate futility of desire. There's still a tired woman in her late fifties who'll give you your change with a muttered 'There you go, sweetheart' and a look in her eyes that suggests this isn't where she thought life would lead her. There are still those funny bingo stalls where you sit on stools and slide little plastic shutters across in the hope of winning a massive teddy bear. Here, it is always just before opening time and a man with a mike is trying to drum up trade with a desultory 'eyes down' and his only customers are two elderly ladies who are in their own way as addicted as a Moss Side crackhead. If I were a French philosopher, I might conclude that amusement arcades were a bit like sex, entered into with youthful brio and enthusiasm but afterwards strangely melancholic and carrying echoes of mortality. Funny people, the French.

Fish and chips on the prom sounded a cheering idea and so it proved to be. My fish was bought from a man who seemed to have arrived that morning from Uzbekistan (so dark and phlegmy was his pronunciation of 'haddock') and was without doubt the fishiest fish I have ever eaten. It tasted rankly and pungently of the sea, which at Blackpool is not always a good idea. Feeling a bit weak, I sat in a bus shelter and marvelled at an advert for an afternoon performance by Charlie Cairoli. Surely not the same one who blighted my Easter Mondays with his sinister, unfunny routines on *Billy Smart's Circus*. He must be a hundred by now. It has to be his son. Maybe his grandson. Maybe a virtual reality hologram.

Cairoli Junior was appearing at Blackpool's famous tower which, as you probably know, is a scale model of the Eiffel Tower. I'd tell you more about this fine landmark structure and its attractions but it was twelve pounds flipping fifty to get in so sod that, I thought. Instead I decided I would spend my money on something that I've always fancied but never done. Something which has haunted my imagination since I were a child. Something a little naughty, wicked even, that my grandma would have shuddered at and ushered me by with alacrity.

Romany Pearl is one of a score of gypsy fortune tellers plying their trade along the Golden Mile. I don't know why I chose her. There were more salubrious, even quite flashy-looking fortune tellers on offer. One had a picture of George Michael and Sandra Bullock outside. They can't have come here, I thought, and on closer inspection they hadn't. Gypsy Petrulengo had simply got their birthdates off the internet and ran up a horoscope. George is going to be the first man on Jupiter and then be eaten by a horse, apparently. Only joking. They're both going to have successful and exciting careers, you'll be glad to hear.

But I picked Romany Pearl's place, accessed directly off the prom through a little curtain next door to a burger bar. In a room the size of a telephone box with a little half-door over which you can look out onto the street, sits Pearl, a woman with a deep leathery tan and a baritone acquired by a lifetime of Embassy Regal. She sits like the Sphinx. The Sphinx with cerise talons and bangles and black candy floss for hair. She may be pushing sixty. But if you told me she was ninety I'd believe you.

I went for palms not tarot. 'One hand or both?' asked Romany. 'What's the difference?' I asked. Two, she said, gives a deeper reading and, crucially, costs a tenner rather than a fiver. Feeling giddy, I opted for the full ten pounds and both hands.

'You've always been lucky,' Pearl tells me in a voice like sifting gravel. 'If you fell in the canal in your old suit, you'd come up in a new one. And you'll never want for money.' Great. Also, I'm not going to die of a disease but of old age. I nearly say that strictly speaking you could say that's a disease. I think better of it in case she changes her prediction to 'You're going to be beaten to death by an irate gypsy of indeterminate age.'

She tells me that in a month's time I'm going to have a really big surprise. A happy one but a big one all the same. Well, the month has gone and I'm still waiting but I'll keep you informed. As I leave, Romany Pearl asks if I want to buy a lucky charm. 'I don't need it, do I?' I laugh at what I think is quite a smart remark. Romany Pearl doesn't seem to get it.

My little session with a palm reader was reassuring but frankly a bit dull, more like going to see a very bland counsellor than a mistress of the dark arts. Part of me would have preferred it if she'd looked into my hand, screamed and said, 'I can do nothing for you, sir. Please be gone,' and crossed herself. In the last analysis, all fortune tellers have one fatal, obvious flaw. If you really could see into the future (a fairly useful skill, I'd have thought), wouldn't you have ended up somewhere a whole lot nicer than chain-smoking cheap fags in a little pavement booth in Blackpool? But maybe I'm misunderstanding the gypsy temperament.

I'm back on the front and looking out to sea. Once upon a time, this whole Fylde coast was an area of impenetrable bog and oak forests. By 1500, this particular hamlet was called simply 'Pul' and later, thanks to its dark, peaty waters, 'Blackpoole'. You can see a kinship with the land across the water, by the way, when you consider that the Gaelic for black is 'dubh' and for pool 'linh'. Hence, Dublin is Blackpool.

The hamlet by the sea grew. By the mid 1700s, there were four hotels to cater for the tourists who came for the invigorating Irish sea air and bathing. There were the beginnings of a promenade, a 200-yard length of grass the width of a goalmouth across which 'a perpetual assemblage of company, when the weather permits, may be seen upon this elegant little walk'. Sea bathing and seawater drinking was a national craze at the time. A bell was rung when it was time for the ladies to bathe, and during this time, any gentleman found on the shore was fined a bottle of wine.

The father of modern Blackpool is one Henry Banks, he who built the first holiday cottages and really got the hotel trade moving. Today Blackpool has more beds for rent than the whole of Portugal. There is, as the brochures have it, 'accommodation to suit every taste and pocket'. At the top end of the scale are the Paramounts and De Veres with saunas, solariums, gym facilities and 'elegant dining'. At the other end, truer I think to the spirit of the town, are countless little family guest houses and B&Bs tucked down every side street where, and I quote from one's literature, 'Your hosts, Daphne and Shane, guarantee your every comfort and the highest level of customer care. No Stag or Hen Nights.'

Such nights are a real bone of contention in modern Blackpool. They bring in the dosh and the bar owners love them but there are many in the Blackpool Chamber of Commerce who pine for the good old days when the town's clientele was decent working families who wanted nothing more than a shared TV room for *Match of the Day* and a choice of Britvic or Sugar Puffs at breakfast. When you've seen a blank-eyed girl in a bridal outfit and L plates urinating in the street, you take their point. Blackpool's traditionalist lobby is resisting moves to build a Super Casino here and turn the resort into the Las Vegas of Europe. 'Casinos will definitely scare all t'families away. Blackpool will lose its old seaside image,' said Pat, who sells sweets on the prom. 'There's enough alcoholics and gamblers anyway in Blackpool.'

Along the crowded front, most of the hotel names I remember from childhood are still here: the Craig Y Don, the Balmoral, the Gainsborough. The Lyndene offers, implausibly, a five-course dinner for £8.95. I'm seeing all this from the window of a tram, the only way to travel in Blackpool, except for donkey, of course, and I'm en route to the Pleasure Beach, where I haven't been in donkey's years. I'm feeling a little bit sick. It could be long-dormant excitement. Or it could be the fish.

The Pleasure Beach is a huge amusement park at the southern end of the Golden Mile. It's Blackpool's Coney Island. You can't go to Blackpool and not go to the Pleasure Beach. It'd be like going to Mount Rushmore and saying, 'Oh, we didn't bother with the big carved mountainside thing. We just had a look in the gift shop.'

You have to pass through a metal detector to get into the Pleasure Beach now. Sad, isn't it? But before I lapse into full 'damning indictment of our troubled society' mode, I should say that fairgrounds have always hung heavy with latent violence. Remember Albert Finney getting duffed up by those squaddies in *Saturday Night and Sunday Morning*? This simmering threat of trouble mingled with a little illicit sex and the hugely amplified sound of The Sweet's 'Ballroom Blitz' from the waltzer is what has always made them so intoxicating to me. One of my favourite photographs ever is found on the back of The Smiths' *The World Won't Listen* album. It shows four teenage girls, circa 1964, hair piled high, faces beautiful and feral, resplendent in their best Rita Tushingham finery on the platform at the side of the waltzer. It is just perfect.

The Pleasure Beach these days promises a more corporate, familial day out. Thanks to the metal detector, I never feel that a

Teddy Boy will razor me at any point. It's twenty-nine quid for a wristband that entitles you to ride the 145 attractions all day. If that's not enough, you can even stay here at the 'chic, modern' Big Blue Hotel where 'each child's bunk bed has its own built-in TV to put an end to fighting for the remote control!' While the kids lie in bed watching TV, slack-jawed with exhaustion and doped on Slush Puppies, Mum and Dad can watch Joe Longthorne do his 'amazingly accurate' vocal impressions at The Paradise Room. These days his act includes him doing the Pet Shop Boys, which actually I'd really like to see. Not as much as I'd like to see him do Captain Beefheart, obviously, but I imagine there's no call for that. According to its promotional material the 'Pleasure Beach® can also offer you a choice of unusual venues to add dimension to your next party, conference, exhibition. Innovative locations in five-star surroundings'. Somehow I can't see the CBI having their next EU trade tariffs debate hanging upside-down from the Pepsi Max Big One or the Irn-Bru Revolution but I'm sure they'd approve of the corporate branding.

In among all this slick innovation, the Pleasure Beach still has much of the trashy, dangerous flavour that made it so thrilling to the youthful Maconie. The whole place is a cacophony of competing barkers, each trying to antagonise slightly drunk men into securing their girlfriends a cuddly toy by throwing darts/knocking coconuts off stands/shooting pop guns. One is a kind of basketball thing in which the prize for a 'hoop' is a giant furry prawn. I can't fathom the basketball/crustacean connection but it at least explains where the girl on the train got hers from.

The Ghost Train looks a little tame now compared to Trauma Towers, and a new ride called Pasaje de Terror, whose poster – a sort of skull-faced monk promising me 'an abyss of pain' – really gave me the willies. Charmingly, there is still a Tunnel of Love, I notice. Who'd have thought that this relic of a bygone age could still survive? I'd imagined most amorous teens would just check into a Travelodge for the afternoon if the sap started rising but, no, there are still some who crave the forbidden thrill of ten minutes with their hands down each other's pants in a rowing boat in a flooded and dimly lit shed.

Disappointingly I discover that the sign reading 'Tunnel of Love' is in fact merely a leftover bit of set dressing from when *Coronation Street* filmed here. It's really just an entrance into that venerable old fave the River Caves. I'm sure you could still get up to a spot of hanky panky here, though, as the ride is rarely crowded. Today's thrill seekers clearly prefer to be catapulted hyperventilating through space rather than taken on a fairly sedate cruise through various grottos, gold mines and at one point, the temples of Angkor Wat. Connoisseurs of fairground architecture will instantly recognise, in the ride's faux-Cubist look, the characteristic style of designers Joseph Emberton and Percy Metcalfe. You can tell that it's an 'old-school' ride by the mannequin of an ebony-skinned native with huge rolling eyes and a bone through his nose, one of several fantastically politically incorrect representations of the peoples of the world. Mind you, the white man doesn't come off much better. I'm sure the British Council of Explorers isn't happy with the depiction of one of its brave members as a goofy midget with a hat made from a coconut.

The Pleasure Beach, I'm happy to say, does have a sense of its own history and the River Caves is one of several rides displaying the fairground equivalent of a Blue Plaque. The Wild Mouse, a mini-version of the Big Dipper, has been rattling the fillings of kids since 1958 and is one of only three wooden Wild Mouse rides in the world. The Log Flume, where generations of Lancastrians have had their best clothes soaked and caught a head cold, was the longest in the world until, as I was putting the finishing touches to this book, it closed down. Sales of Lemsip and poultices will surely suffer.

To the dismay of my health-conscious friends, another thing I love about fairgrounds is what the Americans call 'Fair Food'. While I yield to no man in my admiration for a nice truffle oil risotto with a parmesan and beetroot foam, there are times when only a Westlers lungburger eaten outside a van will do. It helps if you're quite drunk. I wasn't but I still couldn't resist the dark, savoury, intoxicating odour of fried onions wafting over the park. Be honest. Can anyone? The Pleasure Beach (I'm quoting again) 'has over thirty-five restaurants and cafés offering an amazing choice of food. From pasta and pizza at the Italian Job to a burger at the largest Burger King restaurant in the UK'. I did, though, spot a worrying trend towards culinary gentrification, with several outlets openly offering skinny decaf lattes and focaccia. And what's that 'over thirty-five' supposed to mean? Do they mean thirty-six?

Sated on a variety of levels, I left the Pleasure Beach and emerged into the demimonde of the South Shore. Even by Blackpool's own standards, the South Shore is sublimely tacky. There's a shop selling 'samurai and other themed swords', presumably for those off to a ritual killing later in the day. One fast-food stall featured a giant-size anthropomorphic hot dog smilingly slathering itself in mustard, a ghastly image of obeisance and self-sacrifice I found hard to shake off.

That was quite near the Laughing Donkey Family Bar, which made my thoughts turn to Blackpool's equine population. They're all still there, slowly pottering up and down the beach, little kids gently swaying on their back, storing up a lifetime's Proustian scent memories of donkey manure, candy floss and seaweed. Two quid seems cheap for such delights. I looked into the donkeys' eyes for signs of melancholy and lassitude but they looked fairly impassive. I imagine it's hard for a donkey to look otherwise.

As I strolled along the prom back to the station I noticed that Madame Tussaud's Waxworks had changed. Madame Tussaud's is a Blackpool institution. A holiday's not a holiday until you've spent an afternoon squinting at ghoulish figurines in semi-darkness going, 'That looks nothing like Virginia Wade.' Anyway, as you may have read in the papers, Madame Tussaud's has bowed to modern mores and renamed itself Celeb City. Now, you can waste an afternoon looking at ghoulish figurines in semi-darkness going, 'That looks nothing like Gordon Ramsay.'

There was a kiosk next door selling rubber Osama Bin Laden masks but I couldn't work up the necessary enthusiasm. Blackpool is rather exhausting after a while and it was time to leave, I thought. While I was mulling this over I noticed a sign outside the Royal Oxford Hotel saying 'Coming Soon: Bernard Manning'. Definitely time to leave, and with not a moment to lose.

Blackpool is unique. Not all the northern coast is like that. Hardly any of it, in fact. Over in the east, the beaches of Northumbria have never seen a donkey and are beautiful and unspoilt. Seahouses and Lindisfarne are almost magical. Further south, Whitby has goths, Robin Hood's Bay is quaint. Filey and Bridlington have some of Blackpool's 'honest vulgarity'™ but feel tangibly melancholic and fading while Blackpool thrusts itself into the twenty-first century in its inimitably coarse way. Scarborough has its share of Blackpool's tacky pizzazz and hen party bacchanals but is altogether more refined, thanks to the Sitwells, Alan Ayckbourn, the grave of Anne Brontë, the lunchtime concerts at the South Bay and the clifftops which add class to any mise en scène.

Blackpool's neighbours on the north-western coast seem to actively stress their difference from that great lurid behemoth of tat. I once lived in Southport and locals ('sandgrounders', as they're known) were always desperate to tell you how much more classy and upscale Southport was as a resort. What they really meant was dull. They even had a Pontin's, the poor relation of the Butlins chain, which had all the latter's *Hi-de-Hi!* crapness but none of its rambunctious allure. I have to say I liked Southport, though, enough to live there for two years as a penurious, epicurean student. We would drink in the bar of the Scarisbrick Arms, have chicken pathia at the Oriental Grill and later go for long moonlit walks out on the beach in the vain hope of ever seeing the sea.

Morecambe was once a rival to Blackpool in the popularity stakes. Then, like New Brighton on the Wirral, it became a byword for faded glamour and slow decline. The art deco masterpiece of the Midland Hotel, where once men in tuxedos and women in pearls would watch the sun go down over the Isle of Man with a daiquiri, was left to moulder, only used as a backdrop in the odd episode of *Poirot*. It once had two piers, the Central and the West End, but both are now gone. Most ignominiously of all, in 1994, Noel Edmonds opened his ill-judged (insane, if you ask me) World of Crinkley Bottom, a theme park based on his reviled but hugely popular Saturday teatime show *Noel's House Party*. Much in evidence was Mr Blobby, a hyperthyroidal psychedelic PVC monster alongside which Barney the dinosaur had gravitas and quiet authority. In a rare but gratifying show of taste, the British public stayed away in droves and it closed after thirteen weeks, although the ensuing Blobbygate legal wrangle between Lancaster City Council and Edmonds went on for some time. Not long afterwards Morecambe's indoor waterpark Bubbles closed, closely followed by Frontierland, its Pleasure Beach. The West End of Morecambe became a slum, in effect, the hotels used as DHSS hostels as house prices tumbled. The grisly, well-publicised deaths of twenty-three Chinese cockle-pickers on the bay's treacherous sands didn't exactly act as a boost to tourism either.

Lately, though, Morecambe has shown signs of a recovery. That self-same dilapidated West End is becoming a desirable address and property prices are on the up. There's a massive redevelopment programme under way and the Midland is due to reopen in 2007. The tourist board are working hard to sell the area by emphasising its gorgeous if lethal bay and its closeness to the Lake District. To be honest, this is a bit like Hull selling itself on its proximity to the Yorkshire Dales but they mean well. And on a clear day the hills of Cumbria, seen across the glittering water, do seem both very spectacular and very near. Near enough certainly to wander off to, lonely as a cloud. And I'd like to take a detour there too.

I say 'detour' because you could fill a decent mobile library just with Lake District literature. Melvyn Bragg and Hunter Davies have written a couple of shelves' worth between them. Hill-walking high priest Alfred Wainwright started a veritable cottage industry in Lakes books and a canon that's been added to by Bill Birkett, Bob Allen, John and Anne Nuttall and many another scribe. One day it might even be added to by me. But for now let me just add a few drops to those brimming reservoirs of Lake District literature.

I love this place. Even though I wasn't born here, it's the landscape I've come to think of as home. Like Wainwright, I was born and raised in a sooty Lancashire mill town but, like him, I fell hard for this landscape; in my case from my first sight of Elterwater on a misty spring evening and the view from Loughrigg Fell in the haze of a warm August afternoon. As a teenager I'd come here in the holidays and camp with mates at Farmer Brass's place near Hawkshead. In the evening we'd nurse a few pints of Hartleys XB in The Outgate or The Sun or The Queen's Head and then, at closing time, we'd skulk off like poachers to the dark wooded shores of Esthwaite Water and cast weighted lines into the deepest parts of the lake, far out in the middle, far beyond the pool of light cast by our Woolies torches and storm lanterns. We'd sit, each in their own circle of battery light, strung out along the shore at intervals of a few feet and wait for the sudden pluck on the line, the thrilling tug that caught up the slack and made the washing-up bottle top we'd clipped across the line dance wildly, the sign that somewhere in the gloomy fathoms, an eel was taking our bait.

Eel fishing is very exciting. Honestly. Why not try it for that special romantic weekend? An eel is, in its purest essence, a thick muscly inner tube with a primitive central nervous system. They give you a hell of a fight and they taste kind of nutty. We ate them for breakfast every morning in the oddest, often least palatable combinations – eels with fusilli pasta, eel omelette, eel kedgeree, eels on toast – until I became so heartily sick of them that one fateful morning I scooped my dish in the campsite bin and had a Variety Pack instead. A passing naturalist remarked, 'They come all the way from their spawning grounds in the Sargasso Sea just so you can do that, mate.' Perhaps because of this but probably more because I was absolutely flipping sick of the muscly, nutty so and sos, I haven't touched eel since 1980.

The Lake District occupies a very special part of the north's actual and psychological landscape. Like Blackpool, every northerner goes there at some point, in fact probably as an antidote to Blackpool. That big blousy fleshpot is only really a few miles south down the coast.

The Lakes, though, despite Jimmy McGovern's best efforts to paint them as a maelstrom of forbidden lust and telegenically unresolved issues in his TV drama of the same name, remain somehow aloof from the strident shore of Lanky to the south. If Blackpool is the north-west's hyperactive huckster super-ego, then the Lake District is its deep-lying and spiritual subconscious. The Lake District is, at least in theory, everything that Blackpool is not. Blackpool is chip fat and sodium lights. The Lakes is crystalline air and twinkling stars. Blackpool is fizzy keg lager, the crash of slot machines and Robbie Williams. The Lakes is real ale, birdsong and Wordsworth. Blackpool is sluttishly demeaning. The Lakes is dreamily uplifting. In theory, anyway; Bowness has become as tasteless as the Carling that flows in gallons there at the weekend, a nasty fragment of Blackpool relocated by a once beautiful lake, now a playground for perma-tanned tossers with powerboats and jet-skis. And Keswick, a charming, almost alpine town nestling between the mighty Skiddaw and the delightful Derwentwater, hasn't got one decent butcher's shop any more but has a thousand identical discount stores selling waterproofs that will leak like a sieve before you've made it to the pay and display machine, let alone Scaféll Pike.

Because of its proximity to big industrial cities like Sheffield and Manchester, the Peak District has always been more of a workers' playground than the Lakes. You can be on the foothills of Kinder Scout and the Dark Peak in forty minutes from dense city estates and suburbs. So there's a long tradition of factory workers hiking out there on their Sundays off, forming societies, cycling and tramping and fell-walking and, as they walked and talked and looked down on the smoking chimneys and the serried terraces and hovels, maybe wondering why some of this beautiful landscape was closed to them, fermenting radical thoughts and eventually and famously trespassing on Kinder Scout in 1932, an act as much to do with class struggle as callisthenics. Out of this came the Ramblers Society, of whom the lazy stereotype is a cuddly sinecure for geriatrics when in fact its true spirit is far more radical and bolshy than any of those Westminster village idiots.

Lakeland's flash of red, though, was more likely to be seen on a huntsman's coat than a worker's flag. The Lake District is wild, high country; compact compared to the Scottish Highlands but still, in British terms, an untamed wilderness with no cities or heavy industry near. Left and right, up and down, from Whitehaven to Wakefield, from Carnforth to Carlisle, it still is all fields around here. And dark, chilly lakes, bleak ridges, shattered peaks and impenetrable forests.

Revolutions, as old Karl Marx pointed out, are very rarely fostered in the milking shed or the top field, and so for centuries Cumbria has been happier wrestling in tights than wresting power from the hands of the establishment. In fact, gentry and peasantry have rubbed along pretty well up here, with a nice lubrication of forelock tugging and nary a Peterloo in sight. The hills are scoured and dotted with evidence of the Lakes' very own light industry – slate and copper mines – where men worked hard day and night miles from civilisation and for a pittance. And yet I can find no record of industrial conflict or unionism. Perhaps working in one of the world's most beautiful landscapes distracted their minds from such things. Or perhaps they were just too tired.

Free of grime and insubordination among its lower orders, the Lake District has always had something of a rarefied air, the domain of climbers, dreamers, poets, teachers and *Guardian* readers rather than the proletariat. When north-westerners get high ideas (in every sense) they head for Cumbria, as this chunk of north-west England has been called since 1974. The newish nomenclature has stuck fairly well, really; it's used reasonably naturally in most people's daily speech as well as more official usages like the BBC's local radio station and local government circles. This may be because the name has a good, solid pedigree. Cumbria, sometimes Rheged, was the name given by the Celts to the kingdom that flourished here between the fall of the Romans and the coming of the Anglo-Saxons. Rheged as a name has reappeared of late as the name of a rather good and very tastefully done mountain exhibition centre cum cinema cum retail and restaurant outlet just off Junction 40 of the M6. Here, if the rain comes as it will, you can buy fabulously decadent home-made chocolates or a Gore-Tex hat and eat and wear both while watching cool stuff about the Himalayas on a massive Imax screen going, 'Ooooh! Look at that crevasse!'

Before Cumbria came into being for a second time, the Lake District as a concept – later enshrined as a National Park – loosely spanned three counties: Westmorland, Cumberland and Lancashire. Yes, Lancashire. One of the iconic Lake District mountains, the Old Man of Coniston, as well as Coniston Water and several fine hills, valleys and tarns lay squarely into north Lancashire, a fact I brandish like a pitchfork whenever someone accuses me of being an offcomer or interloper. Westmorland sits between Lancashire, Yorkshire, County Durham and Cumberland and claims most of the well-known beauty spots while Cumberland, which will tell you over a pint of Jennings that it's the real Cumbria, curves around the north of the district and has its most unspoilt tracts. There is a faint but readily discernible rivalry and suspicion between these different Cumbrians. For a week's walking, I once rented a house in Broughton-in-Furness from a local builder. As he was showing me around, he asked me convivially what I was hoping to do here. 'Well, climb those for one,' I said, pointing out the dramatic skyline of the Buttermere valley, the mountain tops of Grasmoor, High Stile and Haystacks, these and more all clearly seen from the upstairs bedroom window. 'Oh, Buttermere. Yes, I've heard about it. Is it nice? I've never been.' I was staggered. Here was a man living within a well-chucked crampon of the most stunning valley in England and he'd never bothered to go, preferring instead to hang around the branch of Spar and the billiard club in Millom and his little corner of north Lancashire. There was, I felt, some deliberate cussedness in his stupidity. Similarly, I once tried to buy a particular knitted garment, a gift for an elderly relative, in the Edinburgh Woollen Mill in Penrith. 'Oh, we don't stock that. Try our branch in Keswick. It's more geared for tourists,' said the country-set lady with a haughty toss of her silver rinse, as if Keswick were Las Vegas and I'd asked for a pair of crotchless panties rather than a nice cable-knit cardie.

The place where all three counties meet is called the Three Shires Stone, a slender rock pillar sitting high above the Wrynose Pass in the heart of the hills and a favourite walkers' haunt. Here, at dusk, you will always find a damp, dishevelled man or woman, tugging their sodden socks off, perched on the boot lip of their muddy estate car and eating the mangled remains of what seems to have become a pork pie and banana sandwich due to rough carriage in a rucksack and drinking hot Nescafé from a thermos. Bliss.

The first tourists did it in rather more style, in frock coats and bumping around in stagecoaches, looking at the mountains backwards through bijou hand-held mirrors because, bless, they were too frightened to look directly at them. They had been inspired by the romantic poets who had decamped here in the early part of the nineteenth century in much the same way as British avant-garde painters went to Cornwall in the 1950s or every addled London dance music bunny went to Brighton in the nineties. The Lake Poets were hardier souls than those first perfumed, salt-smelling, shrinking violets of tourists, I'm glad to say. They could certainly hold their laudanum, and Coleridge,

the best and boldest of the lot, made the first recorded ascent of
Scaféll Pike, England's highest mountain, in the dark without an
anorak – a century and a half too early, sadly – but with a quill
pen and writing desk. Read his account. It's utterly thrilling. He
would also think nothing of walking the thirteen or so miles over
Dunmail Raise from Keswick to Grasmere to see his mates the
Wordsworths. Dorothy W. would walk halfway back with him at
night and I'm pretty sure Coleridge used this time profitably in
trying to put his hand up Dot's skirt but clearly I can't be defin-
itively sure. Wordsworth, an altogether more boring fellow in his
middle age, skulked around at home, perhaps writing one of his
thirty-two sonnets about the River Duddon. I love Wordsworth
and he is a genuine poetic revolutionary but like Prince, who
shared his dress sense too, he wrote too much and was woefully
inconsistent. 'The Prelude' and the 'Lyrical Ballads' changed
English poetry forever but he could also come up with this
clunker in 'The Thorn', the best example of bathos I know:

> *And to the left, three yards beyond,*
> *You see a little muddy pond*
> *Of water, never dry;*
> *I've measured it from side to side:*
> *'Tis three feet long, and two feet wide*

For me, the quintessential Lake District writer isn't one of those
opiated and dissolute romantics, geniuses though they were, but
a squat bloke from Blackburn who seemingly wore the same
anorak for twenty years. The aforementioned Alfred Wainwright,
'the blessed AW' as some but not all of the walking fraternity
refer to him, came with his cousin to Windermere in 1952 and
climbed Orrest Head overlooking the district's largest lake on its
eastern shore. It was love at first sight. 'Those few hours on

Orrest Head cast a spell that changed my life,' he later wrote. The die of the rest of his long life was cast.

Orrest Head is a tiddler really compared to the big Lakeland hills. You won't get rime clinging to your beard here or ever use your ice axe in anger. It doesn't even make it into AW's own canonical list of Lake District summits, being relegated to his *Outlying Fells* volume of strolls for oldies. But Orrest Head turned Wainwright's head completely. He devoted the rest of his life to walking and writing about the Lake District fells, taking a pay cut in order to become borough treasurer in Kendal and thus closer to the landscape that had ensnared him.

He was a good borough treasurer by all accounts: stolid, a little frightening, genial enough in his old-fashioned way. But he lived a double life. For thirteen years, he spent every non-working hour composing, setting, drawing and writing by hand the seven-volume study of the Lake District mountains that are his master-piece and, for me, one of the great works of English literature.

They are truly beautiful things, recognisably and obviously stunning even if you've no interest in the Lake District. Passion, care and attention to detail ring out from every hand-measured indentation to every pencilled hatching on every cliff face. As Hunter Davies once put it, 'Not merely guidebooks, but philo-sophical strolls, personal outpourings of feelings and observa-tions, written and drawn by a craftsman, conceived and created as a total work of art.' Wainwright himself called them 'love letters' and because of that he refused to take money for them, giving it instead – well over a million – to an animal rescue centre.

As I write these words, I am also preparing to give the annual Wainwright Society lecture at that Rheged centre. I'm honoured to have been asked as Wainwright has perhaps given me more pleasure than any other writer; certainly taken me to more wonderful places and got me out of any number of hair-raising scrapes. Even though the books are now rather out of date – Wainwright steadfastly refused to update the routes though one Chris Jesty has now undertaken this – Wainwright is a good man to have in your inside pocket when the fog comes down on Striding Edge and sheer drops are all around.

But Wainwright was a complicated man and my relationship with him is just as complicated. In his early work, *Pennine Journey*, he is worryingly ambivalent about Hitler and if anything he moved rightward as he aged. By *Fellwanderer* in the seventies, he was calling for the birching of criminals until 'they scream for mercy' and for the castration of football hooligans. He clearly adored women on some romantic level but his attitude to them was archaic and bigoted even by the standards of the thirties. His first marriage was as arid and loveless as his second was tender and passionate. He could be warm and generous; a pledge in his book on the Pennine Way to pay for a half-pint of beer at the Border Hotel in Kirk Yetholm for any walker who completed the Way cost him an estimated £15,000. But misanthropy was never far away. He hated being recognised on the fells and would turn away and pretend to urinate if anyone approached him. When sales of his books were about to pass the million mark, his publishers persuaded him to agree to have dinner with whoever bought the specially signed millionth copy; he panicked and made a hundred-mile round trip and scoured the relevant book-shops to buy the marked copy himself.

Some of his often silly and sometimes disturbingly illiberal views are lauded as 'old-fashioned common sense' by cultees. But not me. It is Wainwright the lover not Wainwright the political philosopher I warm to. I'd rather remember him as the man who could write 'The fleeting hour of life of those who love the hills is quickly spent, but the hills are eternal. Always there will be the lonely ridge, the dancing beck, the silent forest; always there will be the exhilaration of the summits.' It's writing like this that calls me into cold desolate crags in mid-winter as well as sunlit uplands in spring.

All things being equal – unless I fall under the spell of Surrey – I intend to move completely to the Lake District one day and I'm aware that I'd better save some words for then and add my half-inch of spine and few hundred pages to the groaning shelves. The fells and the lakes and the ridges and forest will still be there. They're not going anywhere.

The Lakes may be as over-exposed as, well, insert name of currently ubiquitous celebrity here if you don't mind doing that bit of work yourself, thanks, but the Cumbrian coast is an enigma. I know it pretty well, thanks to my enthusiasm for the county and its awesome landscapes (using the adjective as Wordsworth might rather than Bill and Ted). But most people, most northerners even, don't know it at all. There are seaside resorts here, or were, at least. Silloth is a compact little Victorian seaside town where Cumbria used to take its holidays up until the coming of the package tour. It has a lot going for it: nice squares, a decent beach, golf courses and an expansive, invigorating curve of seafront where you can get comprehensively battered by the wind off the water. Stunned and sitting on a bench, you feel that you could reach out and touch that big round hill across the Solway Firth even though it's actually in another country – Criffel in Dumfriesshire to be precise. A little north of Silloth lies Skinburness, which is a bleakly attractive bird reserve though it sounds like some terrible affliction of the epidermis.

This West Cumberland coast has suffered as much as anywhere from the vicissitudes of the British economy these last forty years. Seaward of Frizington and Cleator Moor, the whole feel of Cumbria changes, from cottages to boarded-up flats, from Gore-Tex and real ale to Burberry and Smirnoff Ice. Maryport was once a bustling port and can still scrub up well, but I once spent as grim an afternoon as I've ever had here, holed up in a dingy, smoky pub eating greasy chips while sheets of rain came in off a churning grey sea. 'Maryport in Cumbria is crap. It has more chavs per head of the population than anywhere else in Britain.' That's how one local resident put it on an internet forum devoted to Britain's worst towns. Civic pride seems in short supply, though the council have made an effort to attract visitors to the town with a series of 'theme' music festivals such as Punk, Sixties, Sea Shanties and Blues. Wonder what BB King made of it?

The big towns on this stretch of coast are Workington and Whitehaven, both former heavyweights who've taken their share of confidence-sapping punches since their glory days. Confusingly, both towns refer to the natives of the other as 'jam-eaters', an insult that has its murky origins in the mines. Apparently one lot had jam on their sandwiches while the others did not. Whether that makes said jam-eaters snobs or peasants, no one seems really sure. I think probably the former; in these parts, where every nightclub bouncer is pumped up on steroids and manliness is highly prized, to be effete or cosseted is the worst insult of all. After all, as one local put it, Workington is a town where 'if you don't like Oasis you are classed as gay' and where the infamous local busker openly drinks petrol in the town square. With its redeveloped harbour and trendy Zest restaurant, which has played host to Tony and Cherie Blair, Whitehaven may be becoming dangerously cosmopolitan, though. I hope they had jam risotto.

The biggest town on this coast was a real mystery even to me. No one I asked had ever been there, even though at one point it was an industrial powerhouse, a huge naval and shipbuilding centre which attracted workers from all across Britain and the world. Now the world thinks of it as isolated, insular and partly abandoned; a hulking town cut off from the mainstream of life at the end of a peninsula where few ever venture. A place that even the locals refer to, thanks to an old Mike Harding routine, as 'stuck at the end of the A590, the longest cul de sac in Britain'.

Barrow-in-Furness is a bloody long way from anywhere. An hour from the nearest motorway, even further from the nearest city. That's a long way for Britain. As the BBC's Cumbria website puts it: 'To get a real understanding of the plight of the Barrovian, you should consider his geographical location. One of the most significant things about Barrow-in-Furness is that only the most hapless, dazed orienteer could possibly visit by accident – you have to have a purpose to get there.' I had just such a purpose. The purpose was Barrow.

Like Iran, this part of the northern coast was once a theocracy. During the Middle Ages it was ruled by the powerful monks of Furness Abbey, just outside modern Barrow. Back then the little fishing hamlet really was cut off, surrounded on three sides by water or the dangerous sands of the Duddon Estuary, and on the other pinned against the sea by the high fells of the Lake District. These days Barrow has adopted 'Where the mountains meet the sea' as a dreamy marketing slogan, gamely trying to make a virtue of what was once a curse.

Then in 1846, usual story, the Furness Railway was opened, connecting Barrow to the national network at Fleetwood, and the town boomed. Iron and steel brought prosperity and the population mushroomed. It wasn't a haphazard development. In America, planned communities are commonplace but Barrow is one of the very few in the United Kingdom, built on the grid system with long tree-lined avenues leading away from central squares. The architect of modern Barrow was one James Ramsden of the Furness Railway Company, who seems to have run the town almost as a fiefdom, owning the town hall, the railway, streets' worth of houses and sitting unopposed as mayor for years. You won't be surprised to hear that he had massive mutton-chop whiskers.

Ramsden, doubtless with his thumbs tucked into his waistcoat pockets, oversaw the building of the docks and the founding of Ramsden's Barrow Shipbuilding Company, which became Vickers in 1897. Barrow became Vickers' town, literally; they built an extension called just that on the adjacent Walney Island in the early twentieth century.

Through a turbulent twentieth century, war brought Barrow prosperity while it brought other cities hell. Barrow built the *Mikasa*, Japanese flagship of the Russo-Japanese War, and the aircraft carrier HMS *Invincible* and a fleet of other floating widow-makers. Later, Barrow became synonymous with submarines. The Royal Navy's first one, *Holland 1*, was built here in 1901, and newer ones such as HMS *Resolution* were developed in the 1960s. The Vanguard class submarines were all built in Barrow. In crowded billets and sweaty hammocks, beneath the inky waters of the world's oceans, Barrow built the sleek and deadly nuclear subs that the cold warriors criss-crossed the globe in.

They were never used in anger, thank God. The thaw at the end of the Cold War might have warmed most of us but it brought a chill to Barrow. There were over 20,000 workers at the shipyard at the start of the 1980s; just 3,000 in 2000. Barrow hasn't had much in the way of good press these last twenty years and, to cap it all, in 2002 it had the grim distinction of suffering the UK's worst outbreak of Legionnaires' disease. Seven people died and another 172 people got sick thanks to a faulty air-conditioning duct at the town's arts centre.

This might have put me in a downcast frame of mind as I made my way along that famous cul de sac, the A590, past Newby Bridge, Broughton and Ulverston, birthplace of Stan Laurel. But I was in a good mood. The sun was shining, the hills were green and sparkling. I had never been to Barrow before and I like adventures, however small. Besides, who can fail to have their spirits lifted by a herd of pink rhinoceroses and elephants pootling about by the side of a major arterial road?

The South Lakes Animal Park was the brainchild of an animal nutritionist called David Gill who runs a similar venture in Australia. You'll see him wandering around the park in a bush hat. From scratch and in an engagingly cranky home-made fashion, he's built what's generally regarded as Britain's best conservation park, a haven for wildlife from around the globe and undoubtedly the only place in the north-west where you're likely to spot a Hamadryas baboon or pygmy hippo or Sumatran tiger or marmoset from the window of your Mondeo as you negotiate a roundabout. Gill is apparently thinking of moving the zoo nearer to the M6 to placate visitors who arrive fractious from the A590 although local rumour has it that Gill just says this periodically to annoy the council. It would be a shame. Barrow folk are proud of the park and its high standing and it would be a shame if it went to some rich metropolitan playground like Witherslack or Ulverston.

Barrovians are proud folk generally, with a fierce sense of community fostered by its geographical isolation. 'It's like an island community, that's the nearest comparison,' says singer and songwriter Chris While, born and raised in Barrow. 'There's water on three sides and hills on the other and there's only one road in or out. So that makes for a fantastic sense of community. People know each other here and share things. In the sixties, some kids would go out to the Twisted Wheel in Manchester and come back and teach the others the new dances. It always felt a really safe and supportive place. Our MP was called Albert Booth and he would march with the CND supporters in the town. There was a sense of solidarity.'

Entering Barrow now, once you've got over the shock of the grazing pachyderms by the hard shoulder, you're struck by the contrasts. Wide, handsome streets and a majestic sandstone town hall alternate with the ubiquitous trappings of urban northern blight, the Golden Megatan with its promise of 180-watt sunbeds, the branches of Greggs, of course, and the drab pubs of which Healey's looks like a maximum security prison with its steel shutters and dearth of windows.

That's the sort of grim pleasure encampment you can find in any tough northern working-class town, though. In general, Barrow's pub life is vibrant though probably not for the faint-hearted. 'You can go out any night and find that the pubs are always hopping,' says Chris. 'I have a guitarist friend who's lived in LA and toured through Asia and he loves and still lives in Barrow because he knows he can stroll into certain pubs where there'll always be a couple of lads with guitars and a musician's culture.'

The flipside of this, though, is that Barrow has a reputation for looking in on itself. 'It is terribly insular,' admits Chris. 'Kids who leave to get an education often never come back once they've had their horizons expanded. It's like a Stephen King town in that respect. My brother thinks that going to Morecambe is like having a weekend ashore.'

If you visit Barrow's Dock Museum (and I really recommend you do) you'll find this very particular sense of place alluded to in what's surely the most candid display currently visible in a UK museum. You're greeted by a board bearing the legend 'It's Grim Up North' and listing some of the choice opinions expressed by locals and some of the received impressions of the town: 'a dump', 'a town doomed to die', 'the largest village in England'. The museum, though, cleverly points out that one person's insular conservatism is another's steadfast independence. Barrow was also known as the English Chicago during the nineteenth century, when it boomed thanks to shipping and steel, and the town was a babel of accents from every corner of Britain and beyond.

As the name suggests, the museum is built into an old dock. You can climb right down into it, stand dryshod where once you'd have been under thirty feet of icy water, and crane your neck at the high walls above you that are still drying out and streaked with green. There was something of an unscheduled distraction during my visit in that a small boy got stuck in the lift – I heard him tapping and moaning forlornly through the frosted glass – and I had to go and seek help from the museum staff. To complicate matters, the attendant vaguely recognised me from the telly and consequently put the rescue into effect with a distinct lack of urgency since he clearly thought it was all some awful Jeremy Beadle-style prank.

This didn't distract me from the opinion that the Dock Museum is really rather classily done. Beautiful scale models of ocean liners remind you that Barrow didn't just make warships and Trident subs but stylish, state-of-the-art floating hotels for the world's leisured elite. Chris While's dad built the bar on the *Oriana*, one of the legendary ships that left the Barrow yard. Many Barrovians can remember the dates of every big launch. They were red-letter days in the town and the kids were given the day off school.

Leaving the museum and walking along the waterfront – a rather quaint little mess of boats and netting in the shadow of the enormous BAE submarine 'yard' – you are at once buffeted by Barrow's legendary local winds. At Christmas 1929, a wind of 115 miles shook the town. Barrow's breeziness is enshrined in an old joke. Two men meet on a still, silent day in the middle of the desert. Both have their hands on their hats. One says to the other, 'Ah sees tha's from Barra as well.'

I'm taking the one road to Walney Island, a lateral spit of land accessed by a single bridge which still occasionally has to be raised to let large boats under. The fact the island only has one way in and out is apparently of major concern to the islanders in the event that, quote, 'there was a major incident'. I'm not sure what that incident would be. Maybe the whole island would get food poisoning from some dodgy lobster at the Chinese restaurant on the beach. Or maybe the sheer ugliness of it – it's built in a disused concrete seventies lido – could cause a mass panic attack. Personally if I were a Walney Islander, I wouldn't care. I'd be more tempted to hoist the bridge up and live here in splendid isolation, between the hills and the wild Irish Sea.

Generations of shipyard workers and their families have lived on Walney Island in Vickerstown, a custom-built estate whose very name reflects Barrow's status as a works town through and through. For many a year, Barrow's day was built around the mournful sound of the Vickers hooter, a muezzin call to work for the town's shipyard thousands. The hooter is long silent now but Barrow still makes ships. Vickers has changed its name more times than Cat Stevens, being at various times Vickers, VSEL, GEC Marine and BAE. But whoever's name is above the door, to the generations of Barrovians who've worked there, and the handful of the new generation who take apprenticeships there, it's 'The Yard', still launching vessels from the Cumbrian coast. Just.

If you ask the people of Barrow, they'll tell you defiantly that the town is on the up. Here on Walney Island, where Barrow meets the sea and where the locals come to enjoy the shingle and grass playground of Biggar Bank, there's talk of a new marina. They're investigating the possibility of an ex-Royal Navy submarine being permanently moored here as a tourist attraction to entice visiting Japanese tourists undersea and away from Beatrix Potter in Windermere. I can't wait. House prices are rising and the tireless local regeneration industry is trying its best to sell Barrow as a destination for luxury cruise ships. It sounds unlikely but you have to admire their conviction as they tell you that, 'Barrow-in-Furness, Britain's newest port of call for cruise liners, is the only deep water port between the Mersey and Clyde and provides instant access to the world famous English Lake District. There are many reasons why Barrow-in-Furness should be your next port of call.' Each year more ships dock at the town. Sneer if you will but it seems to be working.

There's one high-profile position being advertised while I'm in town: King of Piel Island. It's a teardrop-shaped chunk of land half a mile out to sea from modern Barrow and reached from the ferryhouse at Roa Island. There's no mains gas or electricity and communication is by ship-to-shore phone. But there are six cottages, habitable only in summer, a castle and a pub. To paraphrase *Le Morte d'Arthur*, whosoever pulleth the draught bitter from this pump at the Ship Inn shall be King of Piel Island.

It's all something to do with Lambert Simnel, pretender to the throne, who arrived there from Dublin on 4 June 1487 trying to pass himself off as Edward VI, King of England, in a sneaky Yorkist plot. The cheek! In Lancashire as well! Somehow this has become a tradition in which the landlord of the Ship Inn is the de facto King of Piel. But during my time in Barrow, the town was suffering its own abdication crisis. It's not as dramatic as that famous one where the Nazi playboy went off with the American bird. All that's happened here is that the landlord fancied a change of career after fourteen years. But that means that as I write, the pub is currently closed and undergoing refurbishment by the council. The Ship Inn needs a new genial host and Piel Island needs a new king. The Ship is a magnet for day-trippers, so with the pub closed, the ferry trade has collapsed. Understandably, the ferryman has applied to be the new landlord.

Piel Island's one irregular 'situation vacant' hasn't really helped Barrow's job market down the years. When the shipyards and steel mills laid people off, thousands of Barrow's workers went up the road in search of work. Literally. Up the very road I'm on now and, I have to tell you, this is a fabulous way to get to the office. As the road and, hopefully the car, hug the contours of the high shoreline, you'll see on your right that the spoilheaps are grassing over and turning green. On your left, though, is a panorama that will stop you mid-suck on your Murray Mint and have your nervous passenger grabbing the wheel and turning your slack jaw to face the road.

The sea fills the low sky westward and a glittering, serpentine arm insinuates its way up the warm, muddy thighs of the Duddon Sands. Behind is the vast whaleback bulk of Black Combe, forgotten giant of the Cumbrian mountains, where you'll walk all day and never see a soul. But your eye is drawn now beyond Black Combe to the distant splendour of the high fells of the Southern Lakes, a vast, rumpled duvet of smudgy blue retreating ridges lit by a watery sun. As a commute, it beats the Circle Line. Even if, some would say, you're off to stoke the pits of hell.

I remember a broadsheet cartoon from the mid eighties that made me chuckle. It was just after the Chernobyl disaster when the story was doing the rounds that Soviet nuclear power chiefs had asked Britain's advice in dealing with the devastated plant. Two white-coated British boffins are reporting back, and one is saying, 'We suggested that they change the name.' The sign on the door reads Sellafield.

The joke being that the world's oldest commercial nuclear power plant began life as Calder Hall, has bits called Magnox and Thorp and changed the name of its main site from Windscale to Sellafield in 1981. OK, so strictly the names apply to different sections but it all added to a perception that there was something sordid and shameful about the place, like a cheap conman with a roll-call of aliases.

Environmentalists and Irish pop stars have a very poor opinion of Sellafield. 'They' say it has become a dumping ground for the world's nuclear waste, which is true even if British Nuclear Fuels Limited dress it up as a 'reprocessing facility'. That waste, by the way, has to be kept away from people for 250,000 years, fifty times longer than the history of the written word. That's a long time. They also say that it accounts for the abnormally high rates of childhood leukaemia along this coast, though British Nuclear Fuels Limited dispute this. They say that it pumps radioactive waste into the Irish Sea, which certainly was true though arguably much less so today. They say that it can't be justified on the grounds of producing clean, non-fossil fuel energy because it doesn't. They're right: it ceased being a power plant in 2003. They say it's a target for a terrorist attack and an accident waiting to happen. That may be the case although that would also apply to most airports, chemical plants and gasometers. There's no two ways about it, though. However gung-ho you are about the place, you'd definitely be happier having a nice cake shop at the bottom of your garden.

The trouble is that when West Cumbria fell on hard times there just weren't enough cake shops looking to take on staff. Sellafield offered a lifeline to devastated communities. Life has been tough enough in Frizington and Barrow and Egremont and Dalton. Without Sellafield, it would have been hell. Sellafield employs 12,000 people in the region and its benefits extend further than this, boosting local service industries and infrastructure. A few years back, I stayed at a very good country house hotel not far inland from the plant nestling by the shores of England's deepest lake, the vast and gloomy Wastwater. On a Monday night, the place was respectably full with smart professional types, clearly not holidaymakers, chatting discreetly over the amuse-bouches. The next day I asked the proprietor what brought these sober industrialists in steel-rimmed specs to Nether Wasdale. 'Sellafield,' was the answer. 'We couldn't survive without it.'

Sellafield doesn't have to convince most West Cumbrians of its importance to their survival. Most will have a family member or a neighbour who either works there or whose job depends on it. But Sellafield knows it has an image problem. At best it's thought of as a necessary evil like septic tanks, maximum security prisons or ear wax. Most view it as a bafflingly enduring but unlovable relic of a bygone age, like Michael Portillo. And those who loathe it think of it as Hades-on-Sea.

So over the last twenty years or so Sellafield has doggedly fought the PR battle. You wouldn't exactly call it a charm offensive – they know that they're never going to make it an ideal destination for a romantic mini-break – but they have at least tried to soften its image. There's an award-winning visitors centre and on arrival at nearby Seascale station on the forlorn coastal branch line that somehow survived Beeching's axe, you should find a couple of courtesy cars waiting to drive you to it.

The centre is open every day of the year but, as I found, having snaked up the coast road behind a tractor, they do shut promptly at five. I got to the massive car park with half an hour to spare, which the smartly dressed ladies in reception clearly didn't think would be enough to fully appreciate its many delights. But I insisted. I think on the whole I was right.

It is a very impressive place: cavernous, ultra-modern and sexily lit, like a Bond villain's lair from which might come global destruction. Maybe not the best of looks for a nuclear plant, I suppose, but I was childishly taken by it. I half expected and secretly rather wanted, to find the place nakedly and unashamedly partisan in its zeal of nuclear power. I looked in vain

for giant figurines of Eileen the Isotope beaming her pale phos-
phorescence down on grateful kids or for posters showing horribly polluted industrial towns where bronchial children wheezed
while their mothers fought hand to hand over lumps of coal
under a slogan reading 'IS THIS WHAT YOU WANT?
BECAUSE THIS IS WHAT WILL HAPPEN! FOSSIL FUEL IS
FOR FOSSILS! EMBRACE NUCLEAR POWER OR DIE!'

There was none of this. Sellafield is more politically correct,
more wincingly guilt-ridden than a *Guardian* columnist defend-
ing her SUV and Umbrian holiday home. Text projections swim
across the floor, walls and ceiling offering competing opinions on
nuclear power, opinions couched in the most placatory, considered tone. 'Nuclear power, it's a bit worrying, isn't it? I don't
really know what to think.' 'Well, perhaps you're right to worry,
Sandra. But I'm sure it's all going to be all right. And after all,
those oil wells aren't going to last for ever, are they?'

OK, these aren't the actual messages. But they're like that.
It's all very civilised and really rather to Sellafield's credit. They
even have a display devoted to the history of anti-nuclear protest;
yellow smiley face badges saying 'Nuclear Power? No Thanks!',
copies of 'Two Tribes' by Frankie Goes To Hollywood, those
scary Protect And Survive videos and CND's response, Protest
And Survive. Sellafield is so relaxed and reasonable about criticism I half expected to see T-shirts in the gift shop saying 'MY
MUM WENT TO SELLAFIELD AND ALL I GOT WAS THIS
LOUSY DEFORMED AND EYELESS SECOND HEAD'.

There isn't really a gift shop but there are lots of feel-goody
things that could be in a gift shop or, more accurately, a nursery.
I have a theory – a fairly crabby one, I have to admit – that Britain
has become a filiocracy. We are increasingly ruled by children in
the sense that everything has to appeal to them or to those adults
that think like them. TV presenters, weathermen, priests; every

one of them talks to you like you're six. Pretty much everything at Sellafield is presented in this way. There are leaflets saying 'Be A Scientist For A Day!' featuring Dad and the kids with ridiculous Albert Einstein specs and moustache ensembles with their hair standing up. There's a sign advertising forthcoming events, obviously aimed at the little ones, that says 'Be A Human Bubble For A Day!' Personally I think Sellafield's PR material should avoid anything that even hints at freakish mutations but that's just my opinion.

At five on the dot I emerge from Sellafield into the deep honeyed light of a late spring afternoon and head north and inland away from the coast through the towns of West Cumbria that depend on Sellafield. Egremont, home of gurning. Cleator Moor where once they made Kangol hats. Frizington where Hunter Davies once asked a local what living there was like and he replied, 'Desperate.' That was in the blighted eighties, though, and maybe life is better now. There are St George's flags fluttering from windows in preparation for the World Cup, some kids and a dog are playing football in the park and the sun glints off a sign standing on the pavement outside the grocers. I squint at it.

It reads 'No Pies Today'. Desperate indeed. And so I leave Cumbria on the Silk Cut Road to the Far East.

The Great North

Sorry, I didn't quite catch that?

Am I a true northerner? I beg your pardon, Tarquin? Perhaps you'd like to ask me that question again in the car park. I'm sure Sebastian here will hold your blazer and your spritzer…

Sorry. Red mist. Conforming to all regional stereotypes, I know. But the cheek. Am I a true northerner? Of course I am. I like pies. I am childishly pleased when Chelsea, Fulham and Arsenal lose. I say 'bath' and 'care' properly. I have my dinner at dinnertime and my supper in my dressing gown. But in my quieter moments, when the fire is guttering and the last dram of the evening has slipped down, I am plagued by doubts. Dark memories return unbidden and with them a sudden chill.

It's the early 1980s and I'm in the college bar one Friday night. My mate Stod from Gateshead enters with two of his friends from home, who are visiting for the weekend. After introductions, one of them hands me a pint and cheerily engages me in conversation. Or rather, tries to.

'Haddaway yous and Newky Broon divna gannin wor marra.'

Pardon?

'Howay the tabs bonnie lad wor Jackie Milburn.'

Sorry?

'Clarty South Shields hinny wor high level bridge down the netty, pet.'

Or something like that. Basically, I can't understand a word he's saying. No, that's not true. I can grasp the odd word here and there, as a drowning man might clutch at a bit of driftwood. But the overall sensation is a torrent of alien sound. It's like listening to a kind of Norse Doppler effect; stretched vowels, random emphasis and arcane dialect flow from his mouth and right over the top of my head. I feel acutely uncomfortable. This is the sort of difficulty an effete fop from Purley or Esher would have but not a kindred spirit. Stod notices my difficulty and starts to translate. All seem amused. I'm mortified and I say so. After all, we're all northern brethren here. A small bout of genial scoffing ensues. 'Nah, bonnie lad, divn't say yor from the north. Yor from the Midlands alreet.'

Lancashire? The Midlands? But this is a cast of mind that these far northerners often take, Cumbrians, Teessiders and Geordies alike. Some even speak of the Great North as in Great North Road and Great North Run. The Great North is England north of Yorkshire and Lancashire, which may look lonely, wild and empty in parts but has a greater population than Wales. They will tell you that the north-east is the real England, that the very word England derives from 'land of the angles' or the north-east. They will tell you that they are Vikings and the rest of us are suburbanites.

The north-east is the bit of the north that I don't really know. Basically it's a long way away – one of the things Philip Larkin loved about it – and it's not on the way to anywhere except Berwick or Oslo via slow boat. If Larkin were alive today, he'd find that thanks to the staggeringly improved East Coast Main Line, he could have breakfast in Hull and still make it to the capital for a bloody good lunch at Claridges with Kingsley Amis. He probably wouldn't have bothered, though. In that, he'd have a lot in common with his adopted kinsmen of the east. They love that East Coast Main Line, not for how quickly it can get them to London but for how fast it gets them back to the north-east. Back to its two and a half million people, its five universities, two major ports, two international airports, and vibrant cities and towns including Darlington, Durham, Middlesbrough, Newcastle and Sunderland, all of which any self-respecting member of the North-East Regional Development Council will tell you about at the drop of a massive Andy Capp-style cloth cap. But for all that they're fiercely proud of their region, Geordies don't display the bellicose mouthiness of the Manc or that garrulous over-confidence of the Scouser. This is why Geordies are the southerners' favourite northerner.

They even sound lovely, while having by far and away the strangest accent in England. It has more to do with the speech patterns of medieval Denmark than modern Didcot, more Eric Bloodaxe than Enid Blyton. In the middle of quite ordinary words like 'market', 'talkative' or 'university', the vowels will 'wow and flutter' as if someone had stopped a vinyl record with a finger and then let it go again. J. B. Priestley hated it, called it 'the most barbarous, irritating and monotonous twang ... and the never-ending "hinnying" of the women seems to me equally objectionable.'

But in this he seems to be completely alone. Major organisations like Orange have rushed to set up call centres here, realising that most callers find the accent warm, friendly and helpful. The Samaritans love Geordie volunteers because their down-to-earth but quietly reassuring tones are proven to turn people's minds away from the gas oven and tablets. For all its alien ring, this fine tongue doesn't sound as disagreeably blunt and aggressive to the people of the Home Counties as the rest of us northerners. Britain has been conditioned via Ant and Dec, James Bolam and Rodney Bewes, Vic and Bob, Steve Cram and Brendan Foster, Kevin Whately and Jimmy Nail, Chris Waddle and Gazza, to think of Geordies as kindly, funny, roguish, tough but not nasty, bluff but warm. They're a long way away, you see, so you're less likely to have one demand a cigarette with menace outside Soho House and thus they are sweet and charming and exotic. Everyone loves Geordies.

Sometimes, though, this benign mask of tolerance slips. Writing in the *Spectator* in 2004, one Rod Liddle wrote a sneering bit of fluff attacking north-easterners. He recounted a story from his time at the BBC when a Newcastle woman was harangued in the supermarket queue by some busybody from Radio 4's *Today* programme, which he edited. Her basket, apparently, didn't meet with the *Today* programme's approval as it had some unhealthy food in it. 'But I don't like healthy food. I like unhealthy food,' she said. This perfectly reasonable remark was seized on by Liddle – no stranger to the family-sized sausage roll himself, by the look of him – as evidence that north-easterners were, quote, 'monkeys' and 'morons'.

Behind the soft soap and patronising cant, here is the real face of the metropolitan Uncle Tom (Liddle was brought up in North Yorkshire); frightened, insecure, a snob. Worse still was the wheedling excuse offered by Stuart Reed, the magazine's deputy editor, claiming disingenuously that 'Rod Liddle's piece has an element of satire about it'. He went on pleadingly, 'We actually admire the common sense of Geordies and think they are far bigger in spirit and have a better sense of humour than to let this type of thing bother them too much.' In other words, it's the Geordies' fault if they can't rise above this glib, unfunny public-school put-down, which was actually some ironic meta-textual thing that they weren't bright enough to get.

Geordies really are big in spirit and humour. A lot of the time, though, they aren't actually Geordies. For instance, Vic Reeves and Bob Mortimer are from Darlington and Middlesbrough. The narrator from *Big Brother*, maybe the most famous 'Geordie' currently on British TV, is actually from Stockton-on-Tees. Most bitter-sweet of all, *Whatever Happened to the Likely Lads*, the finest evocation of Geordie life and for me the best British comedy series ever, is almost Geordie-free. James Bolam is from Sunderland, Rodney Bewes is a Yorkshireman. Even Brigit Forsyth, the lovely Thelma, is from Edinburgh.

The Great North is riven with factionalism. Tribes proliferate, they lurk in every corner, they give each other odd, colourful, mildly disparaging names. There's Geordie, of course, and then Mackem and Sand Dancer, which are themselves quite prosaic next to Monkey Hanger, Pit Yacker and Smog Monster. Let's begin with the most intense bit of tribal rivalry, the one between Newcastle and Sunderland or Geordie and Mackem. It's now chiefly football-related but it goes back centuries. Back to when a midfield general really was a general in the middle of a field and all police leave was regularly cancelled for those fierce local derbies between the Cavaliers and the Roundheads.

In 1642, before the Civil War had kicked off in earnest, King Charles I awarded all east of England coal trading rights to the merchants of Newcastle. This gave them a monopoly on coal, and the rest of us a proverb on the futility of taking coals to Newcastle. It also put their counterparts in Sunderland out of business.

Perhaps in gratitude, Newcastle and most of the north-east supported the King during the Civil War with the sole exception of Sunderland, which acted as a supply base for the Scottish army, also siding with Cromwell. Two years later when Newcastle was attacked by the Scots, Sunderland helped the Jocks and it was a combined Scottish/Mackem army which defeated the forces of Newcastle and County Durham at the Battle of Boldon Hill. Newcastle was subsequently captured by the Scottish with Sunderland's help. Keen as I am on football, that certainly beats a disputed offside decision as a way to start a rivalry.

Make no mistake, though, football is a very big deal here and has been for a long, long time. In 1290 the first recorded mention of football hereabouts concerns a man who was killed at a match near Morpeth. The north-east still regards itself with some justification as the football heartland of Britain, the breeding ground of most of our finest talent through different eras and styles, from Wilf Mannion's widow's peak to the Brylcreemed Jackie Milburn through Chris Waddle's disastrous mullet to Gazza's thuggish number one.

While there's some truth in this, cynics from the rest of the north will often chunter into their half-time Bovril about Newcastle United's absurdly inflated sense of self-importance. This is a team, after all, who haven't won a domestic trophy for half a century and have spent the GNP of several African states in the not winning of anything. According to the 'Toon Army', the self-mythologising name they've given themselves, Newcastle United are a 'massive club'. You hear this time and time again and frankly no one outside the NE postcode seems to know what that means. It seems to mean, as it does with Manchester City, 'used to be quite good'.

If, as those cynics suggest, there is monumental self-delusion at work here, it gets stoked regularly. Chairman Freddy Shepherd's claim that the Newcastle job is 'one of the biggest in world football' shows a loyalty to the club somewhat undermined by his comments that Geordie women football fans were 'dogs'. Former Magpies striker Micky Quinn once claimed that 'Newcastle is a bigger job than England', which is the football equivalent of saying that the horn section of Dexys Midnight Runners are controlling the weather through people's televisions. Geordies may be everyone's favourite northerners but a sneaking resentment of the Magpies is fermenting of late. You may be wondering, though, why I haven't mentioned Tony Blair's infamous 'lie' about watching Jackie Milburn from the

Gallowgate End (he would have been four at the time and living in Australia). Well, if he'd said it, it certainly would have been as grievous an untruth as any about Saddam's weapons of mass destruction. But he didn't say it. He said that he became a supporter 'after Jackie Milburn' and it was twisted by Tory columnists. From the south of England, naturally.

My theory is that this exaggerated self-belief comes from the fact that Newcastle is a big city with only one football club. In Manchester, Sheffield, Glasgow, Liverpool, Bristol, Nottingham and even Northwich, there's a healthy competition and a sense of balance. Everyone in Newcastle supports the Magpies with a unity of purpose that borders on mass hysteria and conveniently forgets that in 1991, when Newcastle were in the old Second Division, average gates slumped to 16,000. They say 'sleeping giant', others say 'dormant under-achievers'.

All of the above would be echoed to the rafters by their nearest rivals in Sunderland, still smarting from all that coal shenanigans and the memory of skewering each other with pikestaffs several centuries ago. My boss at Radio 2, controller Lesley Douglas, is a Geordie who supports Sunderland due to family history and is by her own admission: 'Not rare – unique. This isn't a friendly local rivalry. It's hatred. The derby game is more important than the rest of the fixtures put together.'

Sunderland, too, has a great football tradition though the team's glory days are even more distant than the Magpies'. They won the FA Cup in 1973 and their manager Bob Stokoe did a funny little dance in a trilby and a flasher's mac that was definitely not Armani. But their halcyon days are as far away as the 1930s when Roker Park roared on Wilf Mannion and Len Shackleton, the 'Clown Prince of Football' who endeared himself to the Mackems by once saying, 'I'm not biased against Newcastle – I don't care who beats them!'

That phrase Mackem is derived from the terms 'mack 'em' and 'tack 'em', dating from the early shipbuilding industry. The folks on Wearside were said to 'mak[e] them' and other people 'tak[e] them' and it began as an insult to the people of Sunderland by the more affluent, canny Geordies. Like many a term of abuse, though, the people of Sunderland have reclaimed the name to be worn as a badge of Wearsiders. If you really want to annoy a Mackem, call them a 'Plastic Geordie' as the Teessiders do, meaning that they sound like Geordies but they're not quite the real thing.

As for 'Geordie', it's the local variant of 'Georgie' or 'George', and there are a couple of explanations as to how it came to mean a Tynesider. One holds that it refers to Newcastle's support for George II during the 1745 Jacobite Rebellion or maybe even of George I during the 1715 Jacobite Rebellion. It's easy to lose track of those Jacobite rebellions. Or they may have got the name from Sir George Stephenson (of 'Rocket' steam train fame) due to local miners' preference for his lamp rather than the safety lamp of Sir Humphrey Davy. I quite like the idea that here in the twenty-first century we still refer to the natives of one of our major cities because of competing fashion trends in underground helmet illumination two hundred and odd years ago. Purists say that a person must be born within the sight of the River Tyne to be a Geordie but a more relaxed definition includes anyone born within the area from Wylam in the west through Newcastle to Tynemouth in the east.

Over the last few years, the rivalry has taken on a new dimension thanks to wildly differing perceptions of the two cities (yes, Sunderland became one in 1991). Newcastle, like Leeds, has acquired a definite air of cool and an already striking city has blossomed, as I'm to find out. News has even reached the salons of London. But Sunderland hasn't had a decent press in years.

That's not entirely fair on the city; some of its failings may just be failings of PR. But there's no getting away from the fact that Sunderland's story was for many years a gloomy one.

In 1834 the yards of the Wear produced more ships than all Britain's other shipyards combined. Sunderland was the largest shipbuilding town in the world. For decades the story was one of continual, unstoppable boom. Sunderland shouldered the burdens of war manfully, producing one and a half million tons of shipping during World War Two. Generations of Wearsiders worked in those yards. The sea and its craft defined the town.

By the 1950s, though, orders for ships were falling. Mass-produced ships from Japan and Korea were cheaper and quicker to acquire than the bespoke one-offs of the Sunderland yards. Over thirty dismal years, the yards of the Wear closed one by one. Finally on 12 December 1988, the last ship built here was launched with little fanfare, a workaday ferry called *Superflex November*. Six hundred years of shipbuilding on the Wear came to an end. The giant yards of Docksford are now silent as cathedrals. There is something ineffably sad about an island race having to buy its ships, no longer having the wherewithal to make the boats to leave its own shores. No, I'd go further than sad. I think it's humiliating. But I'm not sure whose fault it is.

If you want a more upbeat view of the region, you should talk to 'Sunderland arc'. They're a 'public-interest, private company with the objective of delivering the regeneration of Wearside … charged with the task of improving Sunderland's economy, infrastructure and quality of life and the creation of a thriving city centre'. You can tell that they're a modern consultancy by the fact that they've forgotten that the word 'arc' in the title should have a capital a.

'Sunderland arc' are doing their bit in a buzz-wordy, power-pointy, send-out-for-sushi Shoreditch-y kind of way (except no

one in Sunderland ever bought a motorised scooter, even ironically). There is a kind of pleasing irony, though, in the fact that
the most powerful and practical jump-start for the people of the
Wear came from the land of the Rising Yen; the very nation
whose cheap mass-production techniques did for Sunderland's
shipwrights.

While I was touring the north-east for this book, Sunderland
was gearing up quietly for a significant anniversary. It was soon
to be twenty years since the first car rolled off the line at Nissan
Sunderland. It was a white Nissan Bluebird. You can see it on
display in the Sunderland Museum and Winter Gardens. It's not
a terribly pretty sight – in fact it's been described as 'the least
attractive car in any British museum'. But that's not the point.
The point is that it was made in Sunderland with pride, reversing
a tide of decline on Wearside for over three decades.

The plant's location isn't conventionally pretty, stuck in a
triangle formed by the A19, the A1231 Sunderland Highway,
and the busy Washington Road. But with a little Japanese
elegance of mind, conservation areas have been developed;
ponds, lakes and woodland, oases of calm. Greener still, in 2005,
six second-hand 200-foot wind turbines were installed smack in
the middle of the site with the expectation of meeting seven per
cent of the plant's overall power needs through wind power and
reducing 100,000 tonnes of carbon dioxide emissions per year.

That first boxy little white car – built on a belt while the
factory transistor crackled to 'Ooh' Gary Davies playing Five
Star, I'll bet – has been followed by 4.3 million others thanks to
a total investment of £2.3 billion. Nissan Sunderland has been
Europe's most efficient car factory for the last eight years. It's
well ahead of its nearest rivals, General Motors' Opel plant in
Eisenach, Germany, Italy's Melfi Fiat factory and the Volkswagen
factory in Navarra. If only Sunderland FC were as formidable in

Europe against Italian, Spanish and German competition, there'd be dancing in the streets of Ryhope.

This success has been built in part on the application of some very Japanese philosophies. Through the doctrine of Kaizen or 'Continuous Improvement', Nissan encourages everyone to make changes in their working environment, no matter how small, in order to make it more productive or workable. That can mean introducing moving platforms so that assembly line workers don't have to walk alongside the car. Or it could mean just storing the Swarfega at head height. Every department has its own Kaizen team.

The JIT or Just In Time philosophy encourages the use of the minimum amount of resources (space, time, material, workers) necessary to add value to a product, while in accordance with the principle of Job Rotation, each worker is competent in at least three different jobs and at least three people are capable of doing each job. In theory, the factory doesn't worry about absence cover; the worker doesn't get bored.

For a nation whose industrial relations tradition often consisted of bricking the boss's Mercedes or burly shop stewards being manhandled into Black Marias, this talk of quiet co-operation and the application of philosophy is rather strange. But just as Skelmersdale people are slow to mock the TM community, Sunderland has embraced their occidental way. East meets east along the Wear, with the philosophies of the Orient applied in the heart of Mackemland. I don't know whether this has led to a boom in sushi bars in Easington or a run on kimonos in Matalan but Sunderland has a lot of reasons to thank Mister Nissan.

His plant thrums with industry, then, though the shipyards are barren and silent. Sunderland's once-proud ships are now being scrapped, which itself has raised a contentious issue for the north-eastern coast. Shipbreaking is in its own way as painstaking as shipbuilding, particularly if you're going to do it right and not contaminate the seashore with oil, wreckage and radioactive crap. Six hundred ships are broken every year, most in Bangladesh, Pakistan, India and China and broken in a way that endangers nature and worker alike. By 2010, there'll be 3,000 ships needing to be scrapped. We can't keep on dumping them on the coast of developing countries. So in November 2003, four giant US warships from the NATO ghost fleet in Virginia were towed into Hartlepool, some twenty miles down the coast, to be expertly dismantled.

They're still there; huge eerie rotting hulks dominating the waterfront. Ships that were once state of the art, our bulwark against the armed might of the Soviet Union, now languish in the maritime equivalent of the knackers yard, waiting for a knacker that never comes. That should be Able UK. They're the company who have won the contract to break the ships but who have been blocked by environmental groups. Greenpeace approve of the ship-breaking, but not Friends of the Earth. They say the ships are toxic and can't be broken in the water and that building a dry dock will ruin a seal breeding ground. And so the ships have rotted and rusted in Hartlepool ever since, the wards of a legal battle as tortuous and slow-moving as Dickens's Jarndyce v Jarndyce.

As we've detoured to Hartlepool, I should mention that the people hereabouts are known as Monkey Hangers though Hartlepool folk themselves are more than a little ambivalent about the term. The story goes that during the Napoleonic Wars, a French ship called the *Chasse-Marée* was wrecked on the coast at Hartlepool. There were no survivors with the exception of a lone monkey wearing a French sailor's uniform; presumably the poor creature having been dressed up to amuse those on ship. Having never seen either a monkey or a Frenchman, the simple locals assumed the monkey was a French spy, an impression compounded by his simian jabbering. The animal was thus sentenced to death and hung from the mast of a fishing boat.

Some in Hartlepool see the funny side of all this. Despite the obvious implication that they are sadistic peasants, the football team Hartlepool United now have a mascot called 'H'Angus the Monkey'. 'H'Angus the Monkey' stood for election as Mayor of Hartlepool in 2002 and the person inside the monkey suit squeaked in on a protest vote, though he later had to back down on an election promise to give all schoolchildren free bananas. The monkey has even got his own statue down at the pretty new marina and is sometimes incorporated into events at the Hartlepool Maritime Experience. A word of warning, though; there are just as many Hartlepool folk who find the term Monkey Hanger insulting and you may find yourself on the receiving end of some robust physical punishment of your own without recourse to even a basic trial on the beach. While we're about it, I'd watch what you're saying just down the coast in Redcar, a tough, grimy seaside town that's reputed to be one of Britain's prime spots to get beaten up in. Even Redcar is trying to clean up its act these days, though. With its big empty beaches and ferocious North Sea winds, it's perfect for the new extreme sport of kitesurfing and a little enclave of enthusiasts is becoming established in the town. You can even see the odd porpoise basking in water that once had a scum of petrol.

Long before Lycra-clad dudes in dreadlocks came to Redcar, this stretch of coast took its fun seriously. In the years before the coming of the package holiday, Geordie, Mackem and Monkey Hanger alike would spend their summers sucking sticks of rock in South Shields, surely one of the few mining seaside resorts in Britain and a kind of Castleford on Sea. South Shields may never give the Cancun tourist board any sleepless nights but the largest town in South Tyneside has its admirers and its delights. Radio 2 controller Lesley Douglas was one of many north-easterners I spoke to who said South Shields had the best fish and chips in England, though I found the absence of steak puddings demoralising. But there's nothing like eating piping hot battered cod yards from its harvesting grounds. Please don't tell me it comes from Netto.

South Shields is the home town of Eric Idle and Ridley Scott but the town's modest reputation as tourist destination these days is largely thanks to having skilfully marketed itself as Catherine Cookson country. Catherine was for many years the most borrowed author from British libraries (it's probably Jordan now) and every year South Shields gets thousands of visitors keen to see where she was born and raised. They're all devotees of her many books or, uncharitably, her many variations of the same book in which a decent Geordie scullery maid is impregnated by her handsome blackguard of a master but triumphs over adversity to become the owner of Jesmond's first 24-hour haberdashery. Catherine was never rated by the literary elite, a criticism she bore stoically as she dined on swan pasties and Château Lafite-Rothschild 1947 in her castle made of emeralds.

Cookson cultists come to the town in their droves. You can do the Cookson trail or even be driven around South Shields on a bus that passes Cookson's birthplace, her former home, the church she attended and then goes on to take in the really exciting stuff for the modern tourist: the locations used in the filming of the highly acclaimed television adaptations of the Cookson novels, like *The Fifteen Streets*, *The Gambling Man*, *The Dwelling Place*, *The Tide of Life* and *The Girl*. Then they eat chips on the seafront, then they go on the dodgems and then they're sick. A perfect day out, I'd have thought.

South Shields has a lot of real history as well as the ersatz variety. Zeppelins raided the Tyne in World War One and the town's seafront amusement park was attacked. Not exactly the Ruhr Dam in terms of strategic importance but maybe the Boche thought that taking out the coconut shy would be a devastating blow to Blighty's morale. More seriously, during World War Two South Shields suffered well over 200 air raids from parachute mines and incendiary bombs and 156 people were killed. One direct hit on the marketplace killed more than forty people sheltering in tunnels below the square. These are statistics to remember next time you watch a programme about the Blitz. It will be about London as always and feature Piccadilly Circus in flames and cheery Cockneys making their way to Tube stations. If you trusted the London media you could be forgiven for thinking that the south won the war single-handed and that northern England was as quiet as Switzerland. It wasn't, as the people in South Shields will testify.

South Shields also has the dubious distinction of hosting Britain's first modern race riot. At the time of the First World War, Yemeni sailors from the British protectorate of Aden flocked here at the encouragement of the government to man the merchant fleet left short-handed by local sailors going off to fight. A small community was established in the Holborn area of town, with its cafés and boarding houses ringing with strange Arab accents and music. The Mill Dam area was thronged each day with these exotic new incomers. It was the largest Yemeni community outside of Yemen.

There'd always been some unease in the town about the influx and this grew worse at the end of the war when returning local seamen found Arab sailors had occupied the vacant jobs. The year 1919 saw the first serious street violence and racial unrest with attacks on the Arab boarding houses and cafés. Through the twenties, you can trace the scent of simmering discontent through the letters page of the local paper. It wasn't just their jobs that the local men felt were under threat; one irate correspondent said, 'These Arabs pick the prettiest girls and the ugly ducklings are left for the white man.'

Popular feeling in the town had turned against the Yemenis; rumours had long circulated around the town that the Arabs used bribery to get work on the ships thus 'robbing' white seamen of jobs. On 2 August 1930, South Shields gained national notoriety after the so-called 'Arab Riot' at Mill Dam on the quay. A mob of white seamen began by roaming the waterfront looking for Arabs and foreigners to attack. A large police presence was drafted in as tension mounted. Around noon, four white men were hired for the steamer *Etheralda*. Ali Hamid, a jobless Yemeni, was heard to shout, 'They work, but there is no work for the black man.'

No one is quite sure if it was this rather mild remark that sparked the resulting trouble but there was soon furious fighting between a group of white seamen and the Arab crowds. Police drew truncheons and charged, only to be met by a hail of stones. Some Arab men drew knives, stabbing four policemen. The riot spilled over into nearby Holborn, injuring dozens of innocent bystanders.

On Monday morning, the public gallery in the Magistrates Court was packed and a crowd of over 1,000 waited outside. Six white men and twenty Arabs were brought from the cells and accused of causing an affray or riot and a collection of knives, sticks, chair legs and other weapons was displayed. All were released on bail of £10 each. With no work and opinion in the town now against them, the Arab community suffered immediately and grievously. Scores were admitted to Harton Workhouse. A hundred innocent Yemenis not implicated in the riots were deported. On 20 November, after a two-day trial at Durham Assizes, all the Arab defendants were given sentences of hard labour, ranging from three to sixteen months. After serving their sentences they too were deported.

These days in South Shields, you'll meet your share of Geordie Ahmeds and Tommy Al-Nazas, little men with thick Tyneside brogues, dark eyes and cinnamon skin. Problematically, South Shields folks are still known in the area as Sand Dancers, a term deriving both from the splendid beaches and an old slur on the Yemeni population. Sand dancing as practised by Wilson, Keppel and Betty was a music-hall amusement act that parodied and caricatured Egyptian and Arab culture and these days describing a South Shields resident as such is rightly considered mildly offensive. Peter Hitchens would call it political correctness gone mad and so I heartily encourage him to get up to South Shields and call someone a Sand Dancer. Then he can have a riot of his own. The sons and daughters of those Yemeni seamen still form a proud enclave in the local community. In the Second World War, 4,000 Tyneside seamen were lost; 800 were Yemeni Arabs.

For many years South Tyneside had the highest unemployment rate in mainland Britain, but between December 2002 and June 2004 unemployment fell by twenty-four per cent, the eighth best performance out of the twenty-three local authorities in north-east England. With the ships and the mines gone, the town today relies largely on service industries, leisure and retail. It's a commuter town too with many residents travelling daily to work in Sunderland, Gateshead and to where eventually all journeys in the Great North will bring you – Nyurcassle upon Tyne. That's the proper pronunciation and the full title. With all due respect to the one under Lyme, the suffix is never necessary.

I felt well disposed towards Newcastle from the moment I booked my hotel room. I was in a hotel myself at the time, actually, a boxy broom cupboard in Kensington courtesy of the BBC. It was the sort of hotel room where you could swing a cat but it would definitely end up concussed, either when it hit the bracket above the wardrobe where the eleven-inch TV was mounted or possibly via a glancing blow to the temple off the trouser press. We had been filming all day, stopping and starting for pneumatic drills, low-flying aircraft, shouting nutters, sirens, Tube trains, the acoustic furniture of London life. The sort of thing *Time Out* would describe as 'edgy', maybe because it makes you feel so on edge you want to swing a cat in your hotel room.

My shoulders unknotted as I spoke to Kirsty at the Vermont Hotel, Newcastle. She had that warm, slightly concerned, vaguely cheeky Geordie lilt to her voice, and the effect was like an ice-cold bottle of Newcastle Brown rolled damply across the forehead. How wrong was J. B. Priestley? At once, the logic of all those executive relocation decisions became apparent. If you had to hear that your train to Bournemouth had been cancelled or that your overdraft limit had been exceeded, you'd want Kirsty to break it to you. The Samaritans were right as well. In extremis, I reckon Kirsty could get your head out of the gas oven too. 'It's very noisy where you are,' she said, as I struggled to make myself heard above the banshee whoop of a Black Maria heading for Shepherd's Bush. I'm in London, I replied. 'Well, your room's booked, Mr Maconie. So you come up to us and have a nice relaxing time in Nyurcassle.'

I put the receiver down gently. I wanted to check out of Room 1109 of the Hilton Kensington that very moment and, pausing briefly to hand back the plastic key card that had never worked properly, trot through twilit Holland Park, left at Bayswater, through St John's Wood to Islington and onto the Holloway Road, all the time quickening my pace, knowing that I now had the A1, the Great North Road, that legendary ribbon of asphalt beneath my feet; onward through Barnet, Potters Bar, Hatfield, Stevenage and Baldock. As dawn broke over

Biggleswade, I would stride the empty miles, my mind fixed only upon Grantham, Newark-on-Trent, Retford, Bawtry, Doncaster, Garforth, Wetherby, Knaresborough, Boroughbridge, Darlington and eventually the fabled Scotch Corner where I would buy a Cup-a-Soup for a passing lorry driver and be delivered at last into silent, sleeping Newcastle and the Vermont Hotel where I'm sure Kirsty had left a chocolate waiting for me on my pillow.

In the end, I waited a week or two and did it by car. If I'd been coming from London I'd have gone by train, since the East Coast Main Line is one of the few unalloyed public transport triumphs in British history, but I came to Newcastle along Hadrian's Wall which, respect due to the Great North Road, is surely the connoisseur's way. But as Hadrian's Wall is the end of the north and as neat a place to finish my ramblings as an artificial earthwork built by an exiled Italian can be, you'll forgive me if we return there in a while. We are, after all, in a rush to get to Newcastle and Kirsty.

Because of the Jarrow March and *When the Boat Comes In* and *Auf Wiedersehen, Pet* and Terry Collier and maybe even, for those handful who remember it, Harry Enfield's Bugger-All-Money, impoverished Geordie counterpart of Thatcherite plasterer Loadsamoney, because of all these things, Newcastle and poverty go together in the British imagination like Liverpool and thievery or Tunbridge Wells and disgust. But when I Googled for 'Newcastle' and 'poverty', hoping to unearth some relevant statistics, all I found were site after site encouraging Geordies to 'Make Poverty History' in Africa and calling for the cancellation of Third World Debt. The north-east, it seems, is too busy helping the world's unfortunates to stop and consider itself poor.

Why should it? Economic growth in the north-east currently exceeds that of London and the south-east and is higher than the national average. The north-east of England has seen year-on-year reductions in unemployment levels since the turn of the century. Since 2000, unemployment has fallen from 108,000 to 64,000. Joblessness in the region is falling faster than anywhere else in the UK. There will not be another Jarrow March any time soon. It's much more likely that Luton will march north.

Denton Burn, though, looked just as drab and uninviting as the outskirts of Luton or Leicester or Liverpool, its streets crowded with all the characterless and ubiquitous furniture of modern urban Britain, the tanning salons, the badly spelt pizza takeaways and mobile phone shops. It could have been anywhere. It could have been Kentucky or Duluth or even Hyderabad, once you take the Westgate Road into the Asian enclave of Benwell Grove.

Here the shops become more exotic: halal butchers and sari shops with windows that are riots of turquoise and peach. There are scores of video stores. Each is festooned with huge posters of implausibly handsome men and hauntingly beautiful women advertising four-hour films where people launch effortlessly into a song and dance number in between snogging on a yacht and assassinating a drug baron. The accent becomes even more outlandish and wonderful than the original Geordie here, the why-ayes and howays now seasoned with spicy dollops of Farsi, Kurdish and Urdu.

Dropping down into the city this way, you don't really see how handsome it is until you're right in the middle of it. Another advantage of coming here by train is that you arch across the Tyne via one of the famous bridges, of which more soon. We sort of sneak in the back way and end up by the remains of the old wooden castle that burned down – unsurprisingly – and prompted the building of a 'new castle'. True to its name, Newcastle has been building them since 1080.

The Vermont Hotel towers like a Gotham City office-block cut into the quayside and overlooking the wide river. As I'm doing all that vital but quotidian stuff at reception about papers and alarm calls and breakfast, a pretty blonde girl emerges smiling from 'backstage'.

'Ah, so you made it. Welcome to Nyurcassle. Colin will show you to your room, and –' She leans in conspiratorially '– we've upgraded you to a suite.' I think Kirsty may be slightly too good to be true. So do you by now, I imagine. But she isn't.

It's dusk and the view from the room is fabulous. Colin, who runs Kirsty a close second in the helpfulness stakes if not the prettiness, tells us that this is the way to see the riverside and its dazzling new acquisitions, the Baltic and Sage buildings, i.e. by night when the sun goes down over Gateshead and the bars begin to twinkle and the Sage resembles a translucent shell of lambent light rather than, as Colin puts it, 'a load of old mirrors'. He joins me at the window and describes with an outstretched arm a walk that will take in the new glories of the Tyne. But that's for tomorrow. Tonight there are other delights of the Toon to experience. Less sophisticated, less aesthetically pleasing, perhaps. But as strong a current in Newcastle's cultural bloodstream as any arts centre, however translucent.

The Bigg Market isn't that big and it isn't really a market, though you can get fruit and veg here three times a week. 'Bigg' is a type of barley that used to be grown locally and sold in this part of the city in the eighteenth and nineteenth centuries. Come to think of it, there's still a hell of a lot of barley sold here in 2006 but mixed with water and hops, fermented and consumed by the pint until the vendee becomes aggressive, morose or nauseous.

The Bigg Market is Newcastle's party quarter, its Reeperbahn, its Golden Mile, its Sunset Strip. It's not much more than a street really and quite pretty in the day but by night and at weekends a gladiatorial arena devoted to orgiastic alcoholic consumption, moral licentiousness and sexual excess. I counted seventeen pubs so you can have a truly brain-scrambling pub crawl without walking more than a hundred yards. On Friday and Saturday, this nondescript little street is awash with premium lagers, Breezers, Archers and Aftershocks as well as blood, urine, vomit and other nameless fluids.

The Rough Guide to England describes the place as 'the largest cattle market in Western Europe'. That seems harsh to me and more than a little insulting to its clientele, however bovine. But I find it hard to get partisan about the Bigg Market. I feel about it a bit like I feel about that other rambunctiously northern playground, Blackpool. I'll defend it to London trendies, whose idea of a good night out is drinking a small bottle of wheat beer in a basement bar modelled ironically on a seventies living room, but I wouldn't want to spend my free time there. Neither does a great deal of Newcastle, preferring to hang out on the Quayside or neighbouring Collingwood Street. But if an unpretentious piss-up – and possibly a fight and a knee-trembler behind SupaSnaps is what you're after – make haste there.

On a cold Thursday in February, it felt distinctly desolate. None of the bars were full and most were showing FA Cup replays on big tellies to prematurely middle-aged men who truly were 'drinking in the last-chance saloon'. The clubby bars with their DJs and little dance floors looked no more appetising, really. The Pig and Whistle boasted 'years of party tradition' but seemed as quiet as Sunderland docks. Another was called Pop World, where a pallid youth with an earring and a phenomenally bad haircut smoked a fag furtively by the bar – perhaps unaware that the pub smoking ban was still a year off – while two blonde girls in black leather hotpants shuffled around with self-conscious and defensive irony to music I couldn't hear. I was outside watching through the window. Which made me even more tragic than them, I guess.

I was outside because I was debating whether to take my gastric system in my own hands and enter the Rupali, the famous curry house run by Mr Abdul Latif, 'The Lord of Harpole'. While I was in Newcastle, a story about cash for peerages rumbled boringly through our media. I found this scandal amazingly unscandalising since, being northern and suspicious, I had naturally assumed all titles and honours were bought and that this was the natural if corrupt order of things. Well, Lord Harpole has a proper heraldic coat of arms above the door and however he got it, I imagine it's as well deserved as the ones acquired by all those toadies and cronies and cattle barons in Westminster. I wonder if he takes his seat.

By the way, my reference to the digestive challenges offered by Mr Latif's fine curry house was not lazy racism. Lord Harpole himself cheerily extols the lacerating properties of his hotter curries and offers free second helpings for anyone asbestos-gulleted enough to finish a first. The Rupali and its fearsome cuisine has become world-famous via the pages of another receptacle of Geordie culture; one which has done its fair share of propagating an image of the city that has made millions snigger but presumably had the north-east development corporation choking on their skinny macchiatos.

Viz magazine – a bracingly rude, trivia-obsessed, nostalgic and sometimes very funny parody of classic British comics – began as a crude (in every sense) stapled photocopy sold in local pubs. The first twelve-page issue was written and drawn by Chris and Simon Donald and friends Jim Brownlow and Hugo Guthrie and sold for 20p (30p to students), and was soon a word-of-mouth cult initially in the north-east before becoming distributed by Virgin as sales grew.

Then in 1987 the Virgin director responsible for *Viz*, John Brown, set up his own publishing company to handle the comic and it rocketed in popularity to the extent that it was briefly the best-selling publication in Britain. A rash of unfunny imitations were launched and quickly and happily died. At one point 1.2 million people bought *Viz*, though that's now down to around 300,000. *Viz* themselves suggest that this might be because it's not as funny as it used to be.

It's still pretty funny, though. *Viz*'s stock in trade has always been obscene and anarchic parodies of DC Thomson's prim house style, wincingly accurate spoofs of tabloid inanities and general mockery of celebrity and media figures. If they could step from the page, many of *Viz*'s characters would make straight for the bars of the Bigg Market. Sid the Sexist, the eternal gamma male, would try and fail to lose his virginity here, no matter how much of his dole money he spent on turbo-charged ciders. The Fat Slags have long since relinquished their virgin status but would stalk the fun pubs in search of scrawny men like boyfriend Baz to have physically improbable sexual congress with. Biffa Bacon will drink here if he ever attains the age of majority and isn't killed by his sadistic, hyper-violent parents. The above are all Geordies and all cretins; violent, pathetic, sexually loose cretins to boot. Add to that other *Viz* stalwarts such as Eight Ace and Brown Bottle, who are essentially hopeless drunks, and it's a vision of the citizenry that only local lads poking fun at their own hometown could hope to have got away with. Of course, it was actually funny, which is why Geordies enjoyed it more than Rod Liddle's article. *Viz* has won some unlikely allies too. Writing of its leftie-bashing strips Millie Tant and the Modern Parents (the least funny things in it, significantly), the *Daily Telegraph* said that '*Viz* offers an honest subversiveness which a conservative newspaper can admire' and talked of it possessing the 'iconoclastic Toryism of Swift'.

Swift, a lover of the grotesque, would adore the Bigg Market on a Saturday night. Then it's 'rammed' with hair-gelled lotharios in short-sleeved Ben Shermans and shrieking lasses teetering on gold stilettos that would be unmanageable even if you hadn't drunk a vat of Archers. This tide of alcohol is stemmed and soaked up by lardy mountains of junk food. In the Bigg Market, if it isn't a bar, it's a take-out offering pizzas, burgers, baked potatoes, chicken wings and kebabs, any kind of food that you can eat on the move while weaving unsteadily along a pavement crowded with other ambulatory diners. If it contains some kind of gelatinous scarlet sauce you can get all over your new white shirt, so much the better. As the *Today* programme would no doubt tell us in its school ma'amish way, none of the above are essential food groups or the cornerstones of a healthy diet. But then who wants a slice of kiwi fruit and a courgette medley when you've been drinking pints of Stella with a dash of vodka for two days straight?

John Betjeman was too busy getting all moist-eyed about Suffolk beach huts and waiting rooms on the Metropolitan Line to write much about the north but he did manage one sentence on Newcastle. He called Grey Street the finest crescent street in England and praised 'that descending subtle curve' which links the old and new parts of town. Ian Nairn, editor of the *Architectural Review*, thinks it better than Regent Street and has called it 'one of the great planned streets of Britain'. In fact, Nairn has described walking through Newcastle generally as 'an ennobling experience'.

At the top of it on Eldon Square is Grey's Monument where Earl Grey, more famous now for poncey tea than electoral reform, gazes down on the late-night revellers, not all of whom seem significantly ennobled at this hour. There are the girls falling from the vertiginous heels of their 'fuck-me' shoes, the haggard men with their Asda bags clinking with tin and glass, the vomiters both quiet and forlorn or loud and proud and the couples making their way from the brightly lit foyer of the

Theatre Royal to their cars or houses or, like us, to the very special hotelish pleasure of crisp laundry, fluffy towels and an absurdly big bed.

The next day I took what we now thought of as Colin's itinerary and something occurred to me instantly. A city really does need a river. The Thames elevates London from stinking megalopolis to seat of empire. The Tiber and the Seine add romance to cities that already have their fair share. Birmingham and Manchester have their canals but, as Liverpool will tell you with a haughty smirk, they are nothing compared to the roguish glamour and breezy adventurism of the Mersey.

The broad, muscular Tyne runs right through the heart of Newcastle and turns a fine city into something quite breathtaking. On that brisk morning, tucking into my bacon baguette in a pavement café overlooking the water, I could only wonder why more people don't bang on about Newcastle. Not about its economic renaissance or its passionate football supporters or its burgeoning status as UK's science and technology capital but just about how bloody good-looking it is. You get a crick in your neck from gazing up at the stunning and lofty architectural wonders. You do really feel a bit ennobled, pet, especially by close contact with its fabulous bridges.

Fans of early seventies progressive rock will know that Newcastle had five iconic bridges since Keith Emerson's first band The Nice – two-thirds of whom were Geordies – made a long concept suite about them, commissioned by the Newcastle Arts Festival. It took up one side of an album and was the sort of thing bearded heads called Trevor would listen to on headphones in a crashpad while mung bean curry simmered on the hob. It was called, though, with admirable succinctness for prog, 'The Five Bridges Suite'. On an album called *Five Bridges*. So you see it wasn't all *Tales From Topographic Oceans*.

The High Level Bridge is my favourite of the original five. It's a proud relic of the days when train companies actually fought like demons to outdo each other in speed, reliability and directness rather than let safety and passengers and everything go hang and merely line their pockets with share options. Can you tell I use the trains a lot?

By the middle of the nineteenth century, the UK rail network extended up the eastern and western sides of Britain. But the operators of the eastern line worried that unless they could offer passengers an unbroken journey from London to Edinburgh the western route would get all the custom. A rail crossing of the Tyne at Newcastle seemed unworkable and the railway authorities were seriously considering bypassing Newcastle until along came local genius Robert Stephenson. He came up with a daring and elegant three-tiered road/rail solution completed in 1849, the first major example of a wrought-iron tied arch or bow-string girder bridge. I have no idea what that means. But it looks ace.

Over a century and a half later, though, like an ageing starlet, you can see wear and tear if you look closely enough. Cracks have appeared everywhere and it has been closed to road traffic since 2005. While I was in town Newcastle City Council admitted that the bridge would be closed 'at best expectations until 2008, but realistically until 2010 and even then with no prospect of traffic ever using the bridge again'. Stephenson would hate this loss of a practical thrust but aesthetically it doesn't matter. Until it falls down, which is surely a long way off, it will always have for me a lordly, almost autocratic might, the same silencing and silent authority as the Grand Canyon, secure in its own potency.

But the newest and sexiest addition to the Newcastle waterfront is the Gateshead Millennium Bridge. Permit me a moment's crassness; if the High Level Bridge is Greta Garbo, the Millennium Bridge is Scarlett Johansson, one a timeless beauty from an earlier age, the other sexy, modern and dazzling. It takes the form of a slender arc, strung like a harp and rising above the water. It was built to a brief by Gateshead Council that the bridge should not obscure the quayside or overshadow the original landmark bridges and that it could open to allow ships to pass. Wilkinson Eyre/Gifford & Partners' winning design succeeds on the first, classily augmenting an already superb riverscape and on the second count, well, it is elegance in metal. The bridge has just one moving part and that is the bridge itself, which opens like the lid of a beautiful eye to allow the ships to pass beneath. In a neat touch, this also sends all the accumulated litter cascading down special traps.

The bridge has already become as loved by Geordies as their old favourites. It acts as a physical and metaphorical link between Newcastle and Gateshead, traditionally two proudly independent entities but increasingly marketed as one brand: NewcastleGateshead. Maybe one day they'll merge like Budapest, that other great river-rent city that unites across the Danube, and Steve Cram and Paul Gascoigne will embrace tearfully halfway across the bridge.

Gateshead lad and Newcastle lass alike is rightly proud of the bridge, particularly after London made such a song and dance about their Millennium Bridge – Richard Rodgers' 'blade of light', which had to close after one day because it wobbled so much pedestrians feared for their life. I walked across that bridge hard-hatted from St Paul's to the Tate Modern for a Radio 4 programme before it was opened to the public and I felt nowt, mate, because I'm from the north. By the way, that radio programme was one of several on national media devoted to London's Millennium Bridge, its design and commissioning, its ignominious close and muted reopening. I never saw one mention of Gateshead's.

The north's Millennium Bridge leads to the door of the

Baltic Centre, another of New Newcastle's gems. It's one of several superb arts spaces in the city, from the Vine to the Workplace to the Biscuit Factory, but it's the Baltic that really takes that biscuit; a disused 1950s grain warehouse mouldering on a largely forgotten bank of the river until a flourish of civic imagination and forty-six million quid or so transformed it into one of Europe's leading modern art venues.

It's a colossal brick edifice which speaks of past commercial glories and days of empire. But sheer cliffs of glass, exposed lifts and dazzling lighting make it feel thrillingly contemporary. Geordies have always prided themselves on their love of art and when the Baltic opened on 13 July 2002, 5,000 people queued to get in. At midnight, if you will, which makes even more fatuous Brian Sewell's remark that 'all the really important pictures should simply be brought down south ... where they would mean more because nothing is made of them in the north'.

Granted, there were a few less than 5,000 waiting to get in on a blustery morning in February but the ones who were there – tourists, kids, genteel Geordie ladies of advanced years – seemed as thrilled with it as I was. The Baltic seems to have a thing about the human body. Its great opening statement was Anthony Gormley's 'Domain Field', where casts were made of thousands of naked forms. On the day I visit the most striking exhibit is a film of Spencer Tunick's celebrated installation of summer 2005 when 1,700 Geordies got their kit off and were choreographed in differing settings and arrangements around the city. The resulting images are startling and strangely moving, a kind of living sculpture where the vulnerability of the naked body is contrasted with the severity of the urban landscape. I'm pretty sure that this or something like it is what the guide was telling two of those aforementioned genteel Geordie ladies of advanced years. Unfortunately, at the first sign of a dangling male member, they threw their hands up in front of their stricken faces and dashed off crying, 'Oh, no, pet, I don't want to see THAT.' I did notice, though, that some others of their number were made of sterner stuff and spent some moments in quiet appreciation.

A little further down the Gateshead Bank is the Sage Centre. It's a state-of-the-art concert hall and exhibition centre that was seemingly playing host to some world gathering of insurance men when I was there so I popped back across the Swing Bridge and said my goodbyes to Kirsty, as I had a date on the outskirts of town with another lovely local girl.

The Angel of the North may not be a girl any more than Gabriel and Michael were but whatever gender, the people it watches over have truly fallen in love with it. I'm a real fan of Antony Gormley's work which, whether it's the hundred silent figures partly submerged in the tide at Crosby or the Iron Man on Birmingham New Street, all seems to have both intelligence and humanity and grace. Of course, those who don't think art has or indeed ought to progress any further than painting some bananas in a bowl will disagree.

But northern folk know what they like and they know about art. They have taken this angel – twenty metres of steel high above the A1 with wings wider than the Statue of Liberty is tall – to their collective heart. They know what it means. To thousands, it's now a landmark that says 'you're home'. A star to navigate by, a friend, a strangely affecting totem of what the north means to us: lonely, loving, free. From Newcastle city centre you can be at the feet of the angel in half an hour, less if you can get past PC World without stopping. (Richard Ingrams said all male writers become fixated with stationery in middle age. Add random computer accessories to this now.) When I get there, the lay-by is full. There's an ice-cream van doing a roaring trade in 99s and Soleros and three generations of an entire Sikh family is piling out of a people carrier to have their picture taken beneath its spreading, protective wings. Some lads are having a kickabout around it and I'm sure all of this is just what Antony Gormley wanted, just what he meant when he said it should have 'a sense of embrace'.

North and east and west of that guiding angel is the wild north, the Beautiful North, if you like; where the cities almost disappear and even the towns thin out, leaving a few gems dotted here and there of which writer Simon Jenkins said, 'The small towns of the far north are unequalled in England.' But Newcastle does have two sizeable neighbours we should mention, both of whom exist in uneasy truce with their grand big brother on the Tyne. They couldn't be more different, one a town of spires and plainsong, the other a town of cranes and football chants, one steeped in incense, the other soaked in diesel, one revered, the other scorned. Durham and Middlesbrough.

I spent a night in Middlesbrough with the pop trio St Etienne once. We couldn't get over how empty it was. The streets seemed utterly deserted and the area around our hotel was so quiet and depopulated it was like we'd walked into Teesside's very own *Day of the Triffids*. At this point readers from Newcastle and Sunderland will surely make a joke about germ warfare or nerve gas or how everyone must have been waiting for the all-clear sirens. Middlesbrough has a reputation as a dirty, polluted, petro-chemical eyesore. Mark E. Smith of The Fall, speaking about East Germany in the *NME* in 1984, said, 'You've got to see it. It's a horrible, horrible way to live. It's like Middlesbrough.'

There's a kernel of acid truth in all this poison cloud of insults. My friend Paula lived here for several years and on her very first morning in Middlesbrough she was woken by the muffled boom of an explosion, the moaning of a warning siren and the barked command via loudhailer: 'CLOSE ALL

WINDOWS AND STAY INSIDE YOUR HOUSE UNTIL YOU ARE TOLD IT IS SAFE TO DO OTHERWISE!'

The reputation for ugliness is partly deserved. The town wasn't planned but thrown up in a frothing zeal of commercialism over iron, ships and steel. That can make a city rich but not necessarily good-looking. The town's best feature, by a long way, is the famous Transporter Bridge, one of only a handful left in the world and by far the longest. There must have been a craze for these oddities once; every one was built was in the twenty-three years between 1893 and 1916.

Middlesbrough's bridge is still going strong, moving passengers, cars and minibuses across the Tees in a travelling gondola in ninety seconds. The 'car' can carry 200 people, nine cars or six cars and one minibus and makes the journey every quarter of an hour for eighteen hours a day. Try it; you haven't lived till you've been swung 170 feet above 'The Gallant Old Lady' herself.

Some people think it's rather tragic that the town has become so proud of the bridge, even adopting it as its civic symbol. Not me. The north should be as proud of its civil engineering as the south is of its thatched cottages or almshouses. It's what we do, and we do it rather well. If you visit Sydney and look up at its magnificent Harbour Bridge you will see the words 'Made In Middlesbrough' stamped on the side. The Transporter Bridge itself was recognised as a Grade II listed building in 1985. That man Pevsner said that it was, 'in its daring and finesse, a thrill to see from anywhere'. In 1993 floodlights were installed. You can spot it in the movie *Billy Elliot*. Middlesbrough is justly proud of it; when my friend Paula left BBC Cleveland, they gave her a framed picture of it which hangs above her fireplace.

The bridge was built in the glory days of steel. When that industry foundered, ICI and the chemical moguls came and ringed the town with huge plants from which gas and smog plumed skyward day and night. Because of them, Middlesbrough has its very own version of the Northern Lights – great blotchy sunsets of ultramarine and crimson. If you don't think too hard about what's making the sky that colour, they're really quite beautiful.

The city's pollution is legendary. It has entered the folklore, even the folk music, of the area. Local act The Teesside Fettlers have a song called 'Gallant Old Lady', which personifies the River Tees. When she begins in the Pennines and jinks through High Force and Teesdale, she's a sparkling, beguiling creature. By the time she reaches Middlesbrough and the sea, she's a filthy, wheezing hag. The football rivalry feeds on these perceptions too. Newcastle and Sunderland fans call Middlesbrough supporters 'smog monsters' and turn up at Middlesbrough's Riverside Stadium wearing gas masks and anti-radiation suits.

Middlesbrough has been easy to mock. Twenty-seven per cent male unemployment in the mid eighties, years of decline, widespread derision over its lack of beauty. But of late the town has begun to walk with a swagger, and that has much to do with Middlesbrough FC now being established as a decent Premiership side and UEFA Cup Finalists in 2006 after years of relative mediocrity. Ask anyone in a Middlesbrough pub or bus stop how this happened and they'll answer with two words: 'Steve' and 'Gibson'.

Steve Gibson is perhaps the only football chairman in England to have his name chanted by the fans in genuine acclaim rather than before the words 'OUT OUT OUT'. They call him the King of Teesside. A local self-made millionaire through his Bulkhaul transport company, he is a genuine fan rather than an avaricious hobbyist. He saved the club from liquidation, built them a new stadium and has bankrolled the purchase of players like Juninho, lured from the beaches of Rio and the cafés of Europe to the muddy banks of the oily Tees. He has been given the freedom of the town and a statue is surely at the planning stage. Unlike most football chairmen, you can actually listen to his opinions for minutes on end without your cerebral cortex liquefying. 'I was reading in *The Times*,' he once said in a *Times* column by Martin Samuel, 'that most people these days regard themselves as middle-class. Not in Middlesbrough they don't. Ask that question up here and ninety per cent of them would say they were working-class... If you look at Middlesbrough and the area around the town, it has one of the worst infant mortality rates in the country, one of the worst percentages of cardio-vascular disease, one of the highest rates of cancer. Then you list the local Members of Parliament: Tony Blair, William Hague, Alan Milburn, Peter Mandelson. There used to be Mo Mowlam too. And while these career politicians are doing their stuff, advancing up the ladder, their constituents are dying young. So do we see ourselves as the flagship for the town? Of course we do.' Can you imagine Robert Maxwell or Malcolm Glaser ever saying that?

Gibson is right too when he says that the townsfolk are 'loyal, hard-working and innately pessimistic'. Middlesbrough has always had it tough. It has the dubious honour of being the first major British town to be bombed by the Luftwaffe. On 25 May 1940, a Heinkel bombed Dickie Walkington's house on Aire Street. In 1942 a Dornier 217 weaved through the barrage balloon defences and blew up the railway station. According to local legend, several of the town's fish and chip shops were destroyed in these raids. If Stan Boardman had come from Boro, he really could have claimed the Fokkers had bombed his chippy.

Durham was luckier. It should have been hit during the Luftwaffe's infamous Baedeker Raids on cathedral cities and places of historic and cultural worth. Durham was scheduled for attack right after Exeter, Bath and York. The *Durham Advertiser* reported in 1945: 'Tensions were high and fears grew as moonlight illuminated the cathedral perched high above the streets on its rock pedestal. And then the sirens screamed their alarm from the battlemented walls of the castle, just as other alarms had been sounded from there to sleeping citizens so many centuries ago. The greatly augmented Fire Service stood by, ready to fill the maze of pipes running by kerbsides to Cathedral Green with water. The hour was at hand.

'Suddenly a warden dashed into his post and cried, "A miracle! Look at the cathedral!" Everyone rushed out and saw with great amazement that the city, which had been brightly moonlit a moment before, now lay under a pall of white mist, completely blanketing the cathedral and the valleys. Soon after, the bombers arrived overhead and the sky throbbed as they droned about looking for the landmarks that would give the city away... The planes droned all over the sky, puzzled by the disappearance of this bomb-aimer's dream target, and at length they flew away without releasing their deadly load.' Well, not over Durham anyway. They bombed little villages of the Derwent Valley instead, killing thirty-six people, many women and children.

'Why did no one tell me about Durham?' wrote Bill Bryson after his first visit, astonished that his fellow Americans weren't beating a path to the north-east, instead of Stratford and the Tower of London and Blenheim Palace. Just like the Luftwaffe, lots of foreign visitors miss out on it completely and go somewhere else.

The truth is, and really, Bill, this is not just a chippy northerner grumbling, if Durham were in Kent or Sussex, we would never hear the last of it. Every foreign visitor to these shores would salivate over its dreaming spires and punts and misericords and blue-stockinged girls on bicycles. 'Dur-Ham' would be said like 'Boiled Ham' by men in shorts from Boise, Idaho. It would have its own boat race and folk festival and its own TV show where an irascible, beer-swilling, opera-loving detective finds corpses in every cloister and bookshop. But Durham is a long way away from London. Way up that long, long A1 and awkwardly situated, horribly undaytrippable, from the Ramada Heathrow. Far enough north for even this Lancastrian to have never visited before and to ask, baffled, 'Why did no one tell me about Durham?'

But it doesn't feel like the north. Durham has always stood apart. After William the Conqueror had relinquished it, the city and the fractious surrounding county were ruled for centuries as an independent fiefdom or palatinate by some chaps called the Prince Bishops; a powerful line of priest/politicians with their own mint, army and legal system. After the reformation their powers naturally waned but they held out until 1836 before finally ceding control to Westminster and the Crown and joining the rest of us subjects. They abandoned Durham Castle, relocating to a palace in Bishop Auckland, and their old home became the seat of the fledgling Durham University. The effect of all this is to leave a literal and metaphorical peninsula of ancient wealth and grandeur in the centre of what is actually a working-class coal town, one that still has a Miners' Gala though the pits have long gone. It is as if Doncaster's sink estates and flyovers suddenly gave way to reveal a Doges Palace, a Notre Dame or a Sorbonne.

Exquisite and genteel, it's much more redolent of Oxford or Cambridge than a northern city. C. S. Lewis preferred Durham to both Oxford and Cambridge but there is a kinship. Also, like Oxford and Cambridge, the antique glories of its ancient heart often obscure the fact that it has pockets of real deprivation as grim as anywhere in inner-city Liverpool or Manchester. This fact can rankle with Geordies, who resent its ever-so-slightly superior mien, its picture-postcard prettiness, its prim bookish air concealing slovenly habits.

Fair enough. But it is gorgeous. Like Newcastle it's best seen first from the train and, naturally, like Newcastle, I arrived by car. Even if you park in the horribly generic Milburngate shopping mall, it's only a stride or two before things improve. You emerge on a balcony above the river where right on cue, a coxless four glide by disturbing a cormorant or grebe posing madly on a rippling weir. Suddenly a song comes back to mind for the first time in thirty years, forgotten since last you heard Ed 'Stewpot' Stewart play it on *Junior Choice*. That song, yes, is Roger Whittaker's drearily mournful 'Durham Town' which, before anyone writes in, I know is actually called 'Durham Town (The Leavin')'. In it, in the midst of a gloomy catalogue of personal disasters only rivalled in seventies balladry by Gilbert O'Sullivan's 'Alone Again Naturally', Roger sings, 'When I was a boy, I spent my time/Sitting on the banks of the River Tyne.' And perhaps he did. But not in Durham. It's on the Wear. Clean those specs, Rog.

Crossing the Wear from the shops you begin to see the real Durham, which is possibly the fake Durham depending on your perspective. If the students are in town, the riverside pizzerias and pubs will be jumping and it won't be long before the gradients let you know that you are climbing to the city's crown jewels, in both the aesthetic and the Sid James sense.

You see, if you look at a map of Durham and you're of a faintly puerile cast of mind, you will be reminded of the diagrams of the male generative organs – at rest, I should point out – that you would find in biology text books. Well, it reminded me, anyway. On this modest lambent willy of a peninsula is all the stuff that gets people excited about Durham: the castle, the cathedral and Palace Green. If you want a slightly more high-minded comparison, try Pevsner: 'Durham is one of the great experiences of Europe to those who understand architecture. The group of cathedral, castle and monastery on the rock can only be compared to Avignon or Prague.'

Climbing from the wooded cliff sides and onto Palace Green is like stepping out of the north of chips, pies and draught bitter and into an episode of *Brother Cadfael*. There should be vans selling mead. It's a lovely spot but, boy, is it ever popular? I was there at Easter and you could barely hear the evensong over the Minolta powerwinders. My ecclesiastical architecture prose critiques leave quite a bit to be desired so let me instead quote you an expert in the field, Alec Clifton-Taylor, who said: 'With the cathedral at Durham, we reach the incomparable masterpiece of Romanesque architecture not only in England but anywhere. The moment for entering provides for an architectural experience never to be forgotten, one of the greatest England has to offer.'

Well, I'd go along with all of that, squire, with the slight proviso that when you've seen one really big cathedral, you've seen them all, unless you can tell a bema from an ambulatory at fifty paces. That said, it is truly stunning. I thought as I always do when entering one of these places of how powerful, how terrify-ing even, the presence of God must have been in the lives of rich and poor alike to make them build these edifices – not just build them, but so skilfully and impressively, that just entering makes you feel oddly godly. The sheer authority of the place almost forces you to your knees, like a giant hand on your shoulder. Durham Cathedral is religious certainty written in unyielding stone and stained glass; a vast, daunting embodiment of an unprovable, abstract idea, I mused in its vaulted silence. For about ten minutes. Then I went off to find the café.

I had a scone and watched a lovely little vignette at the next table. A delicate, mousy girl in a sweatshirt and round glasses was chatting to a chubby, gentle-faced young man with an untidy beard and a rucksack full of theology books and a different livery of sweatshirt. They were both what I would call 'churchy' and clearly at the very earliest stages of mild courtship. He would say something, possibly a joke about the Venerable Bede, who's buried next door, and she would laugh until her teacup shook and her long, pale face coloured slightly. It was quite the sweetest thing I have ever seen. I do hope they're together now, if that's what they wanted. Or at least I hope they had a really good time finding out that it wasn't quite what they wanted. I finished my scone, bought some pamphlets and left Durham to them and the tourists and the last, liquid honey of the afternoon sun.

If you're hereabouts, drop in at Hexham but try not to approach from the west, where the grim vista of the Waste Transfer Plant and a sprawling industrial estate will make you doubt the guidebook stuff about 'handsome market town'. Hexham is undeniably northern in latitude but Latin in attitude in that it seemed to be having a siesta when I arrived.

I arrived at the Wentworth Café just as they were swinging round the 'Closed' signs and was told there was no food with a look that suggested only a pervert ate between noon and six. I asked the nice lady at the tourist information shop where I could get a bite and she told me to try 'Phat Katz Café'. I liked the way that she spelt it out with a shudder of contempt so went off up the hill to give it a go. Britain's cafés have come a long way in the last twenty years. But at Phat Katz I encountered the classic British look of the dismayed and panicked waitress who fears that the unwanted arrival of customers will throw the whole system into disarray. Nervously, I ask for a toasted teacake. She shakes her head.

'All the machines are switched off; it would take a few minutes.' I wonder whether to tell her about the great advances that have been made in toaster technology since the last war but think better of it. In the end I sip my tea and try to puzzle out any kind of theme in the curious bric-a-brac décor. There's a dulcimer, a skeleton, a trombone, an American pedestrian crossing sign and a Sopwith Camel. Perhaps it's based on a particularly freaky acid trip the owner once had in Kathmandu. That would account for his atrocious spelling as well.

Having seen it on a leaflet in a cathedral café, I drove across country to the Beamish Museum of Northern Life, a replication of the shops, streets, schools, mines and railway stations of bygone generations, a celebration of local life in the centuries past. Most of it was shut, though, still gearing itself up for the tourist season. No matter. The name was revealing enough. Not North-Eastern Life, Northern Life. That feeling again that we Mancs, Scousers and tykes are somehow deluding ourselves if we think that we're northern. No, son, this is the north, it seems to say.

In fact, this is the ending of the north, a notion I was acutely aware of as we toured these last outposts, not just of the north but of England, back and forth along Hadrian's Wall in that lonely, lovely last corridor of England that lies roughly alongside the A69 from Carlisle to Newcastle. The actual wall though stretches from one coast to the other, from Bowness on Solway in the west to Wallsend in the east. It is the most remarkable Roman monument in the country and there's nothing quite like it anywhere else in the former Roman Empire.

We dropped in at Greenhead, where they offer a virtual tour of the wall for £7.50 although the actual wall (free) would seem much better value. Like Wallsend, Walltown may not be imaginatively named but at least you know exactly where it is. Here I went all gooey over a red squirrel. Well-meaning but misinformed *Guardinista* mates have tried to convince me that my dislike of the grey squirrel and zeal for its extermination is somehow analogous to Slobodan Milosevic's ethnic cleansing policy but I'm just not having it. Red squirrels are shy and lovely and they are ours. If we could have both, I'd be happy (though I'd prefer reds), but you can't. Thanks to human stupidity and a disease called Parapox, there won't be a red squirrel left in England in twenty years and another little bit of joy will have passed from the world. Any day you see one is a real red-letter day.

I saw it on Walltown Crags and almost as striking was another sighting there of a gentleman in khaki combat hat of what looked like the Latvian Home Guard. With him was a teenage girl dressed in pink picking her way gingerly in unsuitable footwear through mud. She would glance occasionally and nervously at her dad's headgear and I recognised the look on her face. It was terror that a school friend might see her.

If anyone knows the information centre here and its toilet block, I'd be grateful if they could explain the curious logo, a relief mural which seemed to show a naked man boxing with a pterodactyl watched by a troll in a bobble hat.

From the turrets of Walltown, you can view the vast empty expanse of Northumbria. Empty undulating ridges and dead straight Roman roads built by men from the Mediterranean who must have shivered in their beds and wondered what kind of godforsaken posting this was. Once the wall was garrisoned by thousands of troops who watched over the northern horizon from turrets and milecastles placed at regular intervals. Due north were the savage hordes and ungovernable expanses of Scotland. Haltwhistle, just down the road, is the centre of Britain. Not England, which is Meriden in the Midlands, but Britain, which should remind the Anglocentrics among us just how big Scotland is.

When not nervously walking along the wall looking for mad jocks bent on slaughter, the legionnaires lived in a series of substantial forts placed at strategic locations. The big daddy of these is Housesteads, where I stump up my quid for parking plus three pound odd for admission. The site is massive and the actual fort is a good fifteen minutes' schlep from the car park. The sky glowered, black clouds and slanting rain interrupted by sudden brilliant sun and gusts of icy wind. Even encased in Gore-Tex it was icy. What must it have been like to kids from the sunny Adriatic dreaming of those 'beakers of the warm south' and dusky maidens? Absolute hell, I would have thought.

There are natives of the north who see it like that as well too. Given the choice they'd rather be dancing to cheesy house music in a sweaty club in Ayia Napa while necking an Aftershock. Each to their own. I like it up here. Bleak, challenging, a little raw but wildly romantic. Northern, I'd like to think.

East of here, the A689 is a trunk road that runs between Alston, a fine, isolated moorland village with a desperate short-age of women, it's said, and Penrith, a cracking market town on the border with the Lake District. In 2001, the AA decided that that very A689 is one of the ten best driving roads in the world. Cross it when the clag and murk are down to the valley floor, when the rain comes in stinging sheets that the wipers can't clear, when the hail pings off the bonnet or the snow blows in off the tops, and you will wonder which AA made this decidedly drunken decision. You'll never forget it, though.

And come in the warm, malt whisky light of a late summer evening or a buttered crumpet of a crisp winter morning or in spring when the sky is alive with larks and there is nowhere better in England. A glorious feeling of well-being will suffuse you, especially as you reach the very top of the pass and find a large squat building that just happens to be the best transport café in the world.

Elton can keep the Ivy; Tony can have his Granita. I'd swap every coulis, roulade and jus in NW1 for dinner (at dinnertime) at the Hartside Café. For years, it was a secret known only to bikers, lorry drivers and walkers with a real sense of adventure. Fog and ice and snow means it can only open half the year or so. But when it does, the smell of the grilling bacon evidently carries across the north and everyone from Barrow to Jarrow heads up here. I'm worried that even writing these words might make it harder to get my steak pie and chips on a Bank Holiday Monday.

But let's not be selfish. Hartside Café should be saved for the nation and celebrated by as many as can fit onto its pine-effect chairs and picnic tables, a national treasure in a way Buckingham Palace will never be; a home from home, a place to dream of when you're lost on the tops with bootfuls of brackish bogwater or trying to refold the soaking map over the bonnet in the rain.

Where else can you eat your sausage buttie (sauced from a plastic tomato) and sip your rich dark tea (sugared if required from a glass sphere with a chrome nozzle) while gazing over glorious, wild landscapes in every direction? East are the brooding, lonely Pennines, highest of them Cross Fell, so high it keeps a shawl of snow across its shoulders till May. Alongside is a summit known as Fiends Fell, ancient haunt of demons and the only mountain in England that's been exorcised. To the west, on a clear day, you might see Ireland and the Isle of Man seemingly afloat in the sky rather than the Irish Sea. Between you and they are the mountains of the Lake District.

Finally above you is Dumfriesshire and the lands of the Tweed. Due north but then again not really north. After the wall, after the Solway Firth, after that bloodstained border country, whatever the map and the GPS tell you, you're not heading north but south. Because south is a cast of mind just like north is; the Scots of Ullapool regard Gretna like Geordies think of Devon. Southern, more civilised, a little warmer and softer. 'Bright and fierce and fickle,' whereas the north is 'dark and true and tender', as Tennyson said in his poem 'O Swallow, Swallow'.

A long way below you, just visible in the gathering blue dusk, is the mighty tributary of the M6 running south and that silvery stream of twinkling light is a continuous phalanx of traffic heading south for rendezvous and reasons that you'll never know, roaring there, in fact, as fast and even faster than the law will allow.

331

So turn up your collar, turn your back and be glad that for the moment, at least, you are not.

Epilogue

The last thing I expected was to fall in love. I didn't plan for it, it didn't fit with my schedules, and now that I have fallen, I don't really know what I'm going to do about it. But I do know that the months I spent wandering the north were some of the happiest times of my life. As I said 100,000 words or so ago, I didn't want to carve out a slice of soft soap. I was desperate to avoid writing one of those books that add to the north's already brimming reservoirs of self-esteem or the sort that you parcel up and send off to Uncle Royston to remind him of the good old days of rickets, gaslighting and Geoffrey Boycott, as he sips Zinfandel in his harbourside flat in Vancouver or Capetown.

I was determined – and believe me, so was my editor – that this shouldn't become some cloying hymn to God's Own Country, one of Bernard Ingham's Rent-a-Rants or a print version of 'Matchstalk Men And Matchstalk Cats And Dogs'. But that didn't stop me going utterly, desperately head over heels. It was a love that I knew had always been there but in the spring of 2006, when I thought I'd got over it or at least got used to it, it came back and knocked me off my feet, like seeing a childhood sweetheart who's grown into a beautiful woman. It would hit me in the chest and grab me by the heart when I least expected it; on Alderley Edge, in Alan's bike shop in Wigan, on Blackpool prom and on Bury Market, on the banks of the Tyne and the Mersey.

But before I get too warm and soppy, I'd like to let off a little steam.

I came to realise, more than a little narked, that when columnists and commentators, poets and pundits sing the praises of things 'typically English', they inevitably mean southern English. They mean thatched cottages and village greens, willow on leather, rolling downs. When John Major made his daft little speech misquoting Orwell on Englishness, he talked dreamily of warm beer and spinsters cycling to evensong. He didn't mention Chestnut Mild, rugby league, high lonely fells or colliery towns, things every bit as quintessentially English – just not the sort of thing that pops up in *Midsomer Murders* or Joanna Trollope. John Betjeman once put together a book called *Betjeman's Britain* which sums up beautifully some southerners' attitude to the north's riches. It's a book about the delights of Britain's cities, towns, villages and landscapes. It's 318 pages long and a mere twenty-two are about what you could generously call the north of England. Ten are about Leeds. Seven, bizarrely, are about the Isle of Man. Nothing on Lancashire or Yorkshire or Cumbria or the great cities of the Great North. It just didn't occur to him.

On a rainy drive across the Lancashire moors, I caught a short Radio 4 'issue-based' story about childlessness but, for me, it was the minor detail that provoked the most thought. The protagonist was an academic with a cut-glass accent. She had lost a daughter called Cordelia and her neighbour was a TV producer. At no point was there any suggestion that these people and this milieu were in any way out of the ordinary. This was incredibly telling, I thought. Most people have never met either a Cordelia or a television producer. But as they discussed their (literally) extraordinary lives in voices of crystalline poshness, their remoteness from life as most of us live it was never acknowledged.

If, however, you turn on a Radio 4 play and the voices are northern, it will inevitably be all about 'being northern'. About how poor or cute or funny or indomitable we are. It will never be simply set in Sheffield or Hull or Wigan because it can be and should be. It will never be about an adulterous dentist who just happens to live in Bootle. It will be in some way about his Scouseness. If it's about a young woman hairdresser in Bury, it will be somehow about the essential good-heartedness of northern lasses or the comically parochial nature of Bury life. Some writers may think this is complimentary. In fact, it's patronising. It's in effect saying that you have to have a strong dramatic reason, a 'hook', in order to set your play outside the M25. The fact that most of the country actually lives there isn't good enough evidently.

While I was writing this book, London Transport decommissioned the Routemaster bus, the big red kind they used to have in London. Hardly anyone outside London has ever heard the name 'Routemaster' but that didn't occur to the many media institutions that talked about its passing as if it were the Flying Scotsman, the jumbo jet or parliamentary democracy. I'm ashamed to say that the BBC joined in all this with gusto and actually devoted a night of programmes to the bus's demise. They seemed unconcerned or possibly unaware that, as many of my friends told me forcibly, 'No one outside London gives a fuck about Routemaster buses, whatever they are.'

Some of the above programmes were commissioned and written by northerners, which brings me to another of my bugbears – and a new one, excitingly. I have come to loathe Uncle Toms; yes, even to the extent of using that expression unironically. When I hear some exiled northerner talking about how he supports Spurs or Arsenal because he used to take his son in the seventies or because he fetched up in Hampstead when he first moved down, my lip curls. Almost as much as when I read some disparaging piece about how small and shabby the old town looked when we took Tabitha and Josh back 'up there' to see

Mum at Christmas. I look at these people and in my mind's eye there forms an image of a stooping figure tugging his forelock and 'massa'-ing in front of the plantation owner. Is this a bit strong? Sorry. If you find my use of the term Uncle Tom over-dramatic and insulting, I apologise. How about 'collaborator'?

I'll be all right in a minute. Hate, said Kurt Vonnegut, is a great motivator, but in the end it's about as nutritious as cyanide. Love and hate, though, as tattooed on a Barnsley Teddy Boy's knuckles, would flare up intermittently.

I love the places and the people in this book. I hate how they've become enfeebled and turned into a nation of reality TV freaks and Trisha-trash but I love their spirit and their humour and their indomitable sense of fun. I hate the way they vomit in the street but I love the energy they bring to their lifelong commitment to fun. I can't put it better than J. B. Priestley did in *English Journey* in 1933:

Far too many opinions about staying quietly at home happened to be expressed by comfortable professional men writing in warm, well-lighted, book-lined apartments thirty feet long by fifteen broad. And again, even if they have pleasant homes, the fact remains that most young people like to go out at the weekend. It is not some temporary aberration of the tribe; such is their nature. They want to go out, to get on with their individual lives, which have a secret urgency of their own ... to join their friends, to stare at and talk and giggle and flirt with and generally begin operations upon the opposite sex... Such is their nature, fortunately for the history of the race.

JB would have hated *Big Brother*, but he wouldn't have minded the Bigg Market, I fancy. He understood that when you worked hard all week in a job that dulls your spirit or chokes your throat or rubs your hands raw, you need the sheer escapism and the capacious bosom of indulgence and excess. I know in my heart that I do. I'm a northerner. If a thing's worth doing, it's worth doing to excess. You're only young, ohh, eighteen or nineteen times. If I die with fifty pence in my pocket, that's bad budgeting. Everything in moderation, including moderation. These are my mantras.

I watched spring come to the north. It burst open across it like blossom on flowers. In his poem 'The Waste Land' T. S. Eliot said, 'April is the cruellest month'. Away with you, man. It's a beautiful month. I watched it come across the north as if God had drawn back the curtains on Winter Hill and Cross Fell and Blencathra. Everywhere I went I saw people who looked glad to be alive. Calderdale – the borough that includes Todmorden, Halifax and Hebden Bridge – has more inhabitants over seventy-five than anywhere else in Britain. It's obvious why. They have more to live for: better beer, better scenery, cleaner air, nicer people. They're dancing in the streets, honest. Get up there and take a look.

If all this sounds partisan and partial, then I'm not sure that northernness is geographical. It's philosophical. I've met people from Devon who had the right stuff and people from Preston who made my heart sink. Just like Doctor Who said, lots of planets have a north. By which I like to think he meant that northernness is a cast of mind, not a set of co-ordinates. It's about appreciating that an afternoon's snow is an excuse for sledging, not a state of emergency. It's about realising that the best place to drive a Range Rover is Cumbria not Islington. It's about embracing that life is short and work is hard and that London is not the answer to everything. I love us being smart and aspirational but I hate the idea that we might turn into the Home

Counties. We are not the Home Counties. We are the far, far away counties and all the better for that.

I've tried not to bang on too much about Mark E. Smith of The Fall but if we do secede, he will be on the banknotes, the proud but self-satirising laureate of 'the northern white crap that talks back', as he once said. One of his finest songs is 'The NIRA' – The North Will Rise Again. But if he were writing that great baleful, bilious anthem of dissent and defiance again, it would be the NIRA. The North Is Rising Again. I know. I was there to see it.

In the end, this is a love letter and a love story. I don't know how it ends. But I know I want to go back and see the north rising and be a part of it. Go 'where the weather suits my clothes', as Harry Nilsson once sang in 'Everybody's Talking', even if I leave my jacket at home in November because I don't want to look soft.

Goodbye Piccadilly. Farewell Leicester Square. I'm packed and I'm nearly ready to leave.

I already have the tabard. And I know where I'm going for my dinner.

Which is at midday, by the way.